SPIRITS OF PLACE IN AMERICAN

LITERARY CULTURE

SPIRITS OF PLACE IN AMERICAN LITERARY CULTURE

JOHN GATTA

OXFORD
UNIVERSITY PRESS

Oxford University Press is a department of the University of Oxford. It furthers the University's objective of excellence in research, scholarship, and education by publishing worldwide. Oxford is a registered trade mark of Oxford University Press in the UK and certain other countries.

Published in the United States of America by Oxford University Press
198 Madison Avenue, New York, NY 10016, United States of America.

© Oxford University Press 2018

All rights reserved. No part of this publication may be reproduced, stored in a retrieval system, or transmitted, in any form or by any means, without the prior permission in writing of Oxford University Press, or as expressly permitted by law, by license, or under terms agreed with the appropriate reproduction rights organization. Inquiries concerning reproduction outside the scope of the above should be sent to the Rights Department, Oxford University Press, at the address above.

You must not circulate this work in any other form and you must impose this same condition on any acquirer.

CIP data is on file at the Library of Congress
ISBN 978-0-19-064654-7

SPIRITS OF PLACE IN AMERICAN LITERARY CULTURE

JOHN GATTA

OXFORD
UNIVERSITY PRESS

Oxford University Press is a department of the University of Oxford. It furthers
the University's objective of excellence in research, scholarship, and education
by publishing worldwide. Oxford is a registered trade mark of Oxford University
Press in the UK and certain other countries.

Published in the United States of America by Oxford University Press
198 Madison Avenue, New York, NY 10016, United States of America.

© Oxford University Press 2018

All rights reserved. No part of this publication may be reproduced, stored in
a retrieval system, or transmitted, in any form or by any means, without the
prior permission in writing of Oxford University Press, or as expressly permitted
by law, by license, or under terms agreed with the appropriate reproduction
rights organization. Inquiries concerning reproduction outside the scope of the
above should be sent to the Rights Department, Oxford University Press, at the
address above.

You must not circulate this work in any other form
and you must impose this same condition on any acquirer.

CIP data is on file at the Library of Congress
ISBN978- 0-19-064654-7

For Julia,
Ever at the heart of my home place.

CONTENTS

	Acknowledgments	ix
	Introduction	1
1.	Houses of the Spirit	15
	Emerson, Thoreau, Hawthorne, Stowe, Cather, Robinson, Gaines	
	Transcendental and Other Soul Shelters in Antebellum America	15
	Nathaniel Hawthorne's Home "Somewhere Else"	22
	Harriet's Houses	29
	When Houses Are No Longer Homes	43
2.	Spirits of Pilgrimage, Peregrination, and Re-Placement	57
	Lopez, Servid, Muir Momaday, Bradstreet, Thoreau, Snyder, Berry, Haskell	
	Moving On and Beginning Again	57
	From Pilgrim's Way to the Open Road	72
	Localism versus Globalism	83
	Two Versions of Globally Engaged Localism	89

viii | CONTENTS

3.	The Place of Imagination	105
	Berry, Whitman, Nelson, Véa	
	The Earthiness of Imagination and a Phenomenology of Place	105
	The Contemplative Reach of Imagination: Poetry of Walt Whitman and Marilyn Nelson	114
	Numinous Layerings of Place as Palimpsest	127
4.	Sacred Sites and Geographies	141
	Thoreau, Tillinghast, Black Elk, Melville, Lincoln, Abbey, Williams, Norris, Day, Baldwin, Kazin	
	Orientations of the *Genius Loci*	141
	Hallowed Battlegrounds and Burial Grounds	158
	The Spiritual Fecundity of Wastelands	167
	City Scenes of Grace	181
5.	Contemplating Site-Based Education and Place-Making	197
	Current Concepts and Practices of Site-Based Education	197
	The Rationale for Contemplative Learning in Place	203
	A Case Study in Localized Learning	209
	Afterword	235
	Notes	*239*
	Bibliography	*263*
	Index	*277*

ACKNOWLEDGMENTS

It is a pleasure to recall here with thanks those whose counsel, encouragement, and example have in diverse ways sustained me throughout my work on this project, whether they ever saw or endorsed the contents of my manuscript. That list includes Parker Bauer, Wendell Berry, Christopher Bryan, George Core, Bill Engel, Julia Gatta, Robin Gottfried, David Haskell, Ross Macdonald, Tom Macfie, Robert MacSwain, Wilfred McClay, Chris McDonough, Deborah McGrath, Marilyn Nelson, Jim Peters, Bran Potter, Mary Priestley, Ross Macdonald, Marilynne Robinson, Sarah Sherwood, Isaac Sligh and Norman Wirzba. Adam Hawkins provided invaluable technical assistance. I also benefited from suggestions offered by anonymous readers for Oxford University Press and from Victoria Danahy's judicious copyediting. I am especially indebted to John McCardell, vice-chancellor and president of the University of the South, for granting me much-needed sabbatical time, following my stint as an administrator, without which I could never have begun or carried forward work on this book.

A portion of the commentary in Chapter 1 has been drawn from my essay titled "Harriet's Houses," first published in the

Sewanee Review 123 (Summer 2015): 493–502, and reprinted here by permission of that magazine. Citations of poetry in "The House on Moscow Street," Diverne's House," "Aunt Annie's Prayer," and " Porter, " from Marilyn Nelson's *The Homeplace*, are printed by permission of Louisiana State University Press. And poetic citations in "The Sweet-Hearts," "Professor Carver's Bible Class," and "Bedside Reading," from Marilyn Nelson's *Carver: A Life in Poems* (2001), are used by permission of Boyds Mills Press.

ACKNOWLEDGMENTS

It is a pleasure to recall here with thanks those whose counsel, encouragement, and example have in diverse ways sustained me throughout my work on this project, whether they ever saw or endorsed the contents of my manuscript. That list includes Parker Bauer, Wendell Berry, Christopher Bryan, George Core, Bill Engel, Julia Gatta, Robin Gottfried, David Haskell, Ross Macdonald, Tom Macfie, Robert MacSwain, Wilfred McClay, Chris McDonough, Deborah McGrath, Marilyn Nelson, Jim Peters, Bran Potter, Mary Priestley, Ross Macdonald, Marilynne Robinson, Sarah Sherwood, Isaac Sligh and Norman Wirzba. Adam Hawkins provided invaluable technical assistance. I also benefited from suggestions offered by anonymous readers for Oxford University Press and from Victoria Danahy's judicious copyediting. I am especially indebted to John McCardell, vice-chancellor and president of the University of the South, for granting me much-needed sabbatical time, following my stint as an administrator, without which I could never have begun or carried forward work on this book.

A portion of the commentary in Chapter 1 has been drawn from my essay titled "Harriet's Houses," first published in the

Sewanee Review 123 (Summer 2015): 493–502, and reprinted here by permission of that magazine. Citations of poetry in "The House on Moscow Street," Diverne's House," "Aunt Annie's Prayer," and " Porter, " from Marilyn Nelson's *The Homeplace*, are printed by permission of Louisiana State University Press. And poetic citations in "The Sweet-Hearts," "Professor Carver's Bible Class," and "Bedside Reading," from Marilyn Nelson's *Carver: A Life in Poems* (2001), are used by permission of Boyds Mills Press.

INTRODUCTION

WHAT MIGHT IT MEAN, EXISTENTIALLY and spiritually, for human beings to inhabit a particular site or dwelling place on this earth? Over the last several decades, particularly in the wake of Yi-Fu Tuan's classic work on *Space and Place: The Perspective of Experience*,[1] this primal question has stirred renewed interest among American academics of varied disciplinary training. Fascination with the distinctive character of humankind's sense of place is likewise apparent in the range of new interdisciplinary courses that have sprung up lately across the nation at many colleges and universities, including my own.

At the same time, of course, prospects for sustaining rootedness in anything resembling a "home place" are threatened now in Western culture as never before. In today's mobile society an appreciable number of Americans, including well over half of those still in their twenties, shift their residence every five years.[2] Powerful economic forces associated with globalism, combined with the disembodied and emphatically unlocalized influence of digital technology, can seem to render concerns about the sense of place dated, if not irrelevant. As two recent commentators on the subject acknowledge, "To say that 'place' matters is, to some extent, to swim against the principal currents of our times."[3]

Such swimming is precisely the exercise I am undertaking in this book. Perhaps, though, it is because of the culturally homogenizing temper of our time, rather than despite it, that so much attention has focused lately on the value of recovering place-centeredness. Social scientists, artists, humanists, agents of public policy, and farmers, among all of whom differences otherwise abound, often share the conviction that "place matters" indeed. They offer several reasons for declining to dismiss regionalism and local allegiances as naively parochial.

Literature offers an altogether fitting and natural medium for reflection on the special character of place-inflected experience. Setting has, after all, been traditionally recognized as an essential element of fiction together with plot and character, though commonly regarded as less meaningful than the other two. What has come to be called "ecocriticism" focuses particular attention on setting, on highlighting the presence of features and creatures in landscape otherwise perceived to be merely background material.

Ecocriticism, a form of literary study I have elsewhere been disposed to practice myself,[4] can thus be regarded as a subset or near-relative of the place-centered inquiry I now want to emphasize here. Consider, for example, the title of one apposite collection of essays published in 2003: *A Place on Earth: An Anthology of Nature Writing From Australia & North America*. The volume's editor, Mark Tredinnick, describes it as a "conversation about belonging on earth" and "a complex essay in bioregionalism."[5] Generally speaking, however, ecocriticism is less concerned with human experience of and within the built environment than it is with rediscovering our relatedness to the land and creatures of what still (albeit problematically) might be called biotic Nature, or "First Nature"—that is, the nonhuman world. Ecocriticism, for the most part, continues to dwell on texts that are otherwise identifiable as "nature writing."[6] My intention in this book is to pursue a variant but complementary form of inquiry, centered on a theology and phenomenology of place, that takes fuller account of the built environment—including the domiciles and other structures found in more settled communities—than ecocriticism typically does.

"Phenomenology of place" is one of those sweeping, philosophically derivative terms whose sense requires some explanation. I take it to define, in essence, that bodily, dynamic interplay between human selves and their setting or dwelling which constitutes our lived experience of emplacement. So it involves at least some degree of consciousness about how and where we are physically situated in the world. But the term, which has lately gained currency in the emergent, transdisciplinary field of place-studies, also calls for critical reflection of the sort I pursue in Chapter 3.

Imaginative literature is a particularly apt medium for such reflection because it typically involves a specified incarnation of ideas about place that can otherwise remain abstractly theoretical. The action unfolded in narrative and dramatic literature takes place, almost inevitably, in an identifiable some*where*. Literature thus, by its very nature, holds the capacity to evoke subjective, emotively colored impressions of place, in contrast to factually objective coordinates in geographic space. For space becomes a place only if and when it becomes endowed with human stories, memories, experiences, and feelings.[7]

Such perceptions sometimes involve the author's attribution of anthropomorphic personality to certain favored sites. John Muir's apostrophic paeans to Yosemite or Henry Thoreau's love colloquies with Walden Pond are cases in point. Although these personalities of place often reflect something of humanity, they may also—as for Thoreau and Muir, or later for the likes of Barry Lopez or Denise Levertov—bear an aspect of sacred divinity. These spirits-of-place, conjured through language, thus become sites of resistance to the otherwise-overwhelming tide of post-Enlightenment rationalism that Max Weber once identified as an all-but-inevitable disenchantment of the world.[8]

And yet, despite the fragmenting force of postmodernity, I believe that an imperative to recover humanity's connection with some form of sacred geography persists in our own time.

It has been argued, in fact, that the health, if not survival, of our increasingly urbanized civilization depends on finding means to reclaim the original ground of our being in spiritually vitalized earth.⁹ So for Gary Snyder, the "real work" falling to inhabitants of the United States is that of "becoming native to North America," learning to accept primary citizenship in "the continent itself," its land and creatures, rather than in the nation state.¹⁰ To feel at home in this land, Snyder insists, one must aspire to know it from the ground up. He believes that "to know the spirit of a place" likewise calls for a realization "that you are a part of a part and that the whole is made up of parts, each of which is whole."¹¹ Curiously, though, this newer ecospiritual¹² emphasis shows itself to be partly an outgrowth of ancient ideas—including the notion, prevalent in the Roman world, of a *genius loci* [spirit-of-place].

Identified with a discrete, unseen guardian spirit felt to inhabit a given locale, the *genius loci* principle affirmed the inherently religious potential of place, within the polytheistic or animistic worldviews of premodern peoples. One might expect to find such a presence dwelling not only around altars, temples, and sacred groves, but in domestic structures as well. In fact, "early popular religious beliefs in Genius" commonly construed the Genius figure as "the begetting spirit of the family embodied in the paterfamilias."¹³ Hence it strikes me as appropriate that the opening chapter of my study should be concerned with domestic structures and with the diverse forms of spirit-presence often attributed to home dwellings. Just as the ancient Romans and others understood their participation in meals as a key feature of domestic worship, sometimes understood as propitiating the household spirit, so also my chapter recognizes the special attention that Harriet Beecher Stowe devotes, albeit within her own Christian context, to rituals associated with food preparation and consumption.

The Romans were also apt to figure the numinous, untamed force of the genius as serpentine. The most familiar example appears in book 5 of the *Aeneid*. Here Virgil narrates an episode in which Aeneas, amazed to see a shining snake gliding among altar and tomb vessels, wonders whether to interpret this reptile as guardian and genius of the place. For ancient Rome, the totemic snake and symbolic cornucopia, two essential figures of the household Genius, were both associated with generative fecundity—and worshipped as such. As one scholar points out, the sexually charged "creative spirit" of Genius was thought to protect "a particular place" whereas "the paterfamilias, responsible for begetting new members, guaranteed the perpetuation of the family stock, the clan."[14]

The reptilian totem bears sacred meaning not only in the animistic atmosphere of ancient Rome, but in other cultural contexts as well. In Hebrew and Christian scriptural settings, for example, the serpent has been variously interpreted as an evil, intrusive presence, construed by later tradition as demonic; as a fearful yet potentially restorative anodyne to ill, epitomized by Moses' ritual crafting of a bronze snake in the wilderness; and as an untamable and inexplicable yet regenerative life force that the author of the Fourth Gospel understands, by analogy with the Mosaic episode, to be responsible for the lifting up of Jesus upon and beyond the cross.[15]

In any case, this archetypal serpent imagery reminds us that the Genius of a place, though ordinarily welcomed as a protecting spirit comparable in Christian terms to a guardian angel or localized patron saint, can also bear a darker and even sinister aspect. To offend the Genius of a place is perilous business. Or else, apart from committing any deliberate misdeed, one might simply lose favor with a capricious mountain god or sea spirit. Nathaniel Hawthorne's lesser-known tale "The Ambitious Guest" shows it is possible for an author to sustain some credence in this primordial notion even in nineteenth-century America. Situated in the Notch of New Hampshire's White Mountains, the story tells of a rock avalanche in which all members of an extended family, together with a young man who happens to have stopped at their cottage for refuge, are suddenly swept to their deaths. But just before the calamity overtakes them, as they hear the ominous overture of a single rock fall, the father of this family remarks, half-facetiously but prophetically, that '"The old Mountain has thrown a stone at us, for fear we should forget him."'[16]

For that matter, one should scarcely suppose all spirits to be benign. In Christian tradition, those third- and fourth-century ascetics who lived alone in the Egyptian desert were intensely cognizant of the threats posed to the soul by evil spirits. Neither is everyone in our contemporary world ready to dismiss the possibility of their existence. Tales about spooky spirits of place continue to be told, in offices as well as around campfires, and fascination with the idea of haunted or horror houses, ghost hunts, and ghost stories persists throughout present-day America.

Consonant with America's mercantile instincts, such fascination has often been exploited commercially. One can today purchase a guided tour of haunted houses not only, and most predictably, in Salem, Massachusetts, but also in cities across the nation, including a full array of southern haunts such as New Orleans, Savannah, Charleston, and Chattanooga. Even in my own small settlement of Sewanee, a few students and others have been keen to preserve and circulate ghost stories, as well as a roster of local sites they presume to be haunted. In our culture dominated by rationalistic skepticism, certain primordial or animistic suppositions seem to endure, sometimes coexisting uneasily with strains of traditionally theistic religious belief. From the first, as is widely known, ancient Rome influenced the shaping of the American Republic in several spheres including architecture, law, urban design, engineering, and government. So Roman and animistic traditions of the *genius loci*, which lie behind some American tales of enchanted dwellings or locales,[17] must be numbered among these influences.

Yet variant conceptions of sacred space, involving manifestations of God's indwelling presence on earth, can likewise be recognized throughout Jewish, Muslim, and Christian tradition. In Genesis 18, for example, the Lord's appearance to Abraham, mediated through three men, is said to occur in connection with the primordially charged natural setting of "the oaks of Mamre." A Christian counterpart to the *genius loci*'s protective properties can be discerned in traditions honoring some localized patron saint or guardian angel.[18]

Even in modern, post-Enlightenment culture, one finds a surprisingly resilient inclination to conceive of place in sacramental terms. As David Brown's analysis confirms, belief that something within or animating the material world nonetheless transcends physical space and materiality is culturally pervasive, extending beyond its "churchy" formulation in Christian doctrine. Such precedent for what Brown terms the "sacramentality of place" can thus be found within the European classical world, as well as elsewhere.[19] In this light, the *genius loci* tradition appears as yet another manifestation of sacramentality. The Christian church's traditional definition of a sacrament as that which presents "an outward and visible sign of an inward and spiritual grace" is extended toward broader recognition that a multitude of signs and sites scattered throughout the physical world can bear numinous potential.

What, then, might reconfigured versions of the *genius loci* tradition come to mean in our own era, particularly as expressed through American literary culture? That is a central question of this book. As theologian Belden Lane reminds us, "above all else, sacred place is 'storied place.'"[20] Yet in adopting for my title the plural "spirits of place," I wanted to acknowledge the multiple meanings that sacred space must bear in our latter-day, pluralist society. Even from the limited perspective of monotheistic religious faith, a Christian version of which happens to accord with my own theology and outlook on life, more than one conception of the sacred can be associated with the same physical locale. An obvious example would be the earthly Jerusalem, held as sacred but in divergent and even competing fashion by Jews, Muslims, and Christians alike.

Not surprisingly, every case I examine in what follows supports the conclusion that place does matter, in one way or another. Yet no place in particular can be said to matter definitively, to define absolutely humanity's place in the world. There remains a provisional aspect of our attachment to every site imaginable. Our place-associations of whatever sort are thus inherently paradoxical—meaningful, to be sure, yet inevitably contingent and transient for all mortals. David Brown observes, for example, that the very notion of pilgrimage implies "a critique against absolutizing place," offers further reason to deny an "idolatry of place." And even Henry Thoreau, wedded to Walden Pond though he is often fancied to be, remarks that "Thank Heaven, here is not all the world."[21]

Thoreau's sympathetic elder, Ralph Waldo Emerson, likewise recognized the paradox whereby sites of Transcendental experience were perceived to be at once significant yet radically contingent. For Emerson, the numinous power accessible through these sites was not inherent "in" the locale itself but derived from the site's interaction with the human soul—and, by extension, the Over-Soul. It is therefore telling that, in the second chapter of Emerson's *Nature*, those episodes of ecstatic revelation and delight he tells us he was graced to receive occurred not in one sublime spot but in two disparate physical settings—in the one case, while "crossing a bare common," in the other, "in the woods." So "It is certain," he insists, "that the power to produce this delight, does not reside in nature, but in man, or in a harmony of both."[22] Even apart from Emerson's Transcendental outlook, it is evident that some investment of human sentiment and meaning is invariably involved in transforming space into place. For Gaston Bachelard, too, it is by virtue of the dynamic interplay between self and surroundings that certain sites become meaningful. Or, as Wordsworth reminds us, our human sensibility is such that we "half create" what we perceive, every place we look.[23]

In reflecting on these matters, I was drawn to order my larger inquiry in accord with a thematic rather than strictly chronological sequence. First, in my opening chapter, with reference to literary examples, I reflect on the spirits and sacramental connotations of home dwellings because domiciles are, in effect, the most fundamental and unavoidable forms of human encounter with place. Apparently antithetical to that, the untethered ethos of pilgrimage becomes a focus of attention in my second chapter. Pilgrimage, or travel narrative more broadly, although never centered in a single locale, suggests fascination with the variability of site-based experience. The implications of relocation—that is, what it means for anyone to find or make a new home place by adoption—is another concern of this chapter.

In the third chapter, I consider ways in which the creative spirit of Imagination, crucial to all artistic endeavor, shapes our perceptions and expressions of placement. As Wendell Berry and others have suggested, our outward apprehensions of place are not only influenced by the mental power of imagination but can also influence, in turn, our very conception of the imaginative faculty. The place-inspired identity that imagination often assumes is especially pronounced in certain forms of literature, including most fiction. So my inquiry focuses on the numinous reach of imagination, as well as on the special role that scene, location, or regionality seems to play in nearly all fictive expression. In a relevant essay, Eudora Welty once encapsulated much of what is at issue in these matters by asking "What place has place in fiction?"[24] A pivotal question indeed. And what I end up highlighting as the "*earthiness* of imagination" has rarely been discussed directly in the manner I attempt in Chapter 3, though I take it to be embodied, or acknowledged at least implicitly, in an appreciable share of Anglo-American writing. I explore here as well the ways in which place can be imaginatively construed as palimpsest. What, in other words, might be the religious implications of considering how place is inevitably mutable, multilayered, constantly being overwritten and altered across time?

From this juncture my fourth chapter sets out to assess, and to visit by way of imagination, diverse sites, geophysical orientations, and structures throughout North America that have commonly been construed as sacred or might be construed as such. Both natural and humanly constructed sites figure in this assessment. On what grounds might it still be possible, in our post-Enlightenment world, to apprehend any physical site as sacred or enchanted? What can literature tell us about prospects for identifying contemporary loci of encounter with numinous reality? Such are among the questions considered in this central chapter, an unusually long one because here I pursue a sustained application of topos readings to numerous American literary texts of diverse character, reflecting an array of faith traditions. And because the sense of place is always colored by human subjectivity, I have along the way interspersed with my critical analysis, notes of personal narrative and reflection.

Likewise in my final chapter, which reaches beyond straightforward literary criticism, I venture to draw on personal experience and observation to consider some practical applications of place-based inquiry. I also wish to take some account here of collegiate courses and programs other than those with which I have been directly involved. What are the peculiar benefits and liabilities of place-based educational programs of the sort that have recently been implemented in US colleges and universities? How might such programs enlarge not only students' awareness and understanding of place, but also their capacity for place-making? And what role might the cultivation of contemplative spirituality play in at least some of these endeavors?

One way I address these questions is to describe my experience as an instructor in our experimental first-year course here at Sewanee, a team-taught offering identified by catalog title in 2015 as "Discovering a Sense of Place: Upon and Beyond the Domain." Those of us collaborating in the course have aimed to approach our common subject with the benefit of local field visits as well as selected techniques of contemplative learning. Partly from what I learned in the process, I consider in this chapter how one might, in the course of educating present-day college students, deepen their apprehension of the ways in which sacral and other notions of place can matter—to them personally, to other human beings, and to the earth. This project assumes special relevance at a time when radically cosmopolitan assumptions, and the ascendency of distance learning, threaten to displace traditionally residential models of higher education. To be sure, it seems ironic in one sense that those of us engaged in the first-year course presume to talk with students about the value of finding their place at the very time when, newly arrived on our campus, they have been freshly uprooted from their places of origin. In another sense, though, it seems all the more appropriate to engage first-year students at this juncture of their lives, when they temporarily perceive themselves to be placeless, in thoughtful analysis of what it means to develop a sense of place. In this context the academic objectives of place-studies shade inevitably into the existential project of place-making. We can be grateful to theologically informed authors such as Craig Bartholomew, Douglas Christie, and Michael Northcott for highlighting lately the indispensable role that place-making must play in human flourishing.[25] And I would hope that, for students enrolled in my section of the course, reflection on literary texts might become integral to the process of learning how to *belong* somewhere, or how, as Gary Snyder would put it, to *become* native to a place that may or may not have been the land of one's birth.

Because my book is largely devoted to academically informed literary analysis, the last chapter is, admittedly, an unconventional culmination. My hope, though, is that ending with a case study of this sort will be revealing for readers beyond the small circle of literary scholars, not despite but rather on account of its textured particularity in relation to my own community of living and learning in Sewanee, Tennessee. I believe it is fortunate, in fact, that we have seen the emphasis in place-studies moving lately beyond the ideal of a purely objectified, endlessly expansive place-knowledge of one sort or another toward place-making—that is, toward learning how to live more fully and productively wherever we find ourselves. For if the sense of place is to mean anything beyond the realm of abstract theory it must be embodied—realized through sensate perceptions of some actualized place on earth. The first-year course in question aims to locate that common ground of understanding where texts, places, and persons come together. And I trust there is nothing like teaching first-year students to ensure that one's speculative musings about place are brought solidly down to earth.

What does it mean to *know* a place, beyond superficial acknowledgement of the space it occupies? How exactly might one learn to encounter what Snyder calls "the spirit of a place"? That became a perennial question for us, both students and instructors, throughout the semester of our course offering. Part of the answer, we knew, had to come from shared walks and other experiences together in the field, across campus, and in surrounding communities. Yet we also found the perspective we brought to such encounters informed by reading selected literary texts. Some of those texts evoked places defined, for the most part, by human settlement. Others aimed to convey a deep sense of wilder sites, occupied largely by nonhuman communities. From this last perspective, here is how noted writer and naturalist Barry Lopez describes authentic knowledge of place:

> To know a physical place, you must become intimate with it. You must open yourself to its textures, its colors in varying day and night lights, its sonic dimensions. You must in some way become vulnerable to it. In the end, there's little difference between growing into the love of a place and growing into the love of a person. Love matures through intimacy and vulnerability, and it grows most vigorously in an atmosphere of trust. You learn, with regard to the land, the ways in which it is dependable. Where it has no strength to offer you, you do not insist on its support. When you yourself do not understand something, you trust the land might, and you defer.[26]

Reading books, including this book, can never substitute for the vitally sensate, affective knowledge of place that Lopez describes. Yet there is reason to believe that reading, reflection, and higher education all contribute to the critical consciousness that must inform such knowing, and that better enables us to discover just where and how we belong.

1

HOUSES OF THE SPIRIT

TRANSCENDENTAL AND OTHER SOUL SHELTERS IN ANTEBELLUM AMERICA

In more ways than one, the *first* space that humans typically understand to be their place on earth is their family's home, a domicile of one sort or another. So it is scarcely surprising that Gaston Bachelard begins his classic if idiosyncratic discourse on "The Poetics of Space" with sustained reflection on the topos of home dwellings. We are apt to regard our house, he observes, as "our first universe, a real cosmos in every sense of the word." For Bachelard, the house figure expresses nothing less than "the topography of our intimate being." Although materially constituted, it embodies transmaterial or spiritual realities in such a way as to offer "ground for taking the house as a tool for analysis of the human soul."[1] More recently, too, Michael S. Northcott calls to mind that much as the ancient Hebrews took the Temple in Jerusalem to be "a microcosm of the macrocosm of the earth . . . designed to uphold the sacred order of Creation," so also it was "a related belief in many premodern cultures that domestic dwellings were the meeting point between their inhabitants and other beings, both earthly and heavenly, and that their aesthetic design should symbolize this sacred purpose . . . ."[2]

On American ground, Ralph Waldo Emerson anticipated such notions by declaring in 1836 that "Every spirit builds itself a house; and beyond its house a world; and beyond its world, a heaven."³ This Transcendentalist motto has far-reaching implications, anthropologically as well as philosophically. Henry Thoreau, who had read and inwardly digested *Nature*, concedes, toward the start of *Walden*, that some form of shelter, whether constructed or discovered, ordinarily ranks among the elemental necessities of life. Frequently, too, even non-human animals are instinctually impelled to create some form of dwelling place. Oliver Wendell Holmes, for example, in his poem "The Chambered Nautilus," analogized the progressive, ever-expanding growth of that marvelous shell where the pearly cephalopod resides to the human soul's potential to shape for itself "more stately mansions," finding thereby "each new temple, nobler than the last." Emerson's seminal pronouncement in *Nature* likewise suggests that our material house should at once embrace yet also transcend our material needs. Ideally, it should define where we locate ourselves in the world, spiritually as well as physically. Although a "shelter" of sorts, the ideal domicile is not a bulwark against nature and the wider world so much as a threshold between Emerson's individuated Me of civilized culture and that wilder expanse of all that is Not Me.

We can begin to understand Henry Thoreau's house-building project at Walden Pond as a practical, almost literalistic realization of Emerson's abstract principle that "every spirit builds itself a house." And by reminding readers that he had with his own hands constructed his habitation by the pond, Thoreau makes good his claim to fulfilling Emerson's call for self-reliance.⁴ His account underscores the point that he builds that habitation, which he characteristically calls a "house" rather than a hut or cabin, as deliberately as he endeavors to construct his Transcendental life and to pursue his spirit-quest at Walden. He approaches each step of house building methodically, with a self-conscious logic he is at pains to share with readers. Acknowledging that "civilization is real advance in the condition of man," though only if selectively appropriated, he endeavors to combine the best of "savage" and "civilized" patterns of life. Accordingly, his doctrine of "simplicity" wedded to "economy" allows for the market purchase of certain foodstuffs and other items, as well for the use of interior furniture—albeit on the very modest scale of three chairs, a bed, table, and desk.

Thus, instead of settling for the most primitive form of shelter or construction techniques, perhaps finding living quarters in a wigwam or cave, Thoreau deliberately exploits certain products of industrial civilization—nails, for example—to build his house. The product of his labor is, to be sure, only a "miniature house,"[5] measuring just 10 × 15 feet and configured as a single room, but a house nonetheless. And by purchasing for secondhand use a number of construction items including windows, bricks, and boards from an Irish laborer's shanty, he practices a form of economy recognizable today as earth-friendly "recycling."

As James Dougherty observes, Thoreau's house, "thoughtfully built and reflectively occupied," figures in religious terms as a *sacramental* vehicle—one of several such nonecclesiastical sacraments observed throughout *Walden*.[6] Thus, reflecting as well the Transcendental principle of organic metaphor, the house structure's outward and visible materiality mediates its inhabitant's involvement with an inward spirituality. "Verily," Thoreau affirmed in his journal for 1845, "a good house is a temple—A clean house—pure and undefiled, as the saying is."[7] Thoreau evidently understands his lakeside house, particularly as conjoined with its natural surroundings, as sacred space. He describes several of its physical features—including its hand-dug foundation, its concentration within a single rather than divided living space, and the centrality of its hearth fire—in a manner that carries spiritual overtones. And he attributes a sacramental character not only to the house as fixed object but also to the process by which he assembles it. It is in and through this progressively creative action that the house builder enacts part of the centering exercise and self-making process entailed in his Walden experiment.

Still, the larger part of Thoreau's self-making and self-discovery at Walden depends, of course, on his interaction with the wilder face of nature, epitomized by the pond. The symbiotic linkage between pond and house, between relatively free-spirited nature and a fixture of civilization, is critical to the soul's realization of what Emerson had called "an original relation to the universe."

Both the southwestern-facing window and the southeastern-facing door of Thoreau's house afforded him a view of the pond. He often took in that view. He tells us, for example, how in the summer dawn he reveled in watching and listening, as he sat with "door and windows open,"[8] to attune his own awakening to that of nature, including the hum of a mosquito touring his quarters. Particularly on such occasions, he liked to regard the house as an exposed threshold into its surroundings, a site porously coextensive with the natural elements that embraced it. Together with the pond and its environs, the house offered him a platform for sustained meditation on his "original relation to the Universe." In *Walden*, this contemplative focus of the house is memorably expressed in Thoreau's description, toward the beginning of "Sounds," of how he sometimes loved to sit in silence on its pond-facing portal:

> I love a broad margin to my life. Sometimes, in a summer morning, having taken my accustomed bath, I sat in my sunny doorway from sunrise till noon, rapt in a revery, amidst the pines and hickories and sumachs, in undisturbed solitude and stillness, while the birds sang around or flitted noiseless through the house, until by the sun falling in at my west window, or the noise of some traveller's wagon on the distant highway, I was reminded of the lapse of time. I grew in those seasons like corn in the night, and they were far better than any work of the hands would have been.

> They were not time subtracted from my life, but so much over and above my usual allowance. I realized what the Orientals mean by contemplation and the forsaking of works. For the most part, I minded not how the hours went. (75)

And yet, though Thoreau saw the house serving for a time as his window on the world, he scarcely regarded it as his primary or ultimate "home." His insistence on preserving a broad margin to life demanded a *lebensraum* [room for life] larger than 10 × 15 feet. Accordingly, he took little interest in housekeeping and spent the larger part of most days sauntering amid Concord's fields and woods. The sacramental centerpiece of his two-year experiment in Transcendental home economics was not the house, after all, but rather the pond and its environs. As Marilyn Chandler notes, for Thoreau "the ideal house would simply be a perching place" because "real living, the best living takes place outdoors, as close to nature as it is possible to dwell."[9] Although Thoreau took pride in having prepared for himself "an airy and unplastered cabin, fit to entertain a traveling god" (57), neither such a god nor he himself—in his pursuit of earthy godliness—planned to remain housebound. He recognized, too, the vanity of presuming to own in perpetuity any form of real estate. Though the plot of land where he raised his house was technically owned by Emerson,[10] Thoreau was content to reside there by squatter's rights. Persuaded that "a man is rich in proportion to the number of things which he can afford to let alone" (55), his ambition at Walden was never to purchase or possess the place, but rather to become possessed by it.

Nowhere is Thoreau's vision concerning the significance of place and of place-centered contemplation better set forth than in the second chapter of *Walden*, titled "Where I Lived and What I Lived For." The linkage signaled in this provocative title says it all. For Thoreau, "Where I Lived" amounts to much more than a physical address. He sees "where I lived" as inseparable, in fact, from the existential question of "what I lived for." "Where I lived" in time as well as space comes to define, more broadly but still in organic relation to the particularities of his locale, nothing less than the essence of his spirit-quest, his interrogation of life's purpose.

How then, exactly, do Thoreau's perceptions of place bear on his Transcendental inquiry into the meaning and purpose of life? Throughout the chapter, Thoreau uncovers this association in progressive stages. Just as Thoreau's reasons for living at Walden surpass his initial plan to finish writing there *A Week on the Concord and Merrimack Rivers*, so also his deep reflection on the place itself—or, in today's colloquial phrasing, on "where he's at" or "where he's coming from"—keeps expanding beyond map space to further planes of perception. But the first stage of his discourse fastens squarely on the physical coordinates of his location. He tells us in some detail about the setting of his experiment: "I was seated by the shore of a small pond, about a mile and a half south of the village of Concord . . . in the midst of an extensive wood between that town and Lincoln, and about two miles south of that our only field known to fame, Concord Battle Ground" (58), and so forth. Encounter with what he subsequently calls the "essential facts of life" must first be grounded, he insists, in the actualities of the physical world, and he tells us features of that world he knows exceedingly well.

But beyond the restricted view available in his immediate setting, he soon extends his vision with the benefit of imagination toward more distant horizons:

> Though the view from my door was still more contracted, I did not feel crowded or confined in the least. There was pasture enough for my imagination. The low shrub-oak plateau to which the opposite shore arose, stretched away toward the prairies of the West and the steppes of Tartary, affording ample room for all the roving families of men. "There are none happy in the world but beings

who enjoy freely a vast horizon"—said Damodara [Krishna], when his herds required new and larger pastures. (59)

In the third and ultimate stage of considering "where I lived," Thoreau looks toward even loftier horizons. "Where do we find ourselves?" Emerson had asked in his essay "Experience." Pondering now "where I lived" in time and amid the expanse of outer space, Thoreau presses that question to its existential endpoint. Somewhat audaciously, he sees himself indwelling a site that qualifies in cosmic terms—as well as any other place imaginable—as the numinous center of the universe, where he can enjoy access to a perpetual morning and the Eternal Now:

> Both place and time were changed, and I dwelt nearer to those parts of the universe and to those eras in history which had most attracted me. Where I lived was as far off as many a region viewed nightly by astronomers. We are wont to imagine rare and delectable places in some remote and more celestial corner of the system, behind the constellation of Cassiopeia's Chair, far from noise and disturbance. I discovered that my house actually had its sight in such a withdrawn, but forever new and unprofaned, part of the universe. If it were worth the while to settle in those parts near to the Pleiades or the Hyades, to Aldebaran or Altair, then I was really there, or at an equal remoteness from the life which I had left behind, dwindled and twinkling with as fine a ray to my nearest neighbor, and to be seen only on moonless nights by him. (59)

Thoreau thus envisions the locus of familiar scenes surrounding his house and the pond as the still point of his interaction with a dynamic, enspirited cosmos.

Present-day visitors to Walden Pond, looking to pay homage to Thoreau's homesite by the shore, are often disappointed to find there only a ring of stone pillars marking the spot. The house is long gone. In fact, it had already been sold and removed from the pond shore, headed soon toward disintegration, by the time *Walden* was published.[11] Pilgrims to Concord searching for houses redolent of the Transcendentalist spirit can still visit Emerson's main residence and museum—which is apt to seem, by contrast with Thoreau's stark quarters at Walden, like one of Holmes's more stately mansions—as well as the Old Manse, where Emerson composed *Nature* and where Hawthorne later resided. But it is probably fitting that just as Thoreau left his house, to continue his sojourning in and beyond the semidomesticated wilds of Concord, so also that building took on other lives before returning to its elemental origins. "Nature is not fixed but fluid," Emerson had concluded. The ecstatic soul that Thoreau discovers and celebrates in *Walden*, in consort with a traveling god, likewise insists on sustaining the fluidity and portability of its place on earth.

NATHANIEL HAWTHORNE'S HOME "SOMEWHERE ELSE"

In Hawthorne's imaginative life, as in much of his personal experience, the prospect of remaining or returning "home" was richly appealing. Yet Hawthorne did not always associate home with a physical structure or single-family home. A rich variety of dwellings appear throughout his fiction. They include a boardinghouse and Coverdale's rustic hermitage in *The Blithedale Romance*, Richard Digby's forbidding cave retreat in "The Man of Adamant," Hester Prynne's modest seaside cottage in *The Scarlet Letter*, and Hilda's living chamber atop one of Rome's medieval towers in *The Marble Faun*. It is telling that, apart from any structural edifice, Hawthorne chose to title his collected series of travel sketches from time spent in England, land of his ancestral heritage, *Our Old Home*.

Despite his time abroad, Hawthorne was indeed, unlike his seagoing friend and adventurer Herman Melville, something of a homebody. He was usually content to live and work in familiar domestic space near his hearth fire, study, wife, orchard, and garden plot, all the while observing the world at a distance. This urge to cultivate his art in domestic seclusion is particularly evident in early sketches such as "Sights From a Steeple" and "Sunday at Home." Many weekdays, too, he was pleased to spend at home. And though he resided during his adult life in several different locales, sites more geographically dispersed than those favored by Emerson or Thoreau, all of those places—aside from his studies in college or travels abroad—lay within the Commonwealth of Massachusetts. Although many of his fictional characters, ranging from Hester Prynne and Clifford and Hepzibah Pyncheon, to Goodman Brown or Ethan Brand, sometimes felt compelled to venture forth into the unknown, they inevitably found themselves driven to return home, whatever the cost or consequences.

Hawthorne shared with his otherwise-suspect Puritan ancestors a reluctance to see sacred space centered primarily within a churchly edifice. New England's Puritan settlers worshipped not in a "church," understanding themselves rather to *be* God's church on earth, but rather in a multipurpose meeting house—as well as in the home, the favored setting for family-based devotional practices. Consistent with nineteenth-century sentiments of domestic piety, Hawthorne, too, sometimes professed heartfelt belief in the sanctity of the American home. Here the fires of a "holy Hearth"[12] could recall the primordial energies of divine creation, could warm the enchanted circle of family members and friends drawn together. In the home, an abode all the more blessed and maintained through a wife's angelic ministrations, souls enjoyed at least a reasonable hope of finding sanctuary from the world's frenetic pace and corruptions.

Such idealized impressions of home life, though scarcely prevalent in Hawthorne's writing, are especially pronounced in his prefatory essay to *The Old Manse*. In these time-hallowed rental quarters overlooking the Concord River, where Hawthorne moved with his bride Sophia in 1842, he spent three years of unusual contentment. Emerson had previously inhabited the "old parsonage," built by his grandfather and originally intended to house the families of ordained ministers. Clerical images and theological books were still omnipresent when its new tenants arrived. Yet Hawthorne, without rejecting the religious, even discernibly Christian potential for worshipful experience he believes the house offers, expresses disdain for its ecclesiastical trappings. It is despite rather than through them that he identifies this house's special access to grace and spiritual inspiration. So he soon strips from its walls their "grim prints of Puritan ministers," replacing these hypermasculine icons with "the sweet and lovely head of one of Raphael's Madonnas."[13] For Hawthorne, the Old Manse's sacramental potency to feed his soul derives largely from the natural beauty and abundance of its setting—the garden, orchard, and river—in which the house is, in Emerson's phrasing, "embosomed."[14]

What Hawthorne valued most about living in the Manse was, in a word, its ready access to grace. And for him "grace" was a word bearing both naturalistic and theological meanings. "I relish best," he confided to his readers, "the free gifts of Providence." The author at home takes delight in gazing on the Concord River, in working his garden a little, but mostly just in watching the squash and other plantings grow. He enjoys standing "in deep contemplation over my vegetable progeny with a love that nobody could share nor conceive of, who had never taken part in the process of creation." In the orchard, he delights in seeing grace bring to fruition that which he alone never could—apples, cherries, currants, pears, and peaches. At the Old Manse he finds inward confirmation of the soul's "infinite spiritual capacity," of a "beneficent God," and of the "saving grace" available even to the unlettered.[15] So for Hawthorne the Old Manse and its grounds held special appeal, even if some of the odd characters he encountered nearby in Concord village did not.

Despite his homing instincts, Hawthorne nonetheless found it hard, over the extended course of his career, to settle permanently at any single location that felt like home. The Old Manse years were an exceptional interlude. As the author's "Custom-House Preface" to *The Scarlet Letter* makes plain, Hawthorne, following his dismissal as surveyor in Salem, felt decidedly estranged from that town: "My native place, though I have dwelt much away from it." While professing that Salem "possesses, or did possess, a hold on my affections," he leaves the place intending never to return, declaring himself henceforth "a citizen of somewhere else."[16] This "somewhere else" locution sounds intentionally indeterminate. Hawthorne would next reside for a time in Lenox. Lenox is indeed "somewhere," a town pleasantly situated in the Berkshire Mountains. And Hawthorne's cottage in Lenox, located today on grounds of the Tanglewood Summer Music Festival, is a place I happen to hold in fond regard after many years of attending concerts performed by the Boston Symphony Orchestra. But Hawthorne never felt quite at home there. After his departure from Lenox he then, once again, occupied a house (The Wayside) in Concord, near the scene of his previous blissful experience as a newlywed in the Old Manse. At other stages of life he lived in Boston, at Brook Farm in West Roxbury, and in West Newton. He died while on a trip to New Hampshire with Franklin Pierce. But once Hawthorne left Salem, his search for a deeply rooted home place "somewhere else" always eluded him. He might well have echoed the sentiment of Hepzibah in *The House of the Seven Gables*, when she confides sadly to her brother Clifford that '"We belong nowhere.'"[17]

Gables, of course, is the fiction in which Hawthorne elaborates most extensively on the figurative significance of houses. As the main character in Hawthorne's favorite romance, this imposing edifice in Salem, built in the seventeenth century, assumes a personality of its own. Its façade is compared to an aged "human countenance" that bears traces of "the long lapse of mortal life, and accompanying vicissitudes, that have passed within" (5).

Yet this house assuredly does *not* qualify as one more domestic shrine or temple of holiness. It remains haunted by evil spirits, despite the piously intended "ceremony of consecration" its Puritan owner arranged to have performed after its completion. For it is built over "an unquiet grave" (11, 9), on land seized by Colonel Pyncheon from Matthew Maule, who had been executed on trumped-up charges of witchcraft. As such, it both embodies and perpetuates this ancestral wrong committed by the House of Pyncheon.[18] It represents the sort of "original sin" that later generations bear when they are unwilling or unable to disavow the material benefits they have inherited from rapacious ancestors.

As such, the house can be read as figure for the whole of America—for the exploitative prosperity of its majority culture, at any rate, insofar as it is erected upon the lands, or wrested from the labors, of displaced peoples—including, of course, the original Indian inhabitants of Massachusetts.[19] Despite the delusions of ownership the Pyncheons had so long entertained, they had become more nearly possessed or imprisoned by their houses than sovereign owners of anything. Colonel Pyncheon's grand edifice, though intended to serve as an impressive showplace, is actually a House of Pride—an image reinforced for Hawthorne by Edmund Spenser's portrayal in book I, canto IV of *The Faerie Queene*. Later afflicted with "both the dry rot and the damp-rot in its walls" (174), this house threatens to become a dungeon. Hepzibah and Clifford, as well as Clifford's malevolent cousin, Judge Jaffrey Pyncheon, all become prisoners in one way or another. In the chapter titled "Governor Pyncheon," a tour de force of sustained satire on Jaffrey Pyncheon's delusions of grandeur, Hawthorne ironically describes the judge ensconced in the oak chair as "keeping house" (268) for the Gables dwelling—though it is *he* who is kept there now, dead and helpless, never to rise again.

After Jaffrey's death, Clifford, during his manic railway flight with Hepzibah, expounds on the folly of attaching oneself to any fixed dwelling place. It is understandable that Clifford, having first been imprisoned for decades, then confined to dark living quarters still under Jaffrey's oppressive sway, should exult in the freedom of movement that his liberation allows. The exhilaration of train travel stirs in him momentary disdain for "those stale ideas of home and fireside,'" renders the prospect of living '"everywhere and nowhere'" appealing (259, 261). The attraction of moving about with unprecedented speed by virtue of new technology, the allure of free-spirited personal mobility—all of this is familiar enough to us in our own day. We can understand why Clifford welcomes the railroad's presumed power to '"annihilate the toil and dust of pilgrimage'" and '"spiritualize travel'" (260). And we understand why Holgrave, described at one point as having been "homeless" (177), had earlier endorsed the Jeffersonian ideal that each generation should build its own houses, dwellings destined to crumble away every twenty years or so. Appreciating the impulse of both characters to shake off the deadweight of the past, Hawthorne reflects partial sympathy for such notions.

For Hawthorne, though, houses that last are well worth preserving, despite the sorrows and crimes their walls have absorbed. Rather than supposing that they and the history they enfold should be annihilated, he brings Holgrave to believe it preferable to renew them periodically, along with their inhabitants, from within. True, his party of sympathetic characters ends up leaving the "dismal" house in Salem, eventually taking up residence at Judge Pyncheon's estate in the country. Yet the House of the Seven Gables has by then served its purpose within Hawthorne's largely secular but partly religious vision of salvation. It is, after all, in and through the Salem house that Holgrave, Phoebe, Clifford, Hepzibah, and Uncle Venner all discover their authentic home.

Hawthorne never attributes to this house an inherently regenerative potency as sacred space. Yet he does see it serving, through the course of his narrative, as a passageway for progress toward personal and spiritual redemption for Clifford, Hepzibah, and Holgrave. Such progress is effected primarily through the providential agency of its angel-in-residence, Phoebe Pyncehon. It is she who brings sunshine and grace into the house, who exorcises its evil spirits, and whose presence counters its gloomy past with hopes of renewal and beauty figured in the garden rosebushes. The story's prosperous conclusion, including its resolution through marriage of the ancient Pyncheon–Maule dispute, raises problems for modern readers.[20] Yet it expresses, as Hawthorne elsewhere sought to verify,[21] some of his core convictions. Technological innovations notwithstanding, he believed that pilgrimage of the heart and soul, if no longer undertaken on the road, was still possible in nineteenth-century America. The spirit of Bunyan and Dante remains vital in this story of Salem, and Hawthorne's romance portrays a transformation of the House of the Seven Gables, once accursed, into a purgatorial passageway toward salvation.

But like Dante, Hawthorne felt acutely estranged from his home town, whose stories he was presuming to tell while himself living in exile. His second full-length romance, despite a playful disclaimer found in its preface, is solidly rooted in the soil and history of Salem, even if the author was not at the time of composition living there but rather in Lenox. And even while a resident of Lenox, he remained at least in part a citizen of "somewhere else." For Hawthorne, finding a home that could serve as an earthly temple of the spirit was an attractive but elusive ideal. So he was otherwise inclined to believe, as his short-story character of Ethan Brand is said to believe at an earlier, reverential phase of *his* life journey, that the human heart is where one might best look to locate a true temple of the divine.

HARRIET'S HOUSES

Like many of us today, Harriet Beecher Stowe relocated several times and inhabited several different houses during her lifetime. Although she was born and died in Connecticut, where she lived longer than anywhere else, she also resided during intervening years in various towns in Ohio, Massachusetts, Maine, and Florida. Moreover, like Emily Dickinson, whose fertile imagination enabled her to "dwell in possibility" well beyond the foundation of her Amherst home, Stowe in her fiction inhabited still other houses and sites beyond those where she had actually slept. Yet throughout it all she affirmed the immense value of finding one's place in a stable, well-ordered home. That conviction is the existential subtext of her writings on domestic economy, including her *Hearth and Home* contributions.

For Stowe and other moderate feminists of her stamp, the nineteenth-century home place was something of a sacred shrine, locus of an intimate fellowship linked to the presiding spirit of Christian motherhood. So I believe it is worth reflecting here on the architectonics of residential structures not only imaginatively, as a telling feature of Stowe's fiction and especially in *Uncle Tom's Cabin*, but also biographically, in connection with home places most familiar to her. Such an inquiry casts light, for example, on the curious fact that the title of her most celebrated work draws attention to a particular dwelling place, more than to any human character or concept.

A logical place to begin this house tour is the site where Harriet herself first drew breath, the church parsonage assigned to Lyman Beecher in what was then the bucolic town of Litchfield, Connecticut. No longer standing, this large, rambling building served as home for the ever-expanding Beecher family but also housed frequent visitors and a number of boarders. In *Poganuc People*, the last novel Stowe wrote, she returned in spirit to acknowledge this first home of hers as "a silent influence, every day fashioning the sensitive, imaginative little soul that was growing up in its own sphere of loneliness there."[22] One room she particularly credited with nurturing her contemplative spirit was her father's study. This book-laden refuge for thought, situated in the uppermost third garret, fed her early fascination with the written word.

Much of the house's influence on the future author was scarcely silent, though, as the place ordinarily bustled with life and sound. Harriet quickly learned to share its space not only with seven other family members who resided there when she was born in 1811 but also with black and white housekeepers, boarders, cats, and scurrying rats. Far from tightly constructed, the Beecher residence encompassed a multitude of rooms, several levels, and a series of outbuildings. Stowe later recalled the place, in the full chapter she devoted to describing it in *Poganuc People*, as "a wide, roomy, windy edifice that seemed to have been built by a succession of after-thoughts."[23]

Such an expansive, complex structure seems at first wholly unlike the rudimentary slave quarters that Tom, Chloe, and their three children inhabit in *Uncle Tom's Cabin*. Stowe credits the housekeepers of both dwellings, though, with maintaining exemplary standards of cleanliness, beauty, and domestic artistry. Stowe portrays even Tom's hewn-log slave cabin as fronted by a flourishing abundance of garden fruits and vegetables and a colorful splendor of flowers, including a "large scarlet begonia and a native multiflora rose."²⁴ The cabin is small, its several functions presumably confined to corners of a single room. But it is well kept, equipped with simple furniture, and adorned with art prints and a portrait. Stowe portrays it as exceedingly modest compared with the nearby Shelby mansion, where a crisis was brewing "in the halls of the master" (26). Yet to some degree she also idealizes Tom's old Kentucky home by way of contrast with the grim quarters or homeless desperation slaves must subsequently endure in this story.

Common spaces of convergence in both dwellings, too, are the hearth fire and kitchen area. As Hawthorne had insisted in his "Fire-Worship" sketch of 1843, the open domestic fire brings "a spiritual essence, into our inmost home." Beyond its practical uses, the "holy Hearth" in his view draws all attention "to one centre." It expresses the very soul of familial life—while displaying indoors something of the elemental "might and majesty" of "wild Nature."²⁵ If Vesta's flame is the soul, then the kitchen precinct, which incorporates the hearth fire of Tom's Kentucky home, corresponds to the communal heart of things. For Stowe the social essence of home life was concentrated in the kitchen. As a child, she enjoyed hearing the lively banter exchanged in the Litchfield home's culinary quarters, where she also gained early exposure to interaction with working-class and African American members of the household. Her fondness for Candace, "our portly old black washerwoman," is reflected in several of her later writings, including *The Minister's Wooing*, wherein a character likewise named Candace plays a maternal and nurturing role for a household in Newport, Rhode Island, comparable to what Stowe had herself known in Litchfield.²⁶ When Stowe moved from Litchfield to Cincinnati, her acquaintance there with household servants of color further influenced her attitudes.²⁷

Tom's cabin is portrayed as an intimate space, largely by virtue of its cramped physical scale. But for Stowe the Litchfield parsonage, particularly in its kitchen bounds, also retained touches of intimacy despite its rambling amplitude. In it were displayed, for example, "little works of ingenuity, and taste, and skill," including needle and embroidery pieces, or "pictures of birds and flowers, done with minutest skill,"[28] wrought by her saintly, departed mother.

It is particularly worth noting how Tom's Kentucky home, which Stowe sometimes calls a "cottage," defines the locus of Stowe's chief convictions for the novel as a whole. This dwelling is the point of departure for Stowe's two main strands of plot development—not only for Tom's forced journey south, as he is cruelly separated from his home and family but also for Eliza's escape to the North and Canada, as she desperately "turns her footsteps" from the cabin just before running away. The atmosphere of human warmth and domesticity that Stowe evokes here encourages an emotional recognition, on the part of her mostly white readership, that commonplace familial and marital ties do indeed matter to African Americans. Such recognition was scarcely to be taken for granted at the time. And in that pivotal early chapter titled "An Evening in Uncle Tom's Cabin," the cottage's portrayal of a richly shared humanity is rendered all the more vivid by the presence there of George Shelby, the familiarity of whose comingling with his family's slaves allows readers to glimpse what a beloved community of multiracial harmony might actually look and sound like.

As it turns out, Tom's cottage serves not only as a home but also as an informal worship space. Its heartfelt Christian liturgy, featuring the "wild and spirited" singing of gospel-inspired texts, draws a "motley assemblage" of cross-generational participants beyond Tom's family. The common prayer enacted here is also, significantly, cross-racial because it includes young George, who is enlisted as a scripture reader and offers some exegetical commentary. But the evident leader of this racially mixed congregation is Tom, acknowledged to be "a sort of patriarch in religious matters," "a sort of minister among them," and a living model of prayer (26). Yet another subtly subversive feature of the domestic scene in chapter four shows George engaged in teaching Tom the rudiments of reading. Such instruction, then discouraged in Kentucky, was strictly illegal in several southern states.

If Tom serves as the high priest of prayer services in this log sanctuary, Aunt Chloe is the presiding spirit of its food preparation and other domestic functions. In *Uncle Tom's Cabin*, as in other of her works, Stowe dwells at length on the rituals associated with preparing and consuming food. Stationed beside the fire, Chloe confidently fulfills her role as head chef, because "a cook she certainly was, in the very bone and centre of her soul" (17). Neither is it coincidental that in the same evening Tom's cottage becomes the site of eating as well as of worship, as Stowe understands both to be sacramental. She portrays shared meals, even if they are other than formally Eucharistic, to be the enactment par excellence of Christian fellowship. The common meal that Chloe celebrates likewise includes Master George, who dines by preference with God's "lowly" brethren rather than in the owner's halls. And in the company of such brethren, he relishes the "smoking batter-cakes" that Chloe heaps on his plate.

A complementary picture of sacramental love emerges several chapters later, when the fugitives Eliza and George Harris are reunited in the Quaker settlement. Here a homey kitchen and dining space in Indiana function as sacred space, the Quaker equivalent of a church temple whose priest is another woman. Rachel Halliday is portrayed as chief celebrant for this sacramental enactment of God's Kingdom, a meal that New England Puritans might well have called a "converting ordinance" by virtue of its effect on George Harris:

> Rachel never looked so truly and benignly happy as at the head of her table. There was so much motherliness and full-heartedness

even in the way she passed a plate of cakes or poured a cup of coffee, that it seemed to put a spirit into the food and drink she offered. It was the first time George had sat down on equal terms at any white man's table . . . This, indeed, was a *home*,—home,— a word that George had never yet known a meaning for; and a belief in God, and trust in his providence, began to encircle his heart, as, with a golden cloud of protection and confidence, dark, misanthropic, pining, atheistic doubts, and fierce despair, melted away before the light of a living Gospel, breathed in living faces . . . . (122)

A few years later, in her third novel, Stowe imagines yet another female celebrant of sacramental domesticity in the person of Mary Scudder, a leading character in *The Minister's Wooing*. Newly married and mistress of a stately new dwelling in eighteenth-century Newport, Rhode Island, this New England woman is presented in the book's closing scene as a "saint" who "has passed into that appointed shrine for woman, more holy than cloister, more saintly and pure than church or altar,—a *Christian home*. Priestess, wife, and mother, there she ministers daily in holy works of household peace, and by faith and prayer and love redeems from grossness and earthliness the common toils and wants of life."[29]

In *Uncle Tom's Cabin*, however, the spiritual solace of a home place is the story's point of departure rather than its endpoint. From the comparative warmth and fellowship of Tom's cottage, this narrative moves swiftly toward a destructive dispersal of black members, tearing asunder all their natural bonds and impressions of "home" while allowing us to glimpse poignant interludes at houses of refuge along the way. One such dwelling, where Eliza and her child are first sheltered after their perilous river crossing, is the Ohio farmhouse of John Van Trompe, owner of a stop on the Underground Railroad and modeled on the real-life John Van Zandt. In Stowe's portrayal of episodes such as this, actuality is strangely interfused with imaginative creation. Stowe's husband, Calvin, had once actually escorted a fleeing servant of theirs to John Van Zandt's cabin. Another leading prototype of Eliza, a slave woman who had actually escaped across ice floes on the Ohio River, found refuge with the Rev. John Rankin, from whom Stowe learned that tale and whose home in Ripley she may have visited. For good reason, though, Stowe avoids all mention of Rankin in her novel.[30] And in yet another actual dwelling that figures in the imaginative weave of Eliza Harris's flight, in this case the Stowe residence up in Brunswick, Maine, where Stowe composed much of her novel, the author, too, had once sheltered a fugitive slave overnight.

While Eliza's story unfolds in the one direction, Tom in the other is temporarily graced with comfortable shelter and relatively benign servitude when he arrives at the New Orleans mansion of his new owner, Augustine St. Clare. St. Clare's home is described as "luxurious and romantic," a kind of semitropical pleasure palace. Constructed in a Moorish mode, with an exotic blend of Spanish and French architectural styles, this mansion is set in marked contrast to the neatly ordered, sober New England farmhouse from which St. Clare's cousin, Miss Ophelia, has come to visit. The mansion's courtyard "had evidently been arranged to gratify a picturesque and voluptuous ideality." This voluptuous impression is heightened by a Poesque blend of "arabesque ornaments" (140–141), Moorish arches, pillars, a fountain, and a colorful array of tropical plants. The St. Clare villa on Lake Pontchartrain suggests an even more appealing taste of earthly paradise, with its "gardens and pleasure grounds" (226), its prospect of glorious summer sunsets over water.

Stowe was scarcely immune to the attractions of living in such settings. The cottage in Mandarin, Florida, that she purchased later in life was a site where she and Calvin enjoyed escaping New England's winters to live in semitropical warmth, amid the lush beauty of orange and olive trees. Ultimately, though, the opulent elegance of the St. Clare mansion is shown to be illusory. Just as its architecture "carried the mind back, as in a dream, to the reign of oriental romance in Spain" (141), so also its claim to legitimacy is a false dream, a culture's self-serving fantasy that the good life, a life of beauty and ease for the few, could be permanently constructed from the slave labor of many. Despite the redemptive presence of Tom and Evangeline as saints in residence, the house's motivating conception is unreal, insubstantial. Its sustaining spirit is transient, as is its master—St. Clare—who is soon to pass from the world.

Thanks to the influence of Tom and Eva, Augustine St. Clare first undergoes a conversion of heart that brings him, on his deathbed, to an assurance that in dying he is "coming HOME, at last" (276). Yet St. Clare's untimely death is so disruptive for Tom that he must live out the remainder of his days in places that are a grotesque parody of home. Accordingly, the building beside which Tom is sold at auction in New Orleans is no house at all but a "warehouse," a kind of whitened sepulcher whose outward face of propriety disguises the abominations enacted within:

> A slave warehouse! Perhaps some of my readers conjure up horrible visions of such a place . . . . But no, innocent friend; in these days men have learned the art of sinning expertly and genteelly, so as not to shock the eyes and sense of respectable society. Human property is high in the market; and is, therefore, well fed, well cleaned, tended, and looked after, that it may come to sale sleek, and strong, and shining. A slave-warehouse in New Orleans is a house externally not much unlike many others, kept with neatness; and where every day you may see arranged, under a sort of shed along the outside, rows of men and women, who stand there as a sign of the property sold within." (282)

Even more ghastly is Tom's final earthly residence, situated on the hellish plantation of Simon Legree. Not only ghastly but for Legree ghostly as well. Cassy and Evangeline, two slaves who persuade Legree that the house is haunted by playing on his credulity, thus engineer their escape from the plantation.[31] And unlike the gracious elegance with which mythology of the Old South is apt to clothe the homes of wealthy planters, Legree's House of Pride is a sinkhole of despair. Instead of whitewashed grand pillars, the edifice displays a thoroughly decayed gentility, a ruin that befits the moral geography of its address in one of the "dark places of the earth":

> The house had been large and handsome. It was built in a manner common at the South; a wide verandah of two stories running round every part of the house, into which every outer door opened, the lower tier being supported by brick pillars.
>
> But the place looked desolate and uncomfortable; some windows stopped up with boards, some with shattered panes, and shutters hanging by a single hinge,—all telling of coarse neglect and discomfort. (298–99)

For Stowe such a place, where Cassy says "'the Lord never visits'" (306), is the antithesis of Tom's aspiration, as memorably phrased in Psalm 23, to "dwell in the house of the Lord for ever." And in the face of Tom's brutal demise, it is worth recalling that he had earlier fixed his mind on the biblical assurance that "in my father's house there are many mansions" (125, with reference to John 14:2)—none of them, presumably, owned or inhabited by the likes of Simon Legree.

Stowe and her Puritan forebears were steeped in the biblical–Augustinian teaching that not only Tom but all humans are transient pilgrims who ultimately own nothing, who possess no permanent home on earth. Prior to the publication of *Uncle Tom's Cabin*, Stowe had never lived in a home that she owned.

While extolling the virtues of home rootedness, she was also being schooled in detachment. The first house that Harriet and Calvin Stowe both designed for themselves and to which they held property title was one where they resided only briefly. They soon had to leave "Oakholm," the dream house in Hartford where they moved when Harriet was already fifty-three years old, because it turned out to be too grand and expensive for their means.[32]

Yet the ideal of a home-place remains pivotal throughout *Uncle Tom's Cabin*. The architectural trajectory of this novel takes us from that early signature scene by the sacred hearth fire of Tom's cottage in Kentucky, through the desolation of Legree's plantation mansion, to a visionary chapter of "Concluding Remarks" situated once again in the fireside solace of a home.[33] Stowe directs her final sermonic exhortation to all America, but especially to its northern white mothers—to "you, who have learned, by the cradles of your own children, to love and feel for all mankind, by the sacred love you bear your child" (384). The author's peroration combines a jeremiad strain of apocalyptic warning, about the horrid wrath to come if her nation refuses to repent its original sin of slavery, with a divine promise of how the Union might still be "saved" (388).

Significantly, that promise of salvation, theologically allied for Stowe to participation in the invisible Kingdom of God, is presented to "men and women of America" not as they are gathered in church or meeting house, but as they sit in fireside reflection at home—to those whom Stowe imagines reading "this book by the blaze of your winter-evening fire" (384). So we can see the author's appeal to an elemental goodness, charity, and sanctity as figured in the familial hearth coming full circle in this book.

But what about the afterlife of Harriet's real-life houses? What further stories might they tell? Some of the homes where Stowe resided during her lifetime still stand today. These structures include the house on 73 Forest Street in Hartford, where she lived for several decades and ended her days. It is now well maintained as a museum and tourist site, adjoining headquarters of the Harriet Beecher Stowe Center with its extensive archives. Her former home in Cincinnati, at 2950 Gilbert Avenue, is another historic site open to the public. The house in Brunswick, Maine, where she wrote most of *Uncle Tom's Cabin* and once sheltered a fugitive slave during her residence in 1850–1851 has undergone several stages of renovation over the years and is not open to visitors. Owned today by Bowdoin College, which had sometimes housed students there (including Henry Wadsworth Longfellow) before and after Stowe's time of occupancy, the building has also served variously as a restaurant, inn, and private residence. Also closed to general visitors is the stone structure in Andover, Massachusetts, that the Stowes renovated before moving there from Brunswick and that today provides student living quarters for Phillips Academy. Andover might qualify, though, as Stowe's final address in America as she is buried in that town.

The later fate of Stowe's birthplace, the Beecher home originally situated on North Street in Litchfield, Connecticut, is especially intriguing. First constructed around 1775, the structure was enlarged considerably by the Beechers after they took up residence there in 1810, shortly before Harriet's birth the following year. Well before Stowe's death in 1896, the house was moved from its original site and became a sanitarium residence. It then served in Litchfield as a dormitory for the Spring Hill School and later for the Forman Preparatory School.

In 1996, after administrators for the Forman School decided they no longer wished to try maintaining the deteriorating structure, they declared it up for sale. But a purchaser would need to remove it from its site on the Forman campus and to face costly repairs. So for a time the house seemed a prime candidate for the wrecking ball. A writer for the *New York Times* reported in 1996 that the Beecher parsonage, birthplace of the famous author who had created Eliza Harris, was now as "defenseless as Eliza crossing the ice."[34]

At this point Mr. Chandler Saint, a preservationist with a background in antique sales, came to the rescue. Zealous to preserve the Beecher–Stowe legacy he saw embodied in the house, he proposed not only to disassemble, move, and restore it, but also to make it the centerpiece of a public museum and educational center. As he envisioned it, such a center would effectively honor and extend in our own day the advances in equal rights that Harriet and her public-spirited siblings had championed. The proposal offered by Saint and his associate, Stephen Solley, was accepted. They took possession of the building for $1. Then, over the course of six months, Saint oversaw the painstaking process of disassembling the entire house, recording in detailed notes just how its pieces would need to be reconstructed, and preserving or uncovering remaining hints of period décor or artifacts.

It was a formidable task, a labor of love for which Saint and his dedicated workers might well have expected public recognition. And in August of 2000, a well-attended, festive celebration of this accomplishment was held in Litchfield. It included a parade, led by horse-mounted members of a Revolutionary War unit specially recommissioned for the occasion by then-Governor John Rowland, musket fire, and a speech by Connecticut Attorney General Richard Blumenthal. Two truck trailers containing disassembled pieces of the house had been moved to the site in Litchfield where Saint planned to reassemble it. Attorney General Blumenthal described the project in glowing terms, praising Chandler Saint as a visionary whose initiative had saved for posterity a building of genuine historical significance.

But certain parties closely associated with Litchfield politics and civic life soon aroused further skepticism about this project and about the reliability of its chief promoter. State officials also began to withdraw their support. Just as *Uncle Tom's Cabin* proved to be enormously controversial but for diverse reasons, both around the time of its publication and subsequently, so also the status of Harriet's house in Litchfield has occasioned several stages of dispute, dissension, intrigue, and legal wrangling lasting more than a decade. Saint has even found himself at odds with bodies such as the Litchfield Historical Society and the Connecticut Historical Commission. Early on, his plan to move the house to a central site in Litchfield's historic district drew heated opposition from residents, complaints so intense that Saint set his trailers full of house parts out on the road and into hiding. The house, he announced, had been sent for its safety on "the Underground Railroad." And he has ever since insisted on maintaining secrecy about the trailers' location.

Saint's detractors have questioned his qualifications, his finances, the undisclosed identity of his financial backers, and what they perceive to be his imperious manner. Some wonder whether the Beecher house, having been so altered over the years and with a dearth of period elements remaining, would have a useful future as an historical museum even if it is successfully rebuilt. Above all, critics objected to Saint's bid to place the house squarely in Litchfield's historic district. Eventually, concerns about zoning or other legal complications, and about the disruption expected to follow from drawing tourist buses into the center of town, stirred enough opposition that Saint felt inclined to seek another site beyond Litchfield. By 2004 it looked as though an agreement had been reached to reconstruct the house, as the centerpiece of an educational venture known as the Beecher House Center for The History of Equal Rights, on land near the University of Connecticut's Torrington campus and in conjunction with the site of John Brown's childhood home in Torrington. But the project would require sizable funding. So this venture, too, has thus far failed to materialize.

Even Chandler Saint's supporters acknowledge his eccentricity. Yet from Saint's point of view, the Beecher House deserves to be restored and preserved for symbolic as well as practical reasons—as something of a shrine to the inspirational values he believes the Beecher family so forcefully embodied. He points out that to honor this dwelling is to honor not only Harriet, who spent here the first formative years of her life until she was thirteen, but also such noteworthy figures as Lyman, Catharine, Isabella, and Henry Ward Beecher. As I know from having met Mr. Saint on more than one occasion, he is a man of intense resolve with considerable knowledge of trade-carpentry lore and historic matters. And having participated in one of his programs on behalf of the Beecher House Society, I must say, too, that his dedication to the cause of moral and historically informed education strikes me as authentic.

Along the way, Saint also enlisted for his cause the support of a celebrated American who had himself once been a resident in the Beecher House. Folksinger and activist Pete Seeger recalled having boarded on the house's second floor in the late 1920s, while a student at the Spring Hill School. In interviews, Seeger testified that the campaign to preserve this house was part of the larger cause—under whose banner both Stowe and he had served—to defend human rights, dignity, and community in America. In this real-life story with a flavor of fiction, the promotional video for the Beecher House Society that Saint sponsored concludes with a clip of Pete Seeger singing—what else?—"We Shall Overcome."

Despite the advocacy of Seeger, who died in 2014, the obstacles to reconstructing and re-siting Harriet's house have yet to be overcome. So the author's original home remains a homeless heap of fragments. Yet it may be fitting that the house itself should have become yet another spirit-wanderer without an address. Such a condition resembles, after all, the homeless state of those slave fugitives with whom Stowe had identified so memorably in her greatest book. So if the author's living soul now resides anywhere on earth, it is probably in that space of imagination that Henry James—an outspoken admirer of *Uncle Tom's Cabin*—called the "house of fiction."

WHEN HOUSES ARE NO LONGER HOMES

In Willa Cather's novel *The Professor's House*, as in Hawthorne's *Gables*, a timeworn domicile steeped in personal and collective memory draws our attention from the first. And Cather's story, like Hawthorne's, illustrates how accumulated wealth can prove to be more of a curse than a blessing to heirs of the deceased. But in Cather's novel the inheritance takes the form of monetary holdings rather than real estate. It derives from a breakthrough in aviation technology achieved by Tom Outland, a young genius and casualty of combat in Flanders during World War I.

And in Cather's story, unlike Hawthorne's, the old house in question is already all but abandoned at the start. Her novel opens, in fact, on a note of melancholic displacement. The story's lead character, Professor Godfrey St. Peter, is slated to move from the midwestern domicile he has occupied for decades into a new house "into which he did not want to move."[35] As Marilyn Chandler observes, the protagonist is torn between the claims of these two houses, which "represent conflicting values and competing ways of life."[36]

The old house offers no glamor or amenities. Poorly designed and in need of repair, this three-story dwelling is "almost as ugly as it is possible for a house to be" (103). Unlike the new house, funded by a history prize Godfrey won for his scholarly *magnum opus* on Spanish adventurers in North America, it was a rental property for which St. Peter's family never claimed legal ownership. Yet long after Godfrey is supposed to have relocated, he insists on continuing to work in his familiar study on the top floor. Under this room, strangely adorned with dressmaker's forms, "was a dead, empty house" (106). Although Godfrey's attic study is drafty and poorly heated by a faulty gas stove, he refuses to leave it behind.

Why this stubborn attachment? What does it signify about Godfrey's sense of place—and sense of self—at a troubled stage of life when relations to his wife, his two adult daughters, and his sons-in-law have all become more or less strained and unsatisfying?

Part of the reason Godfrey feels "doggedly anchored" (264) to the old house, even when it is no longer a home, is attributable to the recollections it holds within its walls. For him, the house is haunted by memories of happier times, past years when his love for his wife, for his daughters, and for his extraordinary student and protégé Tom Outland retained a vibrancy he has long since lost. No longer engaged by the warmth and beauty of feminine associations that once fed his psychic anima, he clings to the company of those dressmaker's forms in his study as meager compensation for that loss.

At one level, then, the vacant house embodies Godfrey's prematurely diminished state of being at the age of fifty-two—Cather's own age at the time of the novel's publication. So it is fair to perceive, on Cather's part, some autobiographical investment in the professor's ennui.[37] Afflicted with a form of late-midlife angst, Godfrey feels he no longer belongs—surely not in the new house, nor in the sustained company of his own family members. He cannot cease grieving the loss of Tom Outland, questions the purpose of his life, and becomes thoroughly absorbed by the prospect of mortality.

But the house, as a repository of memory and dreams, also holds a strain of favorable meaning. Godfrey St. Peter, whose disposition might be self-defined by means of his Christian name as one "free of God," shows no overt sign of piety or religious practice, despite the exemplar of faith recalled in his surname. Yet his study space is the closest thing he knows to a *sanctum sanctorum*, and he cherishes the house's "walled-in garden," which he tends religiously, as "the comfort of his life" (105). Even as he feels more and more fatigued, engulfed by the sea of worldliness, avarice, and strife rising around him, he treasures the house—especially his attic study—as a contemplative island of repose. Ironically, the upstairs room offers him domestic refuge from the otherwise oppressive drama of domestic life. He feels safe behind his study desk, in this "hole no one could creep into" (196). Only there can he enjoy ample space to think, to order his thoughts, to ponder and prepare Tom Outland's diary for publication.

He also feels in this house, the scene of many visits he and his family members had once shared with Tom Outland, all the more connected to the spirit of his dead friend. In a letter Cather wrote in 1939, she observes that it was "Because Tom Outland was in the Professor's house so much during his student life" that Godfrey perceived his life with Outland to have been "just as real and vivid to him as his life with his family."[38] The house thus becomes, for Godfrey at least, a palpable memorial of his friend. It stands in reproachful contrast to the new home that one of his daughters and her husband have built and named "Outland," intending the place to become something of a '"memorial to him'" (121). For Godfrey, such designation for a building Tom could never have known about or visited is misplaced reverence, verging on sacrilege.

And Godfrey understood that for Tom Outland '"a reverence for this place'" (234) is precisely what the young prodigy had felt about his discovery of several ancient, cliff-hung villages hidden away in the Blue Mesa territory of New Mexico. This sighting had evidently been a defining episode of Tom's life. It remained for him thereafter a luminous experience, despite the failure of governmental agencies and others to recognize the find's larger significance. Sheltered within two other sections of Cather's narrative, "Tom Outland's Story" suggests that coming upon this marvelous site offered Tom a glimpse of the numinous. Tom, after he "began housekeeping" (227) with his companion inside the Cliff City and absorbed more of its atmosphere, confesses thinking of this settlement no longer as "an adventure," but as evocative of "a religious emotion" (253). Here, if anywhere, he perceives the residual presence of a *genius loci*.[39]

The people who once inhabited the place had suffered extermination, the artifacts and structures of their well-developed civilization having been preserved unseen for centuries in an isolated, presumably inaccessible canyon. This radical seclusion certainly enhanced the sense of sacred enchantment Tom perceives there—as does Godfrey, albeit mostly at one remove. It is a place whose silence and stillness still resonates, even for those who only read about it. Its participation in the "calmness of eternity" is unforgettable. Tom reports that after climbing atop the mesa, he had "the glorious feeling that I've never had anywhere else . . . in a world above the world." And he recognizes the great round tower rising out of the city of stone as a "fine thing," expressing the lofty aspirations of an extinct people. Father Duchene, a Belgian-French priest who had served as Tom's language tutor and assists in the excavation project, observes that "Wherever humanity has made that hardest of all starts and lifted itself out of mere brutality, is a sacred spot" (234, 221, 246). It is in such a transcendent space that Godfrey, ensconced in his study, still imagines Tom residing—along with part of himself. Especially the part that cringes to think of beginning a new life in a new house (Figure 1.1).

Tom—along with Godfrey, by imaginative extension—cherishes that ancient abode of cliff dwellers not only as a

HOUSES OF THE SPIRIT | 47

FIGURE 1.1 Anasazi Cliff Dwellings in Bandelier National Monument, New Mexico. P. Shaw, Shutterstock. Photo.

sacred sanctuary but as the closest thing to his own home place. Tom points out that, as soon he and his partner finish building their cabin shelter on top of the mesa, they hasten to begin what he calls "housekeeping" (227). The mesa terrain, though not the land of Tom's birth, evidently becomes by adoption his true country, his *patria*. In this light one should recall Cather's remarks in her earlier novel *My Ántonia*, in which her narrator understands Virgil's claim in the Georgics to have brought the Muse into his country—*in patriam mecum*—as referring not to "the capital, the *palatial Romana*," but rather with localized affection "to his own little 'country'; to his father's fields, 'sloping down to the river and to the old beech trees with broken tops.'"[40] Likewise in *The Professor's House*, when Tom visits Washington DC to report on his archaeological findings, his instinctual reverence for the larger nation's capital soon evaporates. At first, stepping "off the train, just behind the Capitol building, one cold bright January morning," he says he had "stood for a long while watching the white dome against a flashing blue sky, with a very religious feeling" (237). But after encountering the city's soulless bureaucracy, he finds he "wanted nothing but to get back to the mesa and live a free life and breathe free air, and never, never again to see hundreds of little black-coated men pouring out of white buildings" (243–244).

The Professor's House does not end on a hopeful note. The only hint of meaning and numinous joy remaining to Godfrey lies in a recollected past and above all through his vicarious participation in "Tom Outland's Story." Cather, too, found access to transcendent meaning or religious experience mediated most reliably at one remove, through artistic expression of the sort embodied in her Outland story—even though she too, like Godfrey, had personally visited scenes in the Southwest. As Godfrey declared in one of his classroom lectures, "Art and religion (they are the same thing, in the end of course), have given man the only happiness he has ever had" (137). His pronouncement corresponds to a central article of Cather's own religious creed.[41]

Despite the impressions of unsettled gloom that surround the novel's close, Godfrey does at least attain a Stoic resolve to accept his lot and confront his mortality. He accepts not only mortality, as he had lately welcomed a deathly release all too readily, but also the need to continue enduring a diminished life. It is worth recalling that, by virtue of his original baptismal name, Godfrey is also a "Napoleon" (198) and ultimately reflects at least one dimension of his namesake's character and circumstance. Not Napoleon as world conqueror or statesman. Rather the man who, after repeated losses and defeat, must now look to conclude his life in secluded exile from the world. The professor knows he does not really belong in the new house and cannot stay much longer in the old. In this regard he mirrors once again something of Cather's malaise about no longer quite belonging in a world she perceived to have broken in two "in 1922 or thereabouts."[42] Moreover, this restless author had, while writing *The Professor's House,* made her home, such as it was, in neither of the two regions where the novel is primarily situated—not on the midwestern plains nor in the Southwest—but in New York City. Still, we are told that Godfrey in the end "thought he knew where he was" (271). He is resigned now to living in the new house—not cheerfully, but likely sustaining a blend of inward detachment and outward civility. Although the affirmation here is soberly tentative, Godfrey's knowing "where he was" suggests that he does manage at last to reclaim a modest place for himself—existentially, at least, if not so definitively within spatial or social boundaries.

Home rootedness and the once-venerated spiritual wellsprings of domestic life are qualities conspicuous by their absence in several contemporary novels. To be sure, a perceived need to escape rather than to seek home shelter has long-standing force in American culture. Fiction prior to our own time presents us with a colorful gallery of free spirits disdainful of domesticity, including Mark Twain's Huck Finn and Jack Kerouac's vagrants on the open road. But the topos of homelessness is especially prominent in contemporary novels. Two such cases might be noted here briefly by way of illustration: Marilynne Robinson's *Housekeeping* and Ernest Gaines's *In My Father's House.*

The pivotal irony of Robinson's *Housekeeping* is that its two central characters, in their instinctual pursuit of the soul's release and self-transcendence, feel drawn to transcend all forms of worldly housekeeping. Sylvie, the narrator's altogether eccentric aunt and guardian, had long preferred to live as a vagrant, "an unredeemed transient."[43] By the story's close, her niece Ruth has likewise embraced homelessness. Both are drawn into the vortex of elemental, chthonic forces, comparable to the floodwaters rising from nearby Fingerbone Lake, that set them at odds with their community's expectations of settled domesticity and social propriety. Linked to the wilder darkness of a forest world, the aptly named Sylvie is aptly described by Ruth as "not a stable person" (82). To most readers, the singularity of her conduct seems by turns comical and unsettling. Sylvie hoards vast numbers of cans and newspapers, boards more than a dozen cats, gathers fish in her pockets, and fails to satisfy what her community considers even minimal standards of household maintenance or parental discipline. She displays a radically contemplative disposition through her preference to sit in silent darkness, to eat only cold food, and to avoid pursuing outside employment or interaction with neighbors. When her guardianship of Ruth is threatened, she torches and abandons their house in Fingerbone, making a perilous escape with Ruth by walking, through a long windy night, across the narrow railroad bridge stretching above Fingerbone Lake.

The house, previously overshadowed by the lake, is now in some sense overpowered by those untamed, potentially destructive forces the lake embodies. Ruth believes that she and Sylvie must abandon for all time not only this house but all forms of domestic rootedness because "Now truly we were cast out to wander, and there was an end to housekeeping" (209).

Despite her oddities, Sylvie embodies the ultimately homeless state of all humanity. Ruth, as she learns to "break the tethers of need, one by one" (204), follows in spirit a *via negativa* path into which Sylvie has led her. Yet Robinson's novel underscores the point that *all* mortal humans must walk at last the way of total dispossession, passage through an abyss as narrow as Fingerbone's railroad bridge. As narrow as the grave. The sorrow of our existential condition, as Ruth perceives it, is that finally "every soul is put out of house" (179). Neither our dwellings nor our bodies are really built to last.

Robinson's outlook coincides, moreover, with traditional Christian and Calvinist reminders that all mortal creatures are transients. No worldly habitation is permanent. In William Bradford's classic account, the Separatist settlers who founded Plymouth Plantation, after taking leave from their households in Holland, felt sorely convicted of this truth. Yet they found some solace in recognizing they had no permanent resting place on earth, because "they knew they were pilgrims, and looked not so much on those things, but lift up their eyes to the heavens, their dearest country, and quieted their spirits."[44]

For Robinson, too, all of us are more wanderers, if not pilgrims, than we may suppose. And passage through a *via negativa* shrouded in divine mystery is ordinarily needed for wanderers, having left their houses, if they are ever to "find a way home" (195). A poetic pronouncement in chapter four of *Housekeeping* captures the essence of this spirituality, centered in the willingness to accept total dispossession and ultimate homelessness:

> Every spirit passing through the world fingers the tangible and mars the mutable, and finally has come to look and not to buy. So shoes are worn and hassocks are sat upon and finally everything is left where it was and the spirit passes on.... (73)

Published in 1978, *In My Father's House* by Ernest Gaines dramatizes even more distressing consequences of exclusion from one's home place on the part of its main characters, father and son. At the outset of the story Phillip Martin, the African American pastor of Solid Rock Baptist Church in a small Louisiana town, is outwardly successful—at the high point of his career, in fact—but ripe for a fall. He loses most everything he cares about when he does fall, a turn of events signaled by his literal collapsing onto the floor of his home after the shock of their reencountering a son he had fathered out of wedlock and then abandoned more than twenty years earlier. A more graphic illustration of what Christian tradition commonly describes as humanity's "fallen" state is hard to imagine.[45]

Phillip now enjoyed an enviable share of material prosperity. His ranch-style brick house was the most elegant and expensive in town. His wife was a patient, loving woman, and he had been blessed with three children, a son and two daughters. Many admired his stalwart leadership of local civil rights activities on behalf of African Americans during a crucial period of social ferment following the assassination of Martin Luther King. Those who regarded him as an inspiring example even took to calling him "Our Martin Luther King."[46] Yet he himself appreciated that it was only by virtue of grace and his conversion to Christian faith that he had managed to leave behind his former dissolute life of drunkenness, womanizing, and gambling.

Or *almost* managed to leave it all behind. Never having come to terms with a past he had thus far willed to forget, Phillip is simply undone when a long-forgotten son suddenly appears on the scene—shows up, in fact, at a party in his own home. Phillip had never acknowledged this young man, whose Christian name he cannot now even recall, as belonging to the "house" or lineage of Martin. Phillip's current family members and neighbors knew nothing of his existence. But his son had now stepped without warning into "his father's house." Why so? Young Etienne, who introduces himself in town as "Robert X," has apparently been driven there by desperation. The anguish he bears is such that "My soul don't feel good ... Like garbage, broke glass, tin cans. Any trash" (25). At night his landlady hears him screaming loudly, pacing restlessly in his room. In response to the ruined life to which he believes Phillip had condemned him and other members of his birth family, Etienne says he means to kill this deadbeat father—but ends up killing himself instead. Yet Phillip, feeling convicted by his past failure to make a place in his life for this son, had become desperate in turn to form a parental bond. In this endeavor, too, he fails, but in the process feels pressured into betraying his leadership of a civil rights showdown in a way that destroys his reputation and alienates him from nearly everyone around him.

These setbacks lead Phillip toward despair. They seriously erode his trust in God, whose silence torments him. And with the loss of his Christian faith, Phillip loses all faith in himself. The story closes without a clear resolution or assurance of this pastor's recovery in future. We can discern less space for encounter with the numinous in Gaines's novel than in Robinson's.

It is telling, though, that the biblical text (John 14: 1–2) Phillip chose for a Sunday sermon he was never fated never to preach so conspicuously recalls the novel's title while affirming the wideness of another Father's welcome into the House of God:

> Let not your heart be troubled; ye believe in God, believe also in me. In my Father's house are many mansions; if it were not so, I would have told you. I go to prepare a place for you. (54).

In the light of Phillip's predictable failure to find a place for Etienne in his own home, is the sense of this allusion purely ironic? I think not. Gaines's portrayal of Phillip is more sympathetic than satiric, despite the minister's self-deception and disastrous misdeeds. But while Phillip goes wrong when he allows himself for personal reasons to betray and deny his people, he does so out of love rather than malice. And while he deserves blame for his faulty parenting of Etienne, both originally and subsequently, there is surely a poignant, Christological resonance in his twice-stated resolve to avoid "denying him twice" (58; see also 41).

When Phillip falls to manic hopelessness in the novel's final scene, his wife and another woman try to console him. Beverly, a woman friend, reminds him of the grounds for gratitude he still possesses, the wife who stands ready to support him, and the service he might still hope to render to others. Above all, in the face of his obsession with earlier progeny and misery at losing his son, she reminds him that "Patrick is your son too, isn't he? Isn't Patrick your son, Reverend Martin?" (213).

Despite everything that has gone wrong, Phillip is indeed still a father, still owner of a house containing several chambers and room for error. For that matter he still is, or might once again perceive himself to be, someone's son—indeed by one account a beloved child of God, invited to occupy the place prepared for him in his Father's house.

Given the tale's ambiguous ending, we are left wondering whether Phillip ever accepts the invitations he is offered for renewal and recovery. To find his way back to spiritual and bodily health, he will need to revise his belief in the once-and-for-all transformation his conversion was supposed to have effected. He will need to curb his fondness for status and wealth, to shed delusions of persevering through his own strength and self-sufficiency so as to rely instead on the grace mediated through members of his community, especially through the caring women who surround him. The way back will be arduous. Recovery remains possible, though, because help for Pastor Martin is at hand if he chooses to use it. Thus, after he finally thinks he can do nothing but confess "I'm lost," it is fitting that Alma, Phillip's long-suffering and aptly named wife,[47] should have the last words: "Shhh," she said. "Shhh, Shhh, We just go'n have to start again" (214).

In these literary frames of reference, someone's house fails either to become or to remain a home. Such is likewise the actual experience of many present-day Americans, of course, as the coherence of communities and ties to extended families continue to erode in this age of heightened mobility. Prospects for claiming "membership" in a community of trust and care, as Wendell Berry names it throughout his fiction, seem less and less promising for each succeeding generation. Berry's novel *Hannah Coulter* dramatizes this point with painful cogency. By now, for good or ill, the once-celebrated American dream of home ownership has also faded for many young adults. And it has been evident for some time that houses here, typically of wood-frame construction, are not built to last in the way European dwellings have traditionally been.

Still, even for those endlessly on the move, the idea or ideal of identification with a home place retains its appeal. And as Bachelard's topo-analysis would suppose, imagination still fastens, even here and now, on the need to find not just physical shelter but a home setting of one sort or another. The homing instinct in play when America celebrates Thanksgiving, that most distinctive and quasi-religious national holiday of ours, with its flurry of migratory motion from far-flung addresses toward something resembling home ground, testifies to this. House structures, whenever they effectively embody our placement in a home, continue to figure as loci of meaning, as sites where spirits reside and memories are housed.

Particularly in the case of older structures, the memories in question are not merely individual recollections, drawn from the experience of current tenants. Old houses often serve as repositories of a broader-gauged collective memory, reaching across generations and beyond anyone's personal lifetime. I think, for example, of all the stories still held within the walls of the colonial-era New England farmhouse, dating from 1732, where I lived for thirteen years just before moving to Tennessee. It is situated in Windham Center, Connecticut, a relatively secluded village that still looks much as it had, at least with respect to outward architecture, prior to the industrial era. For many years, the house had served as a vicarage for the Episcopal Church, immediately adjacent, that my wife served as pastor. So it was, in fact, another "old manse," a home we did not own, with artifacts from that clerical past still strewn about in the attic, basement, and wall spaces. Like Hawthorne's Old Manse,[48] it even held on a pane of period window glass someone's fondly etched message.

Although I am not particularly superstitious, I could not help feeling that a dwelling such as this, which had seen a multitude of births and deaths and lives transpiring within it, continued to be haunted—in the mostly benign sense—by such spirits from the past. As I have reason to believe, this house had also absorbed into its walls a good deal of earnest prayer. The same is true, so far as I can determine, of my current home in Sewanee, Tennessee. Built around 1871 at the initiative of William Mercer Green, first Episcopal bishop of the Diocese of Mississippi, the house's earliest residents were all associated with the Confederacy—a circumstance that called for some adjustment, from an unreconstructed Yankee like me, after I first took up residence in the South. Yet the presence of a saintly woman who had lived here for decades, from 1967 to the close of the century, still permeates this space, partly by virtue of the stories about her that older neighbors have shared with me. T. S. Eliot, in the concluding poem of his *Four Quartets*, writes of how an encounter with sacred space, particularly some historically hallowed site "Where prayer has been valid," can open toward transcendent experience. For Eliot personally, the chapel he once visited, preserved from Nicholas Ferrar's seventeenth-century community of Little Gidding in Cambridgeshire, was one such place.

Yet private homes, no less than churches, have long been favored sites for spirits to dwell, settings "where prayer has been valid." Such is the point Stowe underscores, as she dramatizes toward the outset of her novel the enspirited life that manages to survive even in a modest slave cabin. Stowe was also cognizant that such a scene reenacts, in turn, the worship once conducted in house churches of the primitive Christian church, or for that matter, the domestic setting of Jewish rituals still practiced today.

2

SPIRITS OF PILGRIMAGE, PEREGRINATION, AND RE-PLACEMENT

MOVING ON AND BEGINNING AGAIN

It can be taken as axiomatic that present-day Americans, more than their forebears, are susceptible to rootlessness and anomie. Particularly for those who pursue higher education, prospects for belonging to any form of traditional village culture are rare.[1] Whatever address we claim, our sense of place is also eroded, or so it seems, by the desire or perceived need to relocate our living quarters every few years. And lately eroded still more by pressures unforeseen only a few decades before. As one cultural commentator observes, "for today's mobile citizens, place matters very little; it is an obstacle that technology painlessly overcomes." Although "you can go anywhere... you can also be found anywhere," so that "the possibility encapsulated in the old form of mobility—the freedom to escape one's past, the chance to start anew—is undermined by the technologies of the new mobility, which make it increasingly difficult for us, even from moment to moment in far-off places, to be free from society, from each other, and from ourselves."[2]

Despite these pressures, a few Americans and even some noted authors have either continued to live near their birthplace or have returned to that place to make a home after venturing elsewhere. Such figures include Emily Dickinson, Henry Thoreau, William Faulkner, Flannery O'Connor, and Wendell Berry. They offer the rest of us an invaluable perspective on what it means to live not only in but *into* a place and to sustain rootedness amid the dislocations of a global age. Wallace Stegner once drew a stark contrast between what he called "stickers"—those Americans committed to settling somewhere, who are willing to invest their identities in a particular community of life—and placeless "boomers" intent on short-term exploitation.[3] The vow of stability traditionally taken by Benedictine monks likewise recognizes the spiritual benefits of committing oneself to a life centered in a single place, among members of one particular community.

For several reasons, though, I believe it would be a serious mistake to overstate or absolutize the merits of maintaining lifelong residency in one's native place. To begin with, even those who decide to stay put during most of their lives, somewhere near their place of origin, usually admit to profiting from exposure to other lands and from the renewed perspective gained through travel. Or else, if they leave but subsequently return to their home place, their relation to it has been reshaped by where they have been in the meantime.[4] In either case, the cloistered virtue of a provinciality that knows nothing of an elsewhere is finally no virtue. Thoreau, for example, whose fondness for traveling much within, rather than beyond, his native Concord became legendary, also learned much from his occasional sojourning elsewhere. His records of visits to Cape Cod, Maine, and Canada confirm this.[5]

For that matter, it is fair to say that none of us alive today—aside from, yet perhaps even including, First Nation inhabitants—is native to North America by natural descent.[6] Hence the familiar motto, sounded by Gary Snyder and others, about our need to embrace the project of *becoming* native to this continent, rather than supposing ourselves to be already such, even if we happen to have been born here.[7]

Moreover, those who do come to *belong* wholeheartedly to some particular place on "Turtle Island"[8] often realize that connection not by birth, but by adoption. Writers who move somewhere new may not only find there a new life for themselves, but may help to re-create the imaginative identity of that place for the rest of us as readers. The impressions that generations of readers have by now internalized of Boston-born Ben Franklin's adopted "country" of Philadelphia, of Willa Cather's Nebraska, or of John Muir's Yosemite are cases in point. It is evident that Muir, for example, though he was born in Scotland and had lived in Wisconsin and elsewhere before finding his way to California, did not discover his true home and land of his heart's desire until he reached Yosemite. And though Cather as a child was initially traumatized by her family's move from Virginia to the seeming bleakness of Nebraska's prairie landscape, this displacement eventually contributed much toward inspiring her fictive imagination.

Even more than nativism, of course, migration and immigration have long figured as core traits of America's cultural identity. Theologically, too, formative influences on that identity from Jewish and Christian tradition offer at least as much endorsement of cosmopolitan or migratory impulses as of fixed residency. To be sure, Jerusalem and its temple once defined in geographic terms the sacred center of Jewish faith. But all that changed with the diasporic necessity of Hebrew religious practices after the Second Temple's destruction in AD 70, just as the origins of Hebrew ethnicity had been closely associated with nomadic tribalism rather than enduring settlements. Significantly, too, Abraham, the eponymous father of faith for Jews, Christians, and Muslims, enters the drama of biblical history by accepting a divine call to abandon his homeland in Ur of the Chaldeans and resettle his family in Canaan. A willingness to move, to uproot oneself from one's place of origins, is thereby extolled as evidence of the believer's trust and commitment to a divinely sanctioned destiny. Early Christianity further discouraged believers from honoring any locale, empire, or geographic center of sacred authority so far as to compromise their primary, decidedly transnational citizenship in the Kingdom of God. This dislocated aspect of Christian faith is displayed, for example, by St. Paul's peripatetic vocation, which for years kept him constantly on the move throughout the known world.

For those who braved the perils of an oceanic crossing to participate in the founding of New England, including Puritans who arrived in the Great Migration of 1630, a willingness to uproot and resettle confirmed one's worthiness to fulfill God's design for His saints. These chosen ones believed themselves called by God to "Plant his churches" in that "place where the Lord will create a new Heaven, and a new earth." Their long journey, though it required death to former attachments and "perpetual banishment from their native soile,"[9] yet offered hope of new birth and deliverance across the water. Their oceanic voyage thus amounted to a spiritually regenerative rite of passage. That sense is reflected, for example, in William Bradford's famous account of landing in Provincetown harbor with his party of Plymouth settlers. Bradford recalls the relief and gratitude members of this holy fellowship had felt, having passed through "the vast ocean, and a sea of troubles before in their preparation." So when they found themselves at last "arrived in a good harbor," he writes, "and brought safe to land, they fell upon their knees and blessed the God of Heaven who had brought them over the vast and furious ocean, and delivered them from all the perils, and miseries thereof, again to set their feet on the firm and stable earth, their proper element."[10]

The persistent references in seventeenth-century Puritan writing to a figurative "planting" of churches and people in New England are paralleled in later writings by non-English emigrants to America. Thus Hector St. Jean de Crèvecoeur, in his *Letters From an American Farmer* (1782), presents a comparably favorable, albeit more secular, interpretation of the prospects awaiting Europeans willing to uproot and move to America. Drawing heavily on the botanical figure of transplantation, Crèvecoeur concludes that "men are like plants." They are bound to wither, "wanting vegetative mould and refreshing showers," in the uncongenial cultural soil of Europe. Yet in the New World, "by the power of all transplantation, like all other plants they have taken root and flourished." Crèvecoeur insists that here "Everything has tended to regenerate them: new laws, a new mode of living, a new social system; here they are become men" whereas "in Europe they were as so many useless plants."[11] For Thomas Jefferson, such agricultural metaphors likewise had a practical meaning and application. He perceived the abundance in America of free lands, to support the livelihood of independent yeoman farmers, as essential to the founding of a democratic nation. Yet fulfilling this vision required an enterprising citizenry willing to move and resettle ever-new lands, a vista soon extended to the continent's westward territories.

So whereas my opening chapter fixed attention on the spiritual inscape of home dwellings, highlighting the value of stasis, this chapter is all about motion and re-placement. The focus here is on travelers, explorers, and would-be pilgrims, as well as on resettlers—that is, those of us who leave one place, starting with our birthplace, to adopt another as our own. A leave-taking and resettlement are apt to be repeated several times in each lifetime. From the colonial era onward, travel writing of various sorts has also been recognized as a familiar subgenre of American letters. And the nineteenth century gave rise to an American tourist industry that was at once profitable, albeit often damaging to its favored destinations, *and* instrumental in attaching a sacred aura to certain sites.[12] Among the many spiritually attuned writers who might be discussed in relation to these topics, I want for the moment to consider just two: Barry Lopez, as exemplar of a contemporary literature of exploration; and Carolyn Servid, author of a revealing nonfictional account of finding and making a new life for herself in Alaska. Within this pairing, Lopez can represent the writer as seasoned traveler, someone who reports what he or she has learned to perceive from personal encounter with numerous lands. By contrast, most of Servid's narrative captures the author's experience of migration from one site and cultural setting to another, underscoring the import of her long-term resettlement in southern Alaska.

Barry Lopez has visited and lived among peoples in a multitude of geographic settings, across the nation and around the world. In 2004, he was elected a Fellow of the Explorers Club, an international society devoted to field research. Best known as the author of *Arctic Dreams* (1986), Lopez has won distinction over the years for his writing of creative nonfiction as well as fiction. And he has been honored over the years by a number of bodies in addition to the Explorers Club. Yet "explorer" strikes me as an unusually apt title for one dedicated to Lopez's distinctive style of place-engaged inquiry. Admittedly, the term in current usage may sound antiquated. For many it calls to mind the sort of rugged adventurer who first discovers—or at least purports to discover, on behalf of another civilization—previously unknown or unmapped territory, of which little presumably remains today on this planet other than the ocean floor.

In its core sense, however, exploration is an enterprise and attribute of the actively inquisitive mind. So explorers should be recognized not only, or primarily, as those who first visit and report on lands previously undiscovered by their cultures of origin. "Explorer" is also a fitting title for the likes of Barry Lopez, someone personally committed to investigating diverse sites in a manner that yields new insight into their complex identity. This field-based inquiry supposes that the selected sites can be apprehended, if never fully known, as places enfolding discrete communities of life, rather than simply spaces on a map. Explorers of such disposition, unlike tourists, are peculiarly gifted to make and to share with others fresh discoveries about places they visit. And though there is some generic overlap between what I am calling a literature of exploration and travel or journalistic writing more broadly, most of Lopez's writing shows a number of distinguishing features.

One of these traits is a concentrated personal investment in the territory under scrutiny. Although well versed in science and natural history, Lopez rejects the Enlightenment era's long-standing supposition that relying solely on dispassionate, objectified modes of study and experimentation enables us to know the world. He advocates instead the rediscovery of other ways of knowing, patterned on the experience of indigenous peoples and the behavior of wild creatures. And the subjectively informed wisdom one can glean from personal involvement in a place depends largely, he believes, on the practice of contemplative awareness.

Lopez recalls that his earlier vocational training as a photographer involved him in "a sequestered exploration of light and spatial volume" and helped him cultivate "a technique for paying attention." As a photographer, he had "wanted to explore a single form, which turned out to be the flow of water in creeks and rivers near my home." He found this sharply focused attentiveness to be revelatory, "since the streaming of water around a rock is one of the most complex motions of which human beings are aware."[13] Such concentration of mind and spirit is likewise a trademark of his descriptive writing, including fictional explorations that are characteristically focused on just one or two characters. Most of his short fiction is also localized, mediated through an intensely reflective center of consciousness, and tonally understated. In a self-descriptive essay titled "The Naturalist," Lopez writes of spending time almost every day, over the course of thirty years, simply sitting to watch the McKenzie River from a forested bank bordering his home in western Oregon. He regards this meditative discipline as part of a "naturalist's spirituality" that yields something akin to numinous insight:

> In all the years I have spent standing or sitting on the banks of this river, I have learned this: the more knowledge I have, the greater becomes the mystery of what holds that knowledge together, this reticulated miracle called an ecosystem. The longer I watch the river, the more amazed I become (afraid, actually, sometimes) at the confidence of those people who after a few summer seasons here are ready to tell the county commissioners, emphatically, what the river is, to scribe its meaning for the outlander.[14]

From the stable base of his home place in Oregon, Lopez has ventured out to explore many far-flung places over the course of his career. The sites he selects for scrutiny sometimes sound exotic. But they are not always unspoiled or scenic in the usual sense, as he is at pains to point out in his discourse on "The American Geographies." One of his explorations even takes the form of flying around the globe on a large air freighter while sidling curiously through the ever-changing mass of cargo merchandise carried in the main hold.[15] In his essay collection titled *Crossing Open Ground* he reflects on varied experiences in settings ranging from southern California, northern Arizona, and Oregon to Alaska and Canada's Yukon Territory.

To cultivate what Lopez calls "intimacy with place" a person need not have been born there or committed to lifelong residency. But for as long as one remains in the place, one must have become fully present to the presence that animates it. This presence is sustained by the dynamic interchange within its community of life, by its invisible and interior features of landscape,[16] and by the stories its human inhabitants may have preserved. "Everything is held together with stories," a Lopez character declares, "that is all that is holding us together, stories and compassion."[17] Thus reluctant to be known as a nature writer fixated on the nonhuman, he considers the understanding of place he gleans from its human inhabitants, past and present, to be indispensable. So in exploring a place that is at first unfamiliar, he relies heavily on those "local tutors" or "local geniuses of American landscape" who have long been committed to living on the land. He values particularly the testimony of native people who are steeped in traditional ways of life and the language of animals,[18] a source of knowledge he supplements with his own field study and extensive reading.

Allied to the contemplative disposition that Lopez brings to his exploration is a sense of reverence before the spirit and mystery he repeatedly encounters at sites he visits throughout the world. As philosopher Paul Woodruff has observed, the ancient civil virtue of "reverence" reflects more of a disposition than a particular belief system.[19] Although often associated with religious rituals and practice, what it chiefly expresses is profound respect—verging on veneration—for the otherness of persons, creatures, and things beyond oneself. For Lopez, the reverence that he believes places and their creatures can inspire in us thus witnesses to a transcendent reality. And though not inclined to identify the spirituality of reverence with any religious doctrine, he affirms the ways in which ritual actions, song, and storytelling help to confirm our perception of meaning and order. "Among the Navajo and, as far as I know, many other native peoples," he writes, "the land is thought to exhibit a sacred order." "That order," he goes on to say, "is the basis of ritual," and "the rituals themselves reveal the power in that order."[20]

The religious anthropology informing such statements is something Lopez has evidently taken to heart. More than once, his writing shows him moved to enact his own practice of a nonecclesiastical ritual or sacramental gesture. Its bodily expression takes the simple form of a bow. In his essay on "The Stone Horse," for example, he describes the way in which he gradually came to feel reverence for a rare artifact, constructed by now-extinct Quechan people some 300 years ago, that he came upon in the desert of southern California. What response could one possibly make to such a discovery? Lopez confides that "With a slight bow I paid my respects to the horse, its maker, and the history of us all, and departed."[21] Likewise in *Arctic Dreams*, he relates how he embodied the spirit of reverence by bowing before birds whose nests are exposed on the tundra during his evening walks. He had first paid homage in this way to a single horned lark, as he discloses toward the start of *Arctic Dreams*. But at the close of this narrative he also offers a grand bow toward the icy waters of the Bering Strait, thereby sealing and extending his spiritual connection to the entire bioregion.

The trajectory of Carolyn Servid's place-based narrative is more straightforward than that represented in most of Lopez's writing. *Of Landscape and Longing: Finding a Home at the Water's Edge* begins with an account of the author's origins and childhood experience in Vengurla, western India, where her parents served as medical missionaries. It includes references to other scenes of Servid's life—spent, for example, in northwest Washington or while visiting a mountain refuge of her husband's family in Colorado. But her tale is mainly about the forms of personal and spiritual renewal she came to feel once she made her home on Baranof Island in southeast Alaska, where she moved in 1980 and has resided ever since.

Servid shares some fond memories of her childhood in Vengurla. She remarks that "few of us live out our lives in the place we were born, but there, on the far side of our earliest memories, are the details of the earth's embrace that first gave us ground." Largely insulated from the poverty and disease around her, she writes of cherishing her association with a few native personalities and with the distinctive smells, sights, textures, and worship gatherings she once knew in Vengurla, "the first place on earth I came to love." Yet she remained acutely aware that, given her American lineage and identity, she never really belonged there. Neither could she suppose, when she later went to study at an Indian boarding school, that she had found a genuine home in that place either, where what she shared with fellow students, likewise children of missionaries, was largely "a sense of uprootedness."[22]

As a young woman, Servid set out with a companion on a hiking and climbing adventure in Alaska that took her through some challenging terrain in Glacier Bay and elsewhere. The experience was not altogether pleasant. She was apt to find the landscape intimidating and her physical limitations humiliating. Yet she testifies that because of this trip "the Alaskan landscape had set something in motion in my life" (44). The impulse would soon draw her back to this land, inspiring her to make it her permanent home. It had stirred in her classic apprehensions of the sacred, introducing her to an otherness at once fearsome yet appealing: "Often my body ached and my heart had been wrenched small, and yet here was a presence I could not face down—powerful, indifferent, complex, staggering, sublime. Its lack of humanness offered a curious comfort, a perspective that let me imagine, for the first time, the boundaries of my life being defined and supported by the earth" (37).

Servid's island homestead is backed by a heavily forested slope that runs to a mountainous summit. The house faces south toward the waters of Thimbleberry Bay, an expansive vista that opens beyond the rocky beach situated not far below. *Of Landscape and Longing* devotes little space to describing Servid's dwelling, her daily routine, or the process of her settling in. It features instead descriptive episodes that for Servid evoke the spirit of the place. So she writes about Sitka's stories, creatures, and human inhabitants, including representatives of the Tlingit people who had been living there since time out of mind. She tells us how she responds inwardly to the presence around her of mountains and humpback whales, hermit thrush, ravens, eagles, Sitka spruce and other trees, and the oceanic immensity she confronts in her small wooden dory, handcrafted by Lowell's Boat Shop back in Massachusetts. Her window on the world reveals as much of seascapes as of landscapes. And in a chapter titled "Consecration by Water," she finds her capacious vision of water's sacramental significance for all living things conjoined with her recollection of Presbyterian baptismal rites she had once seen performed in India.

A religious conception of place-rootedness, albeit one of unspecified doctrinal character, thus informs many of the reflections expressed in *Of Landscape and Longing*. And Servid understands the mysterious topophilia that inspires such "longing" to be something of a holy hunger. She cites with approval the conclusion of theologian Walter Brueggemann that "A sense of place is a primary category of faith" and goes on to explain that "Rootedness in place provide an essential context and coherence that allows us to know who we are, that allows us to act, to move our lives into their own significance" (18). So although topophilia might be manifested in terms of human psychology, with its materialist origins largely attributable to evolutionary biology, it is also for Servid a spiritually implanted impulse with teleological force. Drawing us toward invisible as well as tangibly visible features of earth's community of life, it is at once a consequence and a source of faith. "The human hunger for place," she opines, "might be thought of as a longing to be reconnected to the very source of our being . . . I believe, too, that our hunger for place is a yearning for a sense of the holy, for home ground sacred enough to sustain our faith, sacred enough that we will not violate it, sacred enough that our commitment to its holiness will not falter" (176–177).

For Servid, authentic connectedness to place also involves accepting a covenant of care for its welfare, "an agreement that I live well in this place in exchange for my respect and regard for the natural communities that surround and support me as well as the shared human community" (177–178). It means a "willingness to accept what is here, to know the place on its own terms," an investment having "more to do with familiarity rather than ownership" (75).

It also means accepting the pain of death and loss that is pervasive throughout creation and confronting the changes and deformations of landscape wrought by human culture. Servid writes of the sorrow she feels when standing to gaze directly at the "gaping wounds" (164) of forest clear-cuts. Primed to witness some sort of numinous revelation in her first encounter with humpback whales, she develops instead over time a subtler recognition of the divine faith and wonder they inspire. Greater familiarity leads her to understand that "they certainly were magnificent but not transcendent." What they reveal to her of holiness flows instead from the grace of their participation in the larger wholeness of life: "Our proximity to them forced us to recognize not some spiritual essence unique to them, but rather the systematic grace of intricate relationships that are the very foundation of our mutual existence, of the natural world. It is this grace that we, as human beings, can choose or not to acknowledge, giving it the reverence that is due" (63).

Learning the practice of due reverence: Such is arguably the governing principle of Servid's earth-grounded ethic and spirituality, as is likewise the case for Barry Lopez and Wendell Berry. Berry testifies that "hovering over nearly everything I have written is the question of how a human economy might be conducted with reverence, and therefore with due respect and kindness toward everything involved." He declares that in this light he has "learned to see my native landscape and neighborhood as a place unique in the world, a work of God, possessed of an inherent sanctity that mocks any human valuation that can be put upon it."[23] These sentiments echo, in turn, the principle of "reverence for life" that Albert Schweitzer—the polymath to whom Rachel Carson dedicated *Silent Spring*—had articulated as early as 1949.

For Servid, too, the exercise of reverence draws forth not only amazement and profound respect, but also love. This insight, applicable to places no less than to persons or creatures, becomes the keynote of her concluding chapter, aptly titled "The Right Place for Love" after a familiar poem by Robert Frost. She begins the chapter by describing how she felt about seeing a thrush die, after it had smashed into a window pane at her home. The blend of fear, tenderness, and introspection that occasion aroused led her to recall a lecture she had once heard. It explained how the four-letter "alphabet" that produces variations in the DNA cells of every living creature also confirms the continuity of all life. Once she realized the import of this genetically coded common language and the impressive proportion of its constituent elements she as a human shared with other creatures, she could appreciate as never before the ground of her kinship with the thrush. She had shared with this animal considerably more than a certain living space on Baranof Island. In this "divine intersection," this previously unsuspected conjunction of "scientific and holy truth," Servid perceived yet another motive for reverence. This nation's tradition of free-spirited individualism may have disinclined us, she muses, to revere anyone or anything beyond ourselves, so that "even something as compelling as the DNA discovery has not prompted us to give that bond the reverence it is due" (172, 174). Yet her book is an expressive attestation to the feasibility, as well as the rewards, of place-directed reverence.

Although the geographic arc of Servid's life story, stretching from Asia to Alaska, is unusually long, experiences of domestic migration and resettlement are plainly more normative than exceptional for present-day Americans. My own stories of relocation, though scarcely unique, may count here as illustrative. The geographic shift that I found to be most unsettling at first, yet finally most rewarding, was one I made back in 2004. That is when my wife and I left a home in southern New England, where we had been pleased to spend the larger part of our adult lives, to settle in a rural university town in middle Tennessee. A promising vocational opening there for my wife had drawn us to relocate.

But as unreconstructed Yankees, we felt some apprehension about the displacement, if not culture shock, that our resettlement on the Cumberland Plateau—demonstrably part of the *real* South—might entail for us. Could we ever hope to belong there? Although entranced by the region's mountainous beauty, we were taken aback by the sight of cotton fields, gigantic retail stores mainly devoted to selling fireworks, and prominent advertising on highway billboards for all manner of firearms. We marveled at the stately, gothic-style campus architecture of the University of the South, where both of us would be employed, but could scarcely forget that the institution's founding traditions were solidly anchored in the Old Confederacy.

Yet we were surprised to discover how swiftly we came to feel quite at home in this new setting. Such rapid and thorough adjustment was effected largely by virtue of the town's remarkable tissues of community cohesion. For all its deficiencies, Sewanee is a place where mutual trust prevails. So buildings, residential or otherwise, are rarely locked. The owner of the town's only filling station simply trusts his self-service customers to report to him how much fuel they have pumped. "Town–gown" conflicts are minimized because the University—where actual academic gowns are still commonly worn throughout the year—is so bound to the surrounding village that this town, figuratively at least, also wears a gown. And the University's chief executive officer serves as the town's de facto mayor. I do not mean to idealize this place, which is certainly too rural, insular, and lacking in urban amenities for some tastes. Campus life, too, reflects its share of academic squabbles, faculty discontent, and student misbehavior. But I think it fair to conclude, from this fairly typical contemporary experience of mine, that the ties one forms to an adopted place may become no less ingrained and significant than those established in a birthplace or some previous home. Such might also, of course, be true for individuals adopted rather than born into the human family they claim as their own.

FROM PILGRIM'S WAY TO THE OPEN ROAD

Pilgrimage, often identified with a long foot-journey from one's home place to some recognizably sacred site, has long been practiced in diverse cultures throughout the world. Viewed as at least an edifying devotional practice in Hindu and Catholic Christian traditions, it is close to obligatory in Islam, which regards the hajj, or pilgrimage to Mecca, as one of the Five Pillars of Faith. Anthropologist Victor Turner describes pilgrimage as a "liminoid phenomenon." As such, the sacred journey offers participants not only involvement in a "mode of social being" apart from their workaday world but a potentially transformative experience of something like "extroverted mysticism." Turner, whose interest was mainly drawn to European sites of pilgrimage, argued that these destinations are all "believed to be places where miracles once happened, still happen, and may happen again." Or he understands them to be, at least, places where religiously significant events have taken place.[24] Even today, sites such as Santiago in Spain, Fatima in Portugal, Walsingham in Britain, or Lourdes in France continue to attract countless pilgrims. Why, then, are traditional sites and practices of pilgrimage so much rarer in the United States than in Europe? Because Europe's culture has been for some time appreciably more secular than that of the United States, this seems to be a fair question.

The most obvious explanation is that Europe's chief pilgrim sites were already well established centuries ago, under the sway of medieval piety and long before the future United States was colonized. Hawthorne, in his Preface to *The Marble Faun*, describes his nation as one with "no antiquity"[25] or sign of age-old structures. But there must be other reasons why pilgrimage is still so much more widely practiced in present-day Europe than in the United States.

Historically, it seems probable that the dominant influence of Protestantism in the early shaping of America's cultural and religious climate is one reason for this difference. Proponents of the Reformation usually scorned the idea of pilgrimage, together with the allied practices of venerating saints and relics, as yet another medieval corruption that needed to be expunged. Not surprisingly, then, two of the most prominent destinations for religious pilgrims in North America today, the shrines of Our Lady of Guadalupe in Mexico and of St. Anne de Beaupré in Quebec, are both located in lands outside the United States, and both are steeped in Roman Catholic piety.[26]

Such remnants of pilgrimage practice as do persist in the United States today commonly take the form of speedily motorized rather than pedestrian travel. As largely secularized outgrowths of tourism, they often focus on sites associated with historical events or with noteworthy literary, political, or social personalities. Two such sites that continue to attract a host of visitors, who may qualify as devotees no less than tourists, are Thomas Jefferson's Monticello and Henry Thoreau's Walden.[27] It is a stretch to call these places religious shrines, and there is no cultus or mythos attached to the process of journeying to reach them.

Yet from the Puritan era onward, American culture has taken to heart the trope of pilgrimage, if not its traditional forms of exercise. This spiritual affinity is evident in the Plymouth colonists' self-understanding as "pilgrims," in the authority and vast popularity that John Bunyan's tale of *The Pilgrim's Progress* held for nineteenth-century Americans, and in Annie Dillard's latter-day account of her experience as a Pilgrim at Tinker Creek.[28] For Puritan settlers as well as for other immigrants, oceanic migration to the New World effectively displaced walking the old medieval "way" as their favored, life-changing version of sacred journeying.

Thus, in practice as well as in literary imagination, American expressions of the pilgrimage ideal have rarely combined the several elements normative in European tradition. That tradition supposes the pilgrim's way to be defined communally rather individually, for example, and to trace a route that is repeatable in ritual fashion. Above all, it supposes that the process by which pilgrims make their way toward some sacred site, usually on foot, is no less consequential than the spiritual observances at their destination, and that a definite *telos* of the journey has been identified from the outset.

American forms of pilgrimage typically illustrate, in various ways, a bifurcated displacement of this ideal. On the one hand, many sites in America have been counted worthy of veneration or special attention, for one reason or another. In Chapter 4, I consider more closely the character and role of these places, some but not all reputed to have been scenes of numinous encounter. On the other hand, stories about existential journeying abound in American culture. Adventures on the open road—whether pursued on foot, by rail, or by motorcar—have long been glamorized as the national epitome of freedom and self-reliance. Yet these celebrations of the unencumbered, peripatetic life rarely conclude with the traveler's arrival at some special, predetermined destination. It is the going, not the getting there, that matters. A century before Jack Kerouac's hipster version of this story, Walt Whitman had already sounded all its notes, presuming a future as unscripted as what John Milton imagined set before our first parents in leaving the confines of Eden:

> *Afoot and light-hearted I take to the open road,*
> *Healthy, free, the world before me,*
> *The long-brown path before me leading wherever I choose.*[29]

The journey's end, in such displaced tales of pilgrimage, is often shown to be anticlimactic. Sometimes, in fact, a bitter letdown. The desultory road wanderings of Kerouac's Sal Paradise end in New York, more or less, but really nowhere in particular. Or consider the pathway John Muir described in his first book. One might have supposed that Muir left Indianapolis to embark on his "thousand-mile walk to the gulf," as he later titled this botanical excursion through several southern states, with a clear intent to complete his journey in the Florida Keys. But such was not the case. Muir indicates elsewhere that his original thought, in responding to queries about where he was going, was to say "Oh! I don't know—just anywhere in the wilderness, southward." His subsequent, ill-conceived plan was to extend his travels all the way to the Amazonian jungle. Only after falling grievously ill with malaria in Florida did he eventually find his way to the High Sierra country of California. The Golden State, which he saw as radiant with "light of unspeakable richness," became thereafter the land of his heart's desire. But it was not the destination Muir actually had in mind when he set forth, "joyful and free," on that long walk or pilgrimage he undertook in his twenty-ninth year.[30]

To reflect once more on the much-debated ending of *The Adventures of Huckleberry Finn*, and the *telos* of travel Twain charts for his lead characters, is also revealing. The well-known joyous passages in that novel dramatize for both Huck and Jim a long-sought liberation of selfhood and soul in the course of their famous raft journey down the Mississippi River. Yet the geographic endpoint of this journey–quest in the wrong direction, ever deeper into southern slave territory, is no holy place but rather a dead end for Jim, despite Twain's notorious *deus ex machina* rescue. And Huck perceives it to be yet another place of threatened confinement, from which he again yearns to escape. Ed Abbey's tale of his own dream voyage in a rubber boat down the Colorado River in *Desert Solitaire* likewise describes a pilgrimage of sorts. Despite the author's professed materialism, he evokes a realm of holy, ghostly, almost-transcendent beauty during this last voyage through Glen Canyon, soon to be dammed and defaced. Yet the trip ends not at a shrine but with a sign. Ending the chapter all too abruptly, Abbey's citation of this construction notice to boats reminds him and us of the canyon's impending doom. Unlike the lyrical flow of feeling that characterizes the rest of the chapter, the sign stands as a cold sentence of extinction. Abbey describes it as "white, rigid, rectangular, out of place."[31]

Even those continental migrations, in the course of American history, that seem to qualify as sacred journeys almost never became ritualized in later practice as routes of pilgrimage. Consider, for example, the case of Mormonism. In accord with the faith's sacred geography, at two least places in America might claim to be revered as holy sites. One is Hill Cumorah in Palmyra, New York, where founder Joseph Smith is presumed to have received his visions and where annual pageants of commemorative history continue to be performed. The other, of course, is Salt Lake City, headquarters of the Church of Jesus Christ of Latter-Day Saints and the place where Brigham Young and other fellowship members settled following their great exodus westward by wagon train from Illinois in the mid-nineteenth century. Yet there is no tradition in Mormonism that expects or encourages present-day believers to pursue their own pilgrimage exercise by retracing the steps of Brigham Young's migration. That sacred trek is indeed honored in memory, but not regarded as repeatable or as a precedent for present-day observance.

In *The Way to Rainy Mountain*, N. Scott Momaday does narrate his experience of retracing the long path of migration that his nomadic ancestors, the Kiowa people, followed over several generations. What Momaday calls "the great adventure of the Kiowas" was "a going forth into the heart of the continent" expressive "of the human spirit." This great migration took them all the way from the Yellowstone Mountains of western Montana, southward into the Golden Age of their horse-mounted culture on the Great Plains, and finally to a landmark knoll in the Wichita Range of Oklahoma. In a multivoiced presentation that combines recollections of mythography and ethnic history with personal memoir, Momaday explains how his grandmother's death stirred him to seek his own connection with ancient pathways of his people: "Although my grandmother lived out her long life in the shadow of Rainy Mountain, the immense landscape of the continental interior lay like memory in her blood.... I wanted to see in reality what she had seen more perfectly in the mind's eye, and travelled fifteen hundred miles to begin my pilgrimage."[32]

Yet Momaday cannot and does not presume that such travel enables him to replicate the spiritual experience of his ancestors from another world and century. Neither does he suppose that his personal journey establishes any ritual pattern of pilgrimage to be followed by others. In sum, the classically integrated model of pilgrimage as shared with others and repeatable, as sacred journeying toward some well-defined and corporately venerated site, is rarely seen in the United States. Here a spirituality of place is commonly associated either with the *going there* or veneration with what's found upon *getting there*—but not with both.

In present-day Europe, by contrast, one can readily find pilgrimage opportunities that give serious attention both to the going and the getting there. A favored route for those desiring such an integrated exposure to pilgrimage is the Road to Santiago. It continues to draw to Spain and France any number of American seekers–adventurers, who reflect disparate forms and degrees of religious faith; and it has won ever-widening contemporary notice through the many books, films, and academic programs that relate some of the personal tales it has inspired.[33]

But Santiago is not the only pathway of integral pilgrimage still extant in Europe. A lesser-known example in Britain is the annual five-mile walk, conducted en masse toward the close of May, from the Cambridgeshire village of Leighton Bromswold to nearby Little Gidding. In 2015 I had a chance to participate in this yearly ritual. It began with a service of Holy Communion at St. Mary's Church in Leighton Bromswold, the edifice that seventeenth-century poet George Herbert as prebend had once raised funds to restore.

As our party of roughly 100 persons then set off on foot and in festive mood toward Little Gidding, along rural paths through the English countryside, the spirit of George Herbert remained in evidence. Periodically, at five stations on the way, a Herbert poem was read aloud by Rowan Williams—former archbishop of Canterbury, himself a gifted writer and eminent scholar. Bishop Williams, designated leader of that year's pilgrimage practice, then offered a personal meditation on each poem. Following a celebration of Evensong at St. Andrew's Church in Steeple Gidding, the walk concluded at Little Gidding Church, where Bishop Williams laid a wreath of flowers on the tomb of Nicholas Ferrar.

In effect, this instance of sacred journeying combined a ritual involvement in several venerated sites with homage to three noteworthy Anglicans. The saintly figure chiefly invoked as inspiration for the annual walk is Nicholas Ferrar, seventeenth-century founder of a nonmonastic community of prayer, education, and charitable works at Little Gidding.[34] But of course the presence of George Herbert always accompanied us as well, by virtue of his friendship with Ferrar and association with the villages we traversed. Yet another personality who figures inevitably in this threefold commemoration is T. S. Eliot, whose portrayal of Ferrar's household circle in the closing poem of his *Four Quartets* effectively memorialized the name of Little Gidding as a place where "prayer has been valid." I take it that it is just such an accumulated investment of life, spirit, poetry, and human history that continues to mark this site as a holy place, as there is otherwise little at Little Gidding Church to impress a tourist as visually remarkable or picturesque.

I know of nothing in America quite like this ritualized "pilgrimage to the tomb of Nicholas Ferrar at Little Gidding."[35] But insofar as a vibrant if incomplete spirituality of pilgrimage continues to flourish on this side of the Atlantic, as I believe it does, it has been enacted chiefly through the practice, cultus, and literature of walking—as an "end" in itself rather than as centered on a destination.

An early literary illustration from colonial New England, the utterly nonutilitarian walk in the woods that Anne Bradstreet describes in her long poem "Contemplations," is a case in point. Bradstreet, unusually for a woman in her time and place, writes about sauntering alone with free-spirited gaze through forestlands and waterways near her home in North Andover, Massachusetts. The excursion offers her occasion to reflect on how her faith in a divine Creator relates theologically and intellectually to the whole of Creation—both nature and human nature. More than that, the walk becomes for Bradstreet a contemplative exercise. The sauntering poet's physical and sensory involvement in her setting, amounting to a Christianized evocation of the spirit of place, presumably touches heart and soul as well as intellect. As such, Bradstreet's excursion reflects a tradition identified in seventeenth-century usage as "meditation on the creatures,"[36] and that Buddhist tradition might recognize as *kinhin*, or walking meditation. In our own time several of Gary Snyder's Buddhist-inflected prose pieces and poems, including his verses on "The Circumambulation of Mt. Tamalpais," draw on this tradition of mindful walking.

Although we have already noted signs of the sauntering sensibility in Whitman's and Muir's works, Thoreau's essay "Walking" remains the essential text for appreciating how the ideal of unconstrained, self-contained sauntering came to replace the traditional model of pilgrimage in American literary culture. Particularly toward the start of his essay, Thoreau insists that one should conceive of "sauntering" as a "noble art"—not a practical necessity, a mode of transport, or healthful means of "taking exercise." Rather than a restorative change from the crucial activities of someone's life, such sojourning should be welcomed as "itself the enterprise and adventure of the day." To undertake it in the right spirit, the saunterer must be wholly unencumbered, detached from all cares and projects. "I think that I cannot preserve my health and spirits," Thoreau reports, "unless I spend four hours a day at least—and it is commonly more than that—sauntering through the woods and hills, absolutely free from all worldly engagements."[37]

Moreover, the goal of sauntering is not to make one's way speedily and directly to some fixed destination but rather to range widely, curiously, open in imagination to whatever may appear. Thoreau believes that townsfolk of his who have been "so blessed as to lose themselves for half an hour in the woods" (95) should count themselves fortunate. And although he usually feels disposed to begin walking in a westerly or southwesterly direction, sensing that "westward I go free" (105) in accord with what he takes to be the cultural progress of humankind, he is otherwise content to allow instinct, or the "subtle magnetism in Nature," to direct his course.

If Thoreau understands the geographic end of sauntering to be indeterminate, he yet sees it satisfying a decidedly spiritual purpose and character. It involves, after all, an inherently contemplative exercise—not only through the meditative rhythm enforced by physical motion of the limbs, but also through its liberating concentration of mental processes. "You must walk like a camel," Thoreau maintains, "which is said to be the only beast which ruminates when walking" (98). He also underscores the contemplative character of walking by indulging in etymological wordplay on what it means to be a "saunterer." "To be a *Sainte-Terrer*," he muses, is from the French to understand oneself as someone headed on foot toward the Holy Land—that is, someone who recognizes the sacred, spiritually illuminating potential of walking. "They who never go to the Holy Land in their walks, as they pretend, are indeed mere idlers and vagabonds," he concludes, "but they who do go there are saunterers in the good sense, such as I mean." Thoreau confides that he is particularly drawn toward the Holy Land of dark forest, or to a thick and dismal swamp, which he claims to enter "as a sacred place,—a *sanctum sanctorum*" (93, 116).

Yet another sense of the saunterer that Thoreau's essay teases out is that of the walker who is "*sans terre*." The *sans terre* adventurer understands himself or herself to be "without land or a home, which, therefore in the good sense, will mean, having no particular home, but equally at home everywhere. For this is the secret of successful sauntering" (93).

This second layer of Thoreau's wordplay underscores the paradoxical spirituality of place embodied in sojourning. On the one hand, walking is a form of travel that sets the self in an unusually immediate, palpably intimate relation to one's physical surroundings. If anything, the prospect of a leisurely walk alone in the woods sounds more countercultural, even more drastically localized, in our own age of jet transport and freeway driving than it could possibly have been in Thoreau's Concord.

Comparatively speaking, walking qualifies indeed as a highly place-specific mode of situating ourselves within a given environment. On the other hand, though, walking—unlike sitting, lying, or standing—is indeed a form of movement. Alteration of place in slow motion, but movement all the same. As such, and particularly because the scale and spatial reach of "place" defies precise definition, saunterers must constantly be abandoning one place and finding another in their course of travel. So although saunterers are more or less grounded in a certain locale, they are also peripatetic, perpetually readapting to new space in a manner that ensures they are "equally at home everywhere." By virtue of their mobile circumstance *sans terre*, they are the less liable to suffer that ill that which David Brown describes as "idolatry of place."[38] Thoreau's saunterer, in other words, is at once immersed in place yet also a pilgrim–wanderer who is thus insulated from place-idolatry or absorption.

There are numerous counterparts, in latter-day American life and letters, to Thoreau's vision of pilgrimage as a form of spirited foot travel without a definite destination. And one version of displaced pilgrimage that has gained special prominence in present-day US culture is the zeal many show to walk the Appalachian Trail (AT). Such walkers include those stalwarts, otherwise identified as "end-to-enders," who are determined to traverse the entire course of roughly 2200 miles stretching from Georgia to Maine. Even Americans who have never set foot on the trail probably realize that it has by now developed something of its own mythology, its own cult of devotees.

Susan Power Bratton, in her recent book on *The Spirit of the Appalachian Trail*, observes that AT trekkers bring a variety of spiritual perspectives and religious beliefs to their adventures on the trail. Hikers range "from individuals who see wilderness as a relief from the pressures of the greater culture, including the pressures of organized religion, to those who find that their denominational background is compatible with natural aesthetics, to the disciplined practitioners of outdoor meditation, who expect to find God in nature, or seek an ambiance favorable for deep, undistracted reflection." Bratton's study finds that experience on the trail tends to reinforce the spiritual attitudes and beliefs hikers packed along with them in the first place. Yet an appreciable number of AT veterans do find their extended time of mindful trail walking to be life changing and inwardly meaningful. As Bratton points out, the attraction to undertake an AT journey often seems to be broadly spiritual, recalling other religious traditions of walking pilgrimage, and "AT thru-hikers sometimes identify their journey as a pilgrimage."[39] And although thru-hikers plainly have a certain destination in mind, depending on whether they begin their journey in Maine or in Georgia, they have no expectation of discovering a shrine worthy of worship at journey's end. The spiritual return of such pilgrimage, insofar as one might be desired or received, evidently lies in the journeying itself.

LOCALISM VERSUS GLOBALISM

As we have seen thus far, there is abundant reason to believe that the need to develop some form of place-rootedness, or at least place-consciousness, is endemic to the human condition. There is surely a homing instinct in all of us, as well as in birds and other animals. Admittedly, migratory and nomadic ways have also figured prominently in the collective life stories of many peoples, past and present. And in preceding sections of this chapter, I hope to have established that the inward benefits of coming to know and care for a place should not be equated with place-idolatry, with a provincialized fixation on one's birthplace or on any other site.

Given all of that, the arguments set forth by Wilfred McClay and others about why localized attachments matter to us, spiritually as well as psychologically, strike me as well grounded. No wonder Simone Weil, a French, Jewish–Christian mystical writer who never found a secure place for herself in war-torn Europe, claimed that "To be rooted is perhaps the most important and least recognized need of the human soul."[40] Likewise for N. Scott Momaday, the value of settling one's soul in some particular plot of earth, imaginatively as well as physically, can scarcely be overstated. For him the particularities of placement matter indeed—whether or not the place in question happens to be one's home place; and whether or not one visits it repeatedly or only occasionally, with benefit of memory:

> Once in his life a man ought to concentrate his mind upon the remembered earth, I believe. He ought to give himself up to a particular landscape in his experience, to look at it from as many angles as he can, to wonder about it, to dwell upon it. He ought to imagine that he touches it with his hands at every season and listens to the sounds that are made upon it. He ought to imagine the creatures there and all the faintest motions of the wind. He ought to recollect the glare of noon and all the colors of the dawn and dusk.[41]

In many quarters, the case for sustaining some such promotion of place-rootedness or consciousness in today's world may seem too obvious to require justification. It is arguably a central theme in present-day ecocriticism, as well as in the bulk of environmental literature that has become a staple of the American canon. Yet it has not gone unchallenged. In her book *Sense of Place and Sense of Planet: The Environmental Imagination of the Global*, Ursula K. Heise presents a forceful critique of what she regards as "an excessive investment in the local" on the part of latter-day environmentalist thinkers and writers. Heise poses several objections to this "marked emphasis in American environmentalist thought on the local as the ground for individual and communal identity and as the site of connections to nature that modern society is perceived to have undone."[42]

The ideal of rootedness in place has been, she thinks, overvalued. It may obscure the role that nomadic restlessness and mobility have played in American culture. Heise maintains that sense of place rhetoric often fails to acknowledge how our conceptions of place, which cannot even be defined meaningfully in terms of spatial magnitude, are culturally constructed. She points out that American environmental writers who extol place-rootedness may also be disposed to romanticize rural ways and values. Their pastoral and Jeffersonian sympathies, together with their Georgic and self-reliant ideology, are often allied with questionable suspicions of modernity. And their attraction to rural or wilderness settings can distract attention from broader environmental issues, particularly those germane to life in America's many urban or settled spaces.

Above all, Heise finds the localized preoccupation of many environmental writers and thinkers lacking in global vision and consciousness. Such ecolocalism she understands to be at odds with today's emerging sense of our planet's holistic identity, the extent to which its tissues of life—social and economic as well as biological—are interlinked and interactive. And she believes that even a noted writer–critic such as Gary Snyder, despite his transnational training and experience or his discourse on bioregionalism, falls short of proposing an environmental vision that is genuinely multicultural and globalized. She argues that for Snyder what remains most determinative of identity, both personal and collective, is locally based. For Wendell Berry such localism seems to be still more determinative. In place of much sense-of-place rhetoric, Heise therefore calls for the development of an "eco-cosmopolitan" form of discourse and understanding. This "deterritorialized environmental vision," would, she proposes, allow for "a more nuanced understanding of how both local cultural and ecological systems are imbricated in global ones."⁴³

Heise's argument offers a useful corrective to the sentimental coloring of much rooted-to-place rhetoric. It is thoughtfully provocative for those of us who nonetheless believe that more rather than less remains to be said about "why place matters," about how best to cultivate the art and practice of connectivity to place in America. Admittedly, too, the xenophobic nationalism, isolationism, and nostalgia for an illusionary past that figured so destructively in UK and US elections conducted in 2016 need to be challenged. I applaud Heise's broadly stated ambition to put "environmentalist reflections on the importance of a 'sense of place' in communication with recent thoughts of globalization and cosmopolitanism."⁴⁴

I would question, though, the oppositional portrayal of "sense of place" versus "sense of planet" that pervades much of Heise's analysis. There are several difficulties here. To begin with, "globalization" is itself a problematic value. Although the notion of promoting a planetary or globalist consciousness sounds attractive, attempts to replace local and national ties with broader allegiances are not always productive. In fact, they can yield distressing economic, social, and environmental consequences. Recent news of the ongoing monetary crisis in Greece, as that nation struggles to remain solvent while renegotiating its larger identity within the European Union, is one of many possible examples. Another is the recurrent protest movement against the International Monetary Fund (IMF) and various forms of corporate capitalism.

Despite worries about "an excessive investment in the local," the main liabilities of place-identified consciousness are not ones of degree but of kind. Not too much attachment to a chosen site, but attachment of the wrong sort. To embrace a localism in which one stands oblivious to a site's broader ecological and social associations is scarcely desirable. Neither is absolute, uncritical loyalty to one's locus of residence, however defined. Yet the aspiration to live not only *in* a place but *into* a place—as fully and deliberately as possible—is something else again. Hence the local, rightly understood, evidently complements rather than conflicts with the global. Bill McKibben, in writing his now-classic jeremiad about climate change in *The End of Nature*, certainly intended his book to reflect a planetary consciousness. His argument is broadly encompassing and globally germane—as much as one could readily imagine. Yet repeatedly throughout the book he situates it within the particular, localized setting of his home in the Adirondack Mountains of upstate New York. And in stating his case he, like Rachel Carson before him, adopts a personal voice. The planetary impact of *The End of Nature* is all the greater, it seems, so far as its generalizing discourse is confirmed by what the author reports seeing and experiencing on his home ground. Significantly, this book concludes with McKibben's account of what he thought and felt while stargazing one night, on a rocky Adirondack peak near his home.[45]

The problem with a "deterritorialized environmental vision" is its inclination toward theoretical abstraction. To be situated psychically everywhere at once is to live nowhere on earth. A "deterritorialized" outlook is effectually disembodied. In welcoming "new forms of culture no longer anchored in place," it would see our palpable engagement with landforms and communities largely replaced by ties to global "territories and systems." And though some might suppose the very notion of "a spiritual immersion in place"[46] to be outdated, if not fanciful and illusory, the spirituality of place that informs writing by several of our most admired environmental authors is far from airily abstract. Instead it is earthy, bodily configured, and physically evocative. From the standpoint of Christian theology, this sensibility could be called "incarnational" and "sacramental," terms often suited to describing as well the literary imagination of non-Christian writers such as Thoreau.

Buddhist-trained Gary Snyder, for example, once cited with approval the testimony of a First Nations elder in Montana who perceived the interfusion of spirits with the land to be quite real, a sensorially felt presence. This Crow leader was convinced that "if people stay somewhere long enough—even white people—the spirits will begin to speak to them. It's the power of the spirits coming up from the land. The spirits and the old powers aren't lost, they just need people to be around long enough and the spirits will influence them."[47]

So for Snyder, too, the spirit-world is evidently real but inseparable from the material world of mountains, rivers, whales, New York bedrock, and the "riprap of things."[48] His sense of "where we live" existentially, to borrow Thoreau's idiom, is at once intensely localized and cosmic. Persuaded of a person's need to form some vital connection to a "home-base on earth," and the corresponding imperative of learning to know and care for a place, Snyder nonetheless recognizes the mutability of place. Although "our place is part of what we are," he points out that "even a 'place' has a kind of fluidity: it passes through space and time—'ceremonial time' in John Hanson-Mitchell's phrase." Snyder's globally expansive survey of how space, place, bioregion, and commons relate to one another acknowledges this fluidity. Understanding the fluidity of place enables us, in turn, to appreciate how "The spirit world goes across and between species." For Snyder, earthy apprehension of the "sacred" is to be identified not only with fixed sites or objects, but with the larger dynamic of natural processes. He writes of "Mountains and waters," for example, as "a way to refer to the totality of the process of nature."[49]

And for Snyder, it seems to me, the most promising way toward global consciousness comes through rather than despite the localized awareness and affection of a place-based identity.

Thus he describes the Chinese Buddhist poet Han-shan as a hermit who made a home for himself in secluded mountain territory yet also wandered there through woods and streams. Although in one sense settled in place, "the veritable model of a recluse," Han-shan inhabits a "spacious home reaching "to the end of the universe." So in imaginative terms he is also "homeless," which "is here coming to mean 'being at home in the whole universe.'"[50] I believe that Samuel Taylor Coleridge, in a poem such as "Fears in Solitude," suggests a comparable interconnection between localized attachments and universal sympathy.[51]

TWO VERSIONS OF GLOBALLY ENGAGED LOCALISM

How, then, should we interpret the place-identified discourse and spirituality of Wendell Berry? Berry's writing, given its strongly agrarian inspiration and values, is evidently less cosmopolitan in texture than Snyder's. Berry, having spent most of his life in the locale of his birth and upbringing, seems to be the ultimate homebody. His poetry, fiction, and essays are all solidly rooted in the soil of Henry County, Kentucky. So bound up with the place that one might wonder: Is the writerly imagination evidenced here *too* localized and nostalgic to afford proper recognition to a "sense of planet" and global citizenship?

Not surprisingly, I think not. To indicate why, I want to consider here some examples from Berry's sizable corpus of writing that particularly bear on this issue.

One revealing work in this regard is Berry's early autobiographical essay titled "The Making of a Marginal Farm." It describes the process by which Berry and his wife, after residing elsewhere for a number of years, eventually returned in 1964 to live in the land of his origins and upbringing in

Henry County, Kentucky. Five generations of his ancestry had lived and worked before him in this same territory. After purchasing a house and an initial twelve-acre plot there in Lanes Landing, he set about repairing the house, acquiring more land, and undertaking some farming on a modest scale. So far this composition looks to be a thoroughly localized and personal story.

But soon it becomes plain that Berry is reshaping his narrative into an emblematic rather than purely personal fable. His essay becomes an extended parable about what it means to discover the difference between a life anchored "in ambition" and one rooted in a person's "origins" and "destiny," between '"having' a subject" and living in a cherished place "that is one's subject."[52] It is likewise a graphically illustrated parable about how either to advance or to lose ground in the holistic project of living responsibly—or, as we're inclined to say these days, sustainably—in whatever place one inhabits.

"The Making of a Marginal Farm" underscores the point that we should not expect simply to *find* our dwelling place on earth. Or to purchase or claim it in perpetuity. Over time, Berry learns instead, through arduous experience, what it means to be engaged—as a cocreator with nature and the Creator—in the process of perpetually remaking it. He is drawn to do so, especially on the larger plot he ends up purchasing, because much of the land he acquires is hilly, is of "marginal" agricultural worth, or has been badly damaged. Some of it had been deformed by a developer's bulldozers. Much of it had been overcleared, overplowed, and eroded. "What we had bought was less a farm than a reclamation project" (333), the author concludes, and seeing that project through would require considerable labor, patience, and resourcefulness. Given the prevailing assumptions of a throwaway society, why not simply abandon the effort to repair such marginal terrain and move on to better soil? For that matter, why commit oneself to pursuing, even on a part-time basis, an occupation that in contemporary American society is perceived to be so marginal as family farming?

Yet Berry finds his long-term restoration project worth the effort because in rebuilding the soil's fertility he had also, with his family, "begun a restoration and a healing in ourselves" (334). At the same time, he understands the larger process of restoring, healing, and remaking to be ongoing—both within and beyond the bounds of his own acreage. He recognizes that his "place" at Lanes Landing is by no means a permanently fixed and isolated enclave. Its fate is tied in countless ways to its surroundings, an influence felt as close to hand as the Kentucky River that runs along its banks. That even this marginal farm remains centrally vulnerable to economic and ecological forces beyond its bounds becomes most apparent in relation to the river. Berry describes how strip mining and other abuses along the Kentucky River watershed have promoted flood damage and serious soil erosion in his own neighborhood downriver. So "Our river bank stands literally at the cutting edge of our nation's consumptive economy," he observes, a sad circumstance "true of many 'marginal places'" as well as of "many places that are not marginal" (340).

Such emphasis on the broader and even global implications of living in place is particularly prominent in Berry's discourses on "economy," a topic discussed explicitly in many of his essays and otherwise reflected in his fiction and poetry.

Essays found in collections of his such as *Home Economics, What are People For?*, and *Sex, Economy, Freedom & Community*[53] make it abundantly clear that for Berry, as for Thoreau before him, "economy" has to do not merely with trade flow or fiscal policy but with developing a sound rationale for all those practical and existentially inflected choices we make, both individually and collectively, about how best to live. Morally, it bears on our approach to household management beginning in the domestic sphere. But it extends from there to our conduct as members of the whole household of creation. Religiously, it extends so far as to describe our participation in an all-encompassing spiritual order that Berry is emboldened to call the Kingdom of God, or the Great Economy. As Jeffrey Bilbro's astute summary would suggest, there is assuredly a planetary if not cosmic reach to Berry's conception of economy insofar as Berry "turns to the 'Kingdom of God' or 'the Great Economy' as the order that names the health of all God's creation. Like Thoreau, who based his economy on the most comprehensive currency he could imagine . . . the economy of the Kingdom of God includes in its accounting all the exchanges of God's abundant life . . . . The Kingdom of God thus includes not only what we typically think of as economic relationships, but also ecological relationships, which both come from the Greek root *oikos* [household]."[54]

Berry himself explains that "the first principle of the Kingdom of God is that it includes everything." Thus "The Great Economy, like the Tao or the Kingdom of God, is both known and unknown, visible and comprehensible and mysterious." But if construing the Kingdom of God this way is all-encompassing and universal in essence, it becomes locally and materially incarnate in practice. "If there is no denying our dependence on the Great Economy," he writes, "there is also no denying our need for a little economy—a narrow circle within which things are manageable by the use of our wits."[55]

For Berry personally, the land near Port Royal he has been given to inhabit and to care for stands at the center of this narrow circle. And at the core of his vision is an ethical and theological conviction that we are to regard the land—broadly speaking—not as a resource or commodity, not as property that belongs to us, so much as a community to which we belong.[56] For as St. Augustine reminds us, we cannot ultimately own or hold in possession anything on this earth. Berry does at times define humanity's ideal relation to the earth, theologically, in what has become the commonplace language of "stewardship," or that disciplined commitment of care he calls "good husbandry." But such language has its limitations. For despite its aptness in other respects, the stewardship model with its managerial overtones *can* suggest—contrary to Berry's deeper beliefs—that finding our way toward a sustainable future is mostly a matter of sound resource management, of learning the most humane and technically feasible strategies for doling out periodically certain portions of earth for human benefit.

What I take to be a fresher, more promising dimension of Berry's theological vision conceives of the land as a divine gift and our intended relation to it as sacramental and participatory rather than proprietary. Hence the straightforward title of an early, biblically conversant essay of his on this topic: "The Gift of Good Land." He concludes that essay with an oft-cited statement that defines the crux of his sacramental, incarnational spirituality within the Great Economy:

> ... we depend upon other creatures and survive by their deaths. To live, we must daily break the body and shed the blood of Creation. When we do this knowingly, lovingly, skillfully, reverently, it is a sacrament. When we do it ignorantly, greedily, clumsily, destructively, it is a desecration. In such desecration we condemn ourselves to spiritual and moral loneliness, and others to want.[57]

In addition to "economy," "membership" is another key term in Berry's discourse that has theological resonance and figures throughout his fiction, essays, and poetry. Such "membership" is again conceived to be localized and incarnate to begin with, yet universal in its reach. Constituted organically by communities rather than institutions, it extends beyond a community's living citizenry to embrace the larger roster of its dead—as well as, ultimately, all those other, nonhuman inhabitants of the household. One of Berry's early Sabbath poems thus envisions a joyful "membership meeting" taking place in the "holy room" of an outdoor plot of earth:

> *The dark around us, come*
> *Let us meet here, together,*
> *Members one of another,*
> *Here in our holy room.*
> . . . .
> *Light, leaf, foot, hand, and wing,*
> *Such order as we know;*
> *One household, high and low,*
> *And all the earth shall sing.*[58]

Another quite recent Sabbath poem provides a revealing elaboration of this theme:

> *. . . it comes to me*
> *that I know at last how all of us*
> *are held in the union, the communion, the assembly,*
> *the great membership of this world's life*
> *that comprehends its numberless becomings and farewells.*
>   *In the Kingdom of God*
> *all who ever lived are living.*[59]

What then for Berry is, or should be, our own place in the world? At base within the Great Economy, it is knowing ourselves to be not proprietors of the earth, nor even stewards of its resources, so much as members of the living body of creation. Berry recognizes *that* meta-organism as comparable to, and indeed coextensive with, St. Paul's vision of our participation in the body of Christ. Some such recognition, he believes, is essential to the survival of creation. His conception of "membership" confirms that we stand in spiritual solidarity with human beings living throughout the world, those who are dead and those still to be born—an expansive fellowship resembling what traditional Christian teaching identifies as the "communion of saints."

More than that, it envisions an organic bond unity between ourselves and the whole community of creation. Renewing our freely awarded membership in the Kingdom of God begins with acknowledging that "We are holy creatures living among other holy creatures in a world that is holy."[60] In Berry's short story "The Wild Birds," the earthy, plain-speaking character of Burley Coulter puts it this way: "The way we are, we are members of each other. All of us. Everything. The difference ain't in who is a member and who is not, but in who knows it and who don't."[61]

A particularly forceful dramatization of what membership might mean and of how it both embraces and transcends localization can be found in Berry's novella *Remembering*. "Membership" assumes several senses here, developed with benefit of some earnest word play that underscores how critically our hopes of belonging outwardly to places and communities may depend on our inward processes of "re-membering." The bodily sense of membership figures here as well. Andy Catlett, the novel's central character and consciousness, is a Kentucky farmer and sometime agricultural journalist who has literally been dismembered after losing his right arm to a corn thresher. The psychic and spiritual dislocation he suffers from this accident is devastating. He becomes mired in self-pity, estranged from his wife and children, existentially lost. From the first, in this novel's multilayered second sentence, we learn that "He does not know where he is."[62] His unsettled state of mind and soul is underscored by Berry's narrative technique, which includes dream sequences, stream-of-consciousness recollections, multiple flashbacks, and nonlinear storytelling. The book's opening scene takes place in 1976, within Andy's San Francisco hotel room, but its action subsequently leaps back and forth to other time frames situated both within and prior to Andy's own lifetime.

Andy's dislocated, dismembered state of mind is likewise mirrored in the geographic span of his wanderings. Before his final, restorative return to his farm home in Port William, Kentucky, he had been attending a dispiriting conference on food production systems and agricultural technology at a large university in the Midwest. From there he had found his way to San Francisco. And during the decade prior to his last, presumably permanent, return to Kentucky, he had searched and traveled still more widely—living for three years in San Francisco, in addition to spending time in Ohio, Pennsylvania, and Chicago.

From this sketch of the novel's overarching shape, its closing account of Andy's homecoming to his farm at Harford Place may seem all too predictable. It is scarcely surprising that Catlett ends up reclaiming rootedness in his birthplace at Port William. And that he learns from various experiences, during his time away, just why he should solidify his commitment to traditionally sustainable agricultural policies. From this bare outline, one might suspect Berry of simply giving voice here, in the guise of fiction, to his own experience and favored values, particularly with respect to agrarianism and the value of staying put. Like Andrew Catlett, Wendell Berry was born in rural Kentucky in 1934, spent some formative years in California, and eventually decided to return to his "native hill." And it is true that Berry's writing, fictional or otherwise, continues to offer more penetrating insight into the circumstances of life and community in rural America than it does into the experience of urban dwellers or suburbanites. That limitation of his outlook and applicability needs to be recognized.

Yet the sense of place that emerges from *Remembering*, by virtue of the novel's embedded subtleties, is finally much richer than the simplistic, go-back-to-the-farm didacticism that my rough plot outline might suggest. Berry elsewhere explains how his own expansive outlook on the world actually derives from, rather than conflicts with, his commitment to abiding in a particular plot of earth. For "When I have thought of the welfare of the earth, the problems of its health and preservation, the care of its life, I have had this place before me, the part representing the whole more vividly and accurately, making clearer and more pressing demands, than any *idea* of the whole."[63] The vision set forth in *Remembering*, a vision that surpasses nostalgic provincialism, likewise has far-reaching implications that lend cosmopolitan depth to this story.

To begin with, it isn't because Andy doesn't know any better that he decides to return home to Port William. It's rather because he has learned from experience to cease longing for some presumably "better" place to live. To suppose there could ever be a better place than wherever it is a person best belongs is mere fantasy.

Thus, in one telling episode, Andy calls to mind a luminous yet commonplace day of bathing in a local creek that Mat Feltner, his maternal grandfather, had once spent with one of Mat's relatives many years ago, before Andy was born. Andy could "remember" this moment of idyllic respite from hard labor only by drawing on the memory of his grandfather, who had told him about that which, in Wordsworthian language, amounts to a nodal "spot of time." Yet Andy comes to share the sentiment Mat had voiced about this moment, to the extent of subsequently remembering and making it his own: '"I thought of all the times I'd worked in that field, hurrying to get to a better place, and it had been there all the time'" (49). The "better place" need not be somewhere else. By contrast Andy has also seen, in encountering air terminals with their "Gate of Universal Suspicion," how vacuous some contemporary faces of the built environment can look. Such uniformly ordered yet sterile and pseudo-utopian space represents "a no place to which all places reach" (79).

It is noteworthy, though, that the process of "long choosing" by which Andy comes to find himself and his place of belonging depends crucially on his taking leave of Kentucky. He does so more than once, and the novel establishes beyond doubt that what he experiences during his last period of voluntary exile, especially, becomes part of his consciousness in a way that contributes substantially to his restoration. It is not by a fixation with and in his birthplace but by venturing beyond it that Andy eventually "reminds himself of himself" (50, 38). Only after leaving and living elsewhere can he appreciate what he already has at Harford Place. Of course this pattern, replicated not only in the author's own life but in the careers of Jayber Crow and other characters in his fiction, is altogether consonant with human psychology. And it has much to do with why *Remembering* deserves to be read as something larger than a provincial manifesto.

Two episodes recalled from Andy's stay in California can be identified as particularly relevant to catalyzing his spiritual turn of heart, or conversion, from despair toward personal salvation. Significantly, both take place in the densely urban setting of San Francisco. One is his glimpse of a sea lion, as he gazes out into the waters of San Francisco Bay. He is moved by the momentary sight of this animal, who "looks around with the intelligent gaze of a man" (42) and, unlike himself, is so evidently at home in that place of beauty it inhabits.

Yet another episode takes place at Washington Square in early morning, near the bench where a homeless person lies sleeping in this city of St. Francis. Andy looks up at Sts. Peter and Paul Church and reads there a famous line from Dante's *Paradiso* engraved on its face: "LA GLORIA DI COLUI CHE TUTTO MUOVE PER L'UNIVERSO PENETRA E RISPLENDE" (39). Berry later provides the main English sense of this text, which speaks of the Creator's "glory that moves all things resplendent everywhere" (49). The engraving still stands on the façade of Saints Peter and Paul Church, an actual San Francisco landmark.

There is therefore at least a touch of urban environmentalism evidenced in this passage and in the chapter's lyrical close, with Andy now at the cusp of deciding to head homeward. At this point, as he recalls an earlier visit to the Bay Area, that motto he had encountered by chance from Dante—another exile from home, from another time and place—begins to resonate more deeply with him. It stirs him to envision his home place not as a uniquely isolated enclave but as another face of that all-encompassing "glory" that is also discernible on the Pacific Coast:

> But the whole bay is shining now, the islands, the city on its hills, the wooden houses and the towers, the green treetops, the flashing waves and wings, the glory that moves all things resplendent everywhere. (49)

The blessed release from anger and despair that Catlett experiences as he finally reenters Port William derives from the expansive view of membership he has by that time acquired. The spirit of Dante still accompanies him, too, in the form of a ghostly guide, "a man, dark as shadow" who walks ahead of him to lend instruction because, like himself, "the place, though it is familiar to him, is changed." Although Catlett remains "dark to himself," still missing an arm, he finds himself made "whole" (100, 101). And the place he encounters now, through a kind of visionary dispensation, reveals itself to him as freshly permeable, through time as well as space. He sees its membership, like the communion of saints,[64] fully embracing the dead along with the living:

> The dark man points ahead of them; Andy looks and sees the town and the fields around it, Port William and its countryside

as he never saw or dreamed them, the signs everywhere upon them of the care of a longer love than any who have lived there have ever imagined.... Over town and fields the one great song sings, and is answered everywhere; every leaf and flower and grass blade sings. And in the fields and the town, walking, standing, or sitting under the trees, resting and talking together in the peace of a Sabbath profound and bright, are people of such beauty that he weeps to see them. He sees that these are the membership of one another and of the place and of the song or light in which they live and move.

He sees that they are the dead, and they are alive. He sees that he lives in eternity as he lives in time, and nothing is lost. (102)

Another work of fiction that illustrates Berry's cognizance of the mutability of place, in time as well as space, is his short story "The Boundary." Outwardly, at least, not much happens in this tale. Eighty-two-year-old Mat Feltner, not long before his death, feels compelled to set out from his home one day on foot to check on the condition of a fence, which also marks a boundary line, located at a distant reach of his property. During the walk, various landmarks he encounters stir his memory of friends and family members—most of whom have since died—associated with these spots. But on the way back he falters and loses his way. His situation becomes perilous until he finally manages to reach a road, where he is lucky enough to be spotted and rescued by persons familiar to him.

Despite the bodily danger he faces, Mat finds this excursion to be revelatory. Even at his advanced age and in "this place that has been his life," he finds there is ample space for new discovery, as he is drawn to recollect the "wild inward presence of the place" and all those he knows have peopled it, in one time and way or another.[65] There is even space enough here in which to get lost. For a time Mat feels the usual boundaries between past and present, life and death, here and there, slipping away, as "The dead come near him, and he is among them" (304). And well before he is assured that he will find his way to safety, he feels an inward peace and blessedness as he contemplates his relation to all those with whom he is bound in spiritual membership:

> A shadowless love moves him now, not his, but a love that he belongs to, as he belongs to the place and to the light over it.... He is thinking of the membership of the fields that he has belonged to all his life, and will belong to while he breathes, and afterward. He is thinking of the living ones of that membership,—at work today in the fields that the dead were at work in before them.
> "I am blessed," he thinks. "I am blessed." (305–306)

True, Berry's tale concludes on an apparently less sanguine note. We are told that on the night of his return, when Mat's wife finds him "wandering in the darkened house, he does not know where he is" (307). This experience of dislocation is arguably, though, more than just a sign of his mental decline. It signals as well Mat's deepening sense of the permeability of place and time as he approaches that ultimate dislocation of his own death.

This story thus dramatizes the liminal character of spatial and other boundaries. The way we typically define places, as delineated coordinates within space and time, has its uses but reflects a practical rather than absolute perception of reality. So Mat Feltner's familiar yet partly unknowable plot of land is, in the Christian idiom, that place where he is destined to work out his salvation. But it is not, in itself, the invariable locus of his membership in the Kingdom of God. To suppose otherwise would be to construe one's relation to land and place as idolatrous rather than sacramental—something Wendell Berry is scarcely disposed to do.

The last literary case of globally engaged localism I want to consider also happens to be an extreme case, insofar as the "place" that occupies its primary attention is no larger than a single square meter. In *The Forest Unseen: A Year's Watch in Nature*, my Sewanee colleague David Haskell fastens his gaze on a minute patch of woodland, situated in an old-growth portion of the University's extensive acreage known as Shakerag Hollow. He continues this close watching, with repeated visits to the site several times a week, through the course of a full calendar year. Here is localism with a vengeance! Yet the resulting account of his observations, which is also informed by a good deal of reflection and reading, amounts to a sustained meditation on the world.

The Forest Unseen is a kind of prose-poem that reveals the wondrous wealth of knowledge obtainable from attending closely to just one square meter of earth–but a microcosm apprehended in the context of a planetary, macrocosmic understanding. This award-winning book thus embodies a "search for the universal within the infinitesimally small." It supposes that the "truth of the forest," and by extension the dynamics of all life across the globe, "may be more clearly and visibly revealed by the contemplation of a small area."[66] Although or because its attention is so narrowly fixed, this book also illustrates how a person might, by combining scientific scrutiny and acumen with spiritual discipline and attentiveness, learn to see many of the otherwise-unseen textures of life on this planet.

Haskell, trained as a scientist but committed to meditative practice, calls the radically confined space he has chosen to study a "forest mandala." He recalls that the Tibetan mandala is classically understood to be a "re-creation of the path of life, the cosmos, and the enlightenment of Buddha. The whole universe is seen through this small circle of sand." Surpassing the limitations of purely objectified science while affirming the amplitude possible within an extreme spatial limitation, Haskell sees himself dedicated to contemplating his own form of sacred mandala. And he does so by mindfully investing himself in that which he observes. His is therefore a religious project, as well as a scientific one. He conceives of his book, articulated in a decidedly personal voice, as "a biologist's response to the challenge of the Tibetan mandala, of Blake's poems, of Lady Julian's hazelnut" (xi, xii).

Haskell witnesses nothing grand or glamorously exotic in his forest mandala, situated on an unexceptional plot of the Cumberland Plateau in rural Tennessee. But his patiently conducted contemplative survey reveals a plenitude of otherwise unseen truths about the many commonplace creatures he observes. He concentrates his gaze, enlarged by reading and long musing, on such things as lichens, snowflakes, fireflies, worms and microbes, turkey vultures, hepatica, Carolina chickadees, and snails. And he describes each of these creatures, and many more, within the additionally limited space of a particular date in time. Like other American naturalist authors before him, Haskell sets his narrative strictly within the frame of a calendar year, beginning with a chapter keyed to January 1 and ending with one for December 31.

Along the way, Haskell also aims to uncover the complex web of interconnections among various life-forms and features of inanimate nature. In his book such imaginative, inherently ecological insight extends beyond the strictly biological realm to address the interplay between nature and the affairs of human nature. It reveals, for example, how the relative dearth of mosquitoes on the Cumberland Plateau relates not only to malarial parasites but also, in turn, to the history of the University of the South and why the institution was originally sited on a particular upland in Middle Tennessee. We humans are "Russian dolls," Haskell declares, because our involvement with the rest of creation is so richly interlayered that we can even glimpse, in the light of science wedded to visionary imagination, how "the heartbeat of humans and the flowering of domesticated plants are one life" (4, 3).

The forest mandala thus constitutes a window "into the ecology of the world." And though Haskell hastens to point out that the patch of old-growth forest he has assigned himself to watch is only one such window, the place serves him effectively as a vantage point for envisioning the planet at large. "The flow of life here is powerfully affected by currents running in from the surrounding landscape," (244, 155) he notes. The same, of course, must be said of what sight and insight together can reveal when applied within the restricted sphere of any number of other mandala-like places.

3

THE PLACE OF IMAGINATION

THE EARTHINESS OF IMAGINATION AND A PHENOMENOLOGY OF PLACE

"Imagination," a word so evidently central to the vocation and sensibility of English Romantic poets, has likewise been invoked frequently as a defining term in American literary history. As James Engell has shown, conceptual interest in imagination had permeated European literature, literary theory, and philosophy well before Wordsworth and Coleridge articulated their own seminal principles of artistic creativity. Thus the idea of imagination, already prominent in eighteenth-century thought and discourse, might be understood as largely a product of the Enlightenment.[1] Or its origins could be traced still further back in time, to Aristotle and to European medieval thinkers such as Bonaventure and William Langland.[2] Yet it is hard to overstate the long-term influence of Coleridge's all-too-familiar pronouncements on the topic.

Framed in relation to a decidedly religious vision, Imagination for Coleridge names that vital, creative faculty of mind by which we envision the wholeness of reality, the often-unseen web of connections that unifies otherwise disparate elements of God's Creation. In contrast to what Coleridge called "Fancy," or unlike exercises in make-believe or esoteric abstraction, Imagination thus enables us to glimpse the fullness of reality. It corresponds, in fact, to what we might describe today as an inherently ecological cast of mind. Highlighting the "esemplastic power" of Imagination, Coleridge declared the "primary IMAGINATION" to be not only "the living Power and prime Agent of all human perception," but a re-creative force, nothing less than "a repetition in the finite mind of the eternal act of creation in the infinite I AM."[3]

Two features of Coleridge's formulation might be underscored here as salient. First, as already suggested, Imagination carries an ecological meaning by way of defining and affirming our participation in a comprehensive community of Creation extending beyond humankind. What the title character of Coleridge's "Rime of the Ancient Mariner" most clearly dramatizes, after all, through his wanton destruction of an animal—that great seabird—with whom he initially recognizes no kinship at all, is a failure of imagination.[4] It is likewise telling that a now-classic work of American ecocriticism by Lawrence Buell bears the main title of *The Environmental Imagination*.[5] The human faculty of imagination qualifies as inherently ecological, in scientific as well as literary terms, because it envisions the otherwise unseen interconnectedness of disparate elements.[6] For Coleridge, Imagination defined not only the organic interconnectedness of all things within the nonhuman order of Nature, but also to a reconciliation of polarities—involving the marriage of humanity's interior, psychic life with the rest of outward creation.[7]

A second point worth underscoring at the outset is the consistently theological character of Coleridgean Imagination—even though this writer's religious orientation shifted over time, from a pantheistic or Unitarian spirituality toward more orthodox, Anglican Christianity. From the standpoint of Coleridge's visionary faith perspective, the generative creativity of "the infinite I AM" can be glimpsed even in and through the artistry of finite humans. Coleridge understood what Engell calls "the god-like human power" of imagination to be "spiritual even as it works through matter, shaping it organically."

In its cosmic scope and truth-seeking potential, Imagination thus reflects something of divine revelation, while in its capacity for symbolic communication it is "strikingly parallel to the Logos or Christ." And the more conscious, willful exercise of psychic powers that Coleridge associated with secondary (as distinguished from primary) imagination seems particularly suggestive of divine intentionality.[8]

That the Imagination might be construed to bear some form of religious meaning and purpose has likewise shaped the poetic of American writers as diverse as Thoreau, Emerson, Muir, and Levertov. Thoreau, for example, in his famous deep-cut passage from the "Spring" chapter of *Walden*, describes the course of creation, witnessed throughout the course of nature, as a divinely engendered, evolutionary process. Marveling at "this hieroglyphic"—that is, sacred script—he finds inscribed in the railroad's thawing sandbank, he declares himself "as affected as if in a peculiar sense I stood in the laboratory of the Artist who made the world and me,—had come to where he was still at work, sporting on this bank, and with excess of energy strewing his fresh designs about."[9]

For Emerson, too, the prophetic inspiration of the creative artist—characteristically named the "poet"—derives from his or her organic participation in "the life of God." Imagination is that which "intoxicates the poet," enabling earthbound humans to act as "liberating gods." Recognition of a religious dimension more orthodox than Emerson's Transcendental faith is still more unmistakable in a critical statement by Denise Levertov, who wrote that "the imagination, which synergizes intellect, emotion, and instinct, is the perceptive organ through which it is possible, though not inevitable, to experience God."[10]

Romantic accounts of the creative imagination tend, however, to emphasize defining characteristics that are universal and abstract, rather than materially localized. There are exceptions, of course, both in the theory and, even more plainly, in the poetic practice of leading Romantic visionaries. In Wordsworth's "Tintern Abbey," for instance, the poet's all-encompassing reflections on nature, imagination, and his own mental processes are evidently rooted in an experience he identifies with a particular place and time. But the prevailing sense of imagination for Romantic theorists had more to do with exceptional qualities of mind, and thus with an interior landscape, than with the vivid apprehension of places on earth.

So the latter-day turn toward ecocriticism in literary studies, by focusing renewed attention on the place-grounded character of imagination, offers what I take to be a worthy qualification or corrective. Such recognition is effectively encapsulated, for example, in the title of a 2010 essay collection by Wendell Berry: *Imagination in Place*. It is likewise represented in the critical volume, edited by George Core and H. L. Weatherby, devoted to *Place in American Fiction: Excursions and Explorations*. Moreover, if what I am calling the "*earthiness* of imagination" is a latter-day coinage, the theme itself had long been anticipated by commentaries such as Eudora Welty's essay on "Place in Fiction" or, for that matter, by memorable lines that Shakespeare's Theseus voices in *A Midsummer Night's Dream*:

> *The lunatic, the lover, and the poet*
> *Are of imagination all compact*
> . . . .
> *The poet's eye, in a fine frenzy rolling,*
> *Doth glance from heaven to earth, from earth to Heaven,*
> *And as imagination bodies forth*
> *The forms of things unknown, the poet's pen*
> *Turns them to shapes and gives to airy nothing*
> *A local habitation and a name. (5.1.2–17)*[11]

Shakespeare's poet reflects something of the lunatic's audacity as well as the lover's urge to embrace worldly particulars.

In response to this almost erotic urge, the poet's Imagination looks to embody what is otherwise formless, situating those airy abstractions within "a local habitation."

According to Eudora Welty, the localizing impulse of imagination is particularly evident in novelistic fiction. Why so? Suspicious of fantasy narratives and appealing to literary history, she argues that it is

> because the novel from the start has been bound up in the local, the "real," the present, the ordinary day-to-day of human experience. Where the imagination comes in is in directing the use of all this. That use is endless, and there are only four words, of all the millions we've hatched, that a novel rules out: "Once upon a time." They make a story a fairy tale by the simple sweep of the remove—by abolishing the present and the place where we are instead of conveying them to us.

Welty conceives of fiction, then, "by the nature of itself," as "all bound up in the local." And the feelings we associate with particular places, she suggests, are intertwined with fictive imagination. "Location pertains to feeling," she writes, just as "feeling profoundly pertains to place," so that "place in fiction is the named, identified, concrete, exact and exacting, and therefore credible, gathering spot of all that has been felt, is about to be experienced, in the novel's progress."[12]

Throughout his essayistic volume devoted to *Imagination in Place*, Wendell Berry likewise underscores imagination's character as "a particularizing and a local force, native to the ground underfoot." Understandably, the ground Berry believes has most decisively shaped—and been shaped by—his own literary imagination is the agricultural community in Henry County, Kentucky, where he and his ancestors long ago set roots, "a place I don't remember not knowing." It has been the seminal locus not only of Berry's fiction, but of his poetic and nonfictional prose composition as well. And it has shaped his ideal of an imagination freighted with earthiness and existential meaning. "By imagination," he writes, "I do not mean the ability to make things up or to make a realistic copy" but "to make real to oneself the life of one's place or the life of one's enemy–and therein, I believe is imagination in the highest sense."[13]

For Berry, imagination also bears a religious dimension. He often describes his place of habitation in sacramental terms, as a divinely gifted land with sanctifying potential. His account of it is at once familiar, concretely evocative and redolent of soil, yet reverential and spiritually imbued. What better place to work out one's salvation than land so earnestly cared about and cared for, a community of life enspirited not only with human members and ancestors but with other creatures both wild and domestic? Having for decades sustained such care for his farm, Berry reports that "By means of the imagined place, over the last fifty years, I have learned to see my native landscape and neighborhood as a place unique in the world, a work of God, possessed of an inherent sanctity that mocks any human valuation that can be put upon it."

The place of imagination is thus defined as locally embodied yet permeated with sanctifying presence—as an earthiness consubstantial, in other words, with that which is unseen, unknown, and transcendent. Berry maintains that imagination in its "high sense" surpasses "the frameworks of realism in the arts and empiricism in the sciences . . . by placing the world and its creatures within a context of sanctity in which their worth is absolute and incalculable."[14]

So although grounded in place and time, earthy imagination also reflects—for Berry, as well as for Shakespeare—the "forms of things unknown," thereby surpassing the bounds of finitude.

Berry recognizes that, even for writers fully attentive to place-grounded features of the visible world, "imagination knows more than the eye sees." He points out that "Imagination 'completes the picture' by transcending the actual memories and probable facts."[15] For as Welty and others have suggested, Imagination can register in words not only sensate textures of reality, but also the presence of feelings, of unseen spirits. And it is not only through direct observation and experience but also through reflection, reading, and encounter with the musings of other minds that writers are enabled to re-create for us places such as Berry's Port William, Faulkner's Yoknapatawpha County, or Welty's worn path along the Natchez Trace.

What contribution, then, might philosophical discourse offer toward clarifying the place-related reach of imagination? What, in other words, might "the phenomenology of place" mean with reference to this study, and how might it apply to the issues and literary examples under consideration here?

One logical point of departure for considering phenomenology is the thought of Edmund Husserl, who took humankind's knowledge of the "external world" to be founded perforce on experiential consciousness. Consciousness is a keyword here. True, Husserl's neo-Kantian inquiry fell short of representing the self as fully situated in a social and natural environment. Still, affirming the intersubjectivity of human perception, Husserl declined to accept a purely idealistic ontology and epistemology. He did at least recognize the defining import of our bodily activity and immersion in a life world bounded by space.[16]

What has come to be known as the phenomenology of place, elaborated through philosophers such as M. Merleau-Ponty and Edward Casey, thus underscores without isolating the place-making role of human perception. It considers how our sense of place derives from bodily embedded experience, particularly that which involves us in commonplace actions and objects. It finds inspiration in Merleau-Ponty's attention to physical space as not merely "the setting (real or logical) in which things are arranged, but the means whereby the positing of things becomes possible," together with his somatic theory of human perception. Hence the philosopher's insistence that "Our own body is in the world as the heart is in the organism: it keeps the visible spectacle constantly alive, it breathes life in it and sustains it inwardly, and with it forms a system." A phenomenology of place likewise aims ordinarily to take full account of the interplay between objective and subjective perspectives on the self's relation to place.[17]

Husserl notes that emplaced perceptions of our environment are apt to be multilayered, apprehended largely through habitual and bodily actions, but may not always present themselves as fully or literally "conscious." "In a *broadest sense*," he writes, "the expression *consciousness* comprehends (but then indeed less suitably) all mental processes" so that "by virtue of extremely firm habits which have never been contravened, we take all these findings of psychological reflection as real worldly occurrences."[18] The workings of imagination likewise reflect something less than total or consistent self-awareness on the part of human agents. For if the creative process indeed requires one's investment of artful deliberation and craft, as acknowledged in Coleridge's account of the Secondary Imagination, it also calls for receptivity to the intuitional self, welling up from the psyche's subconscious depths.

Another trait of phenomenology germane to place-studies is the preoccupation with language evident in the writings of a philosopher such as Martin Heidegger. Heidegger's influential essay titled "Building Dwelling Thinking" suggests that more than physical materials are needed for any mortal to build an authentic dwelling place on earth. Expounding on multivalent meanings of the German words *Bauen* and *Wohnen*, denotatively equivalent to "building" and "dwelling," Heidegger argues that it is largely through language that we define our very being and construct a place to abide in the world. "It is language," he insists, "that tells us about the essence of a thing, provided that we respect language's own essence." Heidegger holds that a linguistic rather than a purely material dynamic shapes the manner in which we dwell in space, and that "Dwelling . . . . is *the basic character* of Being, in keeping with which mortals exist." He takes language therefore to be inseparable from all determinations of human identity and ontology. Moreover, the vision set forth in "Building Dwelling Thinking" affirms that mortal humans dwell in a space so cosmically expansive as to extend not only across the earth and under the sky, but also "before the divinities," those immortals whom the philosopher identifies as "beckoning messengers of the godhead."[19]

Whatever moral questions must arise in connection with Heidegger's biography and current reputation,[20] the theological tenor of such a statement—though existential rather than metaphysical for Heidegger—is apparent. In its poetic medium, its representation of humanity's dwelling place as an ordered space at least metaphorically infused with divine presence, Heidegger's formulation bears some resemblance to the more metaphysically shaped sentiments voiced in our time by Christian theologians and philosophers concerned with the sacramentality of place.[21]

For such Christian theologians and philosophers, as outward and visible signs of an invisible, unfathomable reality, sacraments enact the interplay between matter and spirit. Unlike scientific materialism on the one hand or religious pantheism on the other, sacramental Christianity posits a dynamically relational worldview in which neither matter nor spirit counts as all-absorbing reality. As John Inge suggests, sacramental theology is not only relational in essence but place-related as well. Sacraments must be constituted, after all, through actions performed within the material setting of a certain place and time. By the same token, epiphanic personal encounters with the divine, including Moses' prototypical revelation from the burning bush, are invariably linked to particular sites, which may thereafter be remembered and honored as holy or "thin" places allied to the spirit-world.

What sacramentality implies, according to Inge, is that humankind may glimpse openings of the numinous on earth only through certain emplaced *events*, in contrast to the questionable presumption "that the world itself is self-revelatory of God in a general and indiscriminate manner."[22] This focus on discrete occurrences in time has an artistic corollary, I believe, insofar as all narrative literature likewise depends on what is disclosed through events or actions of one sort or another. And even in some post-Christian literary contexts, a writer may construe the existential quest to conjoin matter with spirit in sacramental terms. Such language, as we have already noted in Chapter 1, characterizes for instance Henry Thoreau's usage in *Walden*. Thoreau's first-person exposition further illustrates how the self's relation to place may be mediated through the meditative praxis of a "placed self," a topic worth exploring with reference to the imaginative sensibility of other American writers as well.

THE CONTEMPLATIVE REACH OF IMAGINATION: POETRY OF WALT WHITMAN AND MARILYN NELSON

Probably influenced by Puritan and Quaker traditions of introspective piety dating from the colonial era, much of America's literary culture, both early and late, reflects a contemplative disposition. That disposition often shapes personal narratives—including those nonfictional, decidedly place-engaged ruminations recorded by figures such as Henry Thoreau, Ed Abbey, Annie Dillard, Terry Tempest Williams, and Kathleen Norris. And it pertains, above all, to poetic literature. For the very nature of poetry seems to require of readers, as well as writers, a willingness to engage in sustained, unhurried reflection. No wonder Wendell Berry invites those who would genuinely appreciate his "Sabbath Poems" to read them slowly, in silence and solitude.[23] Present-day notice of a "poetry slam," imaging the spectacle of a loudly pugnacious contest, therefore strikes me as a contradiction in terms.

Poetry of meditation, which is often, if not always, religious in orientation, has figured prominently throughout our literary history. Its practitioners have included writers ranging from Edward Taylor and Anne Bradstreet in colonial New England to the likes of Emily Dickinson, Wallace Stevens, T. S. Eliot, Gary Snyder, Denise Levertov, Wendell Berry, and Mary Oliver.[24] If "contemplation" best describes a disposition or mode of being, commonly identified with the wordlessly unitive endpoint of the mystical way, "meditation" refers instead to an activity, the exercise of some mental and spiritual praxis—not unlike the discipline involved in poetic composition. Mainly an interior process aimed at psychic integration, the meditative activity in question may be accompanied by bodily motion in the form of walking meditation, Hatha yoga, or paced and mindful breathing. But its chief aim is to recollect the self, to combine rational and subconscious qualities of mind—including those inward faculties sometimes identified, following St. Augustine's classic Trinitarian formula, as memory, understanding, and will.

In any case, meditation always amounts to an activity, something that (unlike idle daydreaming) one sets out to *do*. Anyone who practices it is always already situated somewhere in an identifiable time and space. Consequently, poetry of meditation often finds matter for reflection through the authorial *persona*'s attentiveness to a particular place or places. One illustration is the series of poetic meditations Denise Levertov composed, from the standpoint of her home in Seattle, as she gazed at and reflected inwardly on distant Mount Rainier.[25] Another is

T. S. Eliot's *Four Quartets*. Its sequence amounts to a sustained meditation on lofty topics such as the meaning of the time, history, art, human mortality, and, above all, the Christian doctrine of Incarnation, expressed as "the point of intersection of the timeless / With time."[26] Yet its exploration of these cosmic themes remains conspicuously place-centered and earthbound because Eliot situated each poem of the sequence at a particular site, laden with personal meaning, either in England or America.

By imaginative extension, place-identified consciousness has played a role in Christian traditions of spirituality even when the exercise's primary focus is scriptural meditation. Toward the start of St. Ignatius Loyola's *Spiritual Exercises*, meditative practitioners are urged to form "a mental representation of the place" portrayed in each relevant biblical narrative. Ignatius thus specifies that "When the contemplation or meditation is on something visible, for example, when we contemplate Christ our Lord, the representation will consist in seeing in imagination the material place where the object is that we wish to contemplate. I said the material place, for example, the temple, or the mountain where Jesus or His Mother is, according to the subject matter of the contemplation."[27]

Among the nineteenth-century works that reward consideration in this light, Walt Whitman's *Leaves of Grass* offers an unusually provocative verse illustration of how one poet's meditative imagination interacts with embodied space—in fact, with a dynamic succession of visualized sites. Take, for example, the startling opening poem of the 1855 *Leaves*, later titled "Song of Myself." At first blush this long, sprawling marvel of declamatory rhetoric lacks any indication of where its author is situated. Whose voice is this? From what geospatial locus does it arise? Evidently someone is loafing somewhere on a field of grass, but the poem in 1855 offers few preliminary hints of its setting on the map or authorial identity. It remains untitled, with the volume as a whole bearing no author's name. Starting from the poem's initial line, "I celebrate myself,"[28] its musings seem lodged, if anywhere, in the consciousness of an untethered, solitary self rather than in any recognizable locale.

But as the poet continues to sound the "barbaric yawp" (85) of his free-flowing verse across the world's rooftops, he offers further clues about his person and place of origin. Eventually he announces himself as "Walt Whitman, an American, one of the roughs, a kosmos" (48) and still more pointedly, in later versions, as a New Yorker, "of Manhattan the son." References to a surrounding seascape, together with animated images of a culturally diverse citizenry at work and play—all of these, too, suggest the poet's primary setting in metropolitan New York.

Yet before long, and especially by the time the poet declares himself "afoot with my vision" (37) in what becomes section 33, his spatial frame of reference expands to limitless proportions. Despite the nation's looming sectional crisis, this work's protean persona counts himself now "a southerner soon as a northerner" (40), a voice qualified to speak on behalf of sundry regions and states throughout the Union and beyond. Place-names abound in the work's sprawling catalog sequences, with the poet walking in an "unending procession" across

> *the roads of Ohio and Massachusetts and Virginia and Wisconsin and New York and New Orleans and Texas and Montreal and San Francisco and Charleston and Savannah And Mexico...*
> *Our swift ordinances are on their way over the whole earth....* (69)

One must wonder, though, whether this claim of ubiquitous consciousness erodes the poem's ability to convey a genuine sense of place. Might readers of "Song of Myself" find, in other words, that this poet abides nowhere on earth by claiming to be everywhere?

Looking at the 1855 Preface to *Leaves* helps, I believe, to explain how Whitman understands the poetics of place in "Song of Myself." From the Preface, where he declares "the United States themselves are essentially the greatest poem" (5), he signals his intention to compose a poem as vital, varied, and imaginatively expansive as the nation to which he gives voice. He presents this chant of a representative American self as his verbal counterpart of the United States. It enacts the nation's motto of *e pluribus unum* [out of many, one] and sets forth a vision of "place" framed in continental than rather than strictly local or provincial terms. The physical scale of place remains, after all, notoriously difficult to define. New York City qualifies as a place, but so does a pinhead, a bioregion such as the Everglades, our Milky Way galaxy, or that spot of earth where the poet lies observing "a spear of summer grass" (25).

"Song of Myself" can profitably be read as an extended meditation on that single spear of grass, revealing its microcosmic and dialectical relation to the whole of life—including the macrocosmic expanse of the American nation. Centering his attention on one green blade, the poet discerns therein a "uniform hieroglyphic" (29) whose import expands to address all of nature and nation. Whitman thus interprets the grass, a Transcendentalist token of all-encompassing Spirit, as what might be deemed a *sacramental* medium. Through his practice of focused meditation, together with bodily mindfulness of his own "respiration and inspiration" (25), he becomes receptive to still-deeper revelation. In what becomes section 5 he testifies to having experienced a mystical epiphany affording him viscerally assured knowledge "that the elderhand of God is the promise of my own" and "that a kelson of the creation is love" (29). For this poet "of the body" (44) no less than of the soul, the role that bodily experience plays toward shaping one's emplacement in the world could scarcely be more graphically illustrated than in that germinal account.[29]

Another of Whitman's poems, first published in the 1856 *Leaves*, offers a more sharply localized account of how spirits of place can be apprehended through a process of imaginatively enlarged meditation. The occasion of "Crossing Brooklyn Ferry" (originally titled the "Sun-Down Poem") was a familiar feature of urban life in Whitman's place and time: the East River boat passage that crowds of passengers took each day, close to sunset, from Manhattan to Brooklyn. But as the poet reflects on his own experience of this crossing, something he had done "many and many a time," he begins to grasp its existential implications. Conducted toward the end of day, the river crossing calls to mind the finite course of Everyman's life journey. The poet ends up perceiving, beneath the surface impression of "crowds of men and women attired in the usual costumes,"[30] a darker reality of mortality and the alienation wrought by mutability and time's passage. Yet by identifying imaginatively with fellow passengers in his own day, as well as with those of future generations, he believes it possible to transcend these limitations, to the point where "it avails not, time nor place—distance avails not" (160). Aiming to bridge the gap between his mortal self and others, he extends his imaginative address even to those members of a future generation—to the likes of *us*, that is—who never took the ferry crossing but can now only read about it in his poem. The haunting immediacy of his address to current readers arises from bodily involvement in the scene he absorbs in New York Harbor yet paradoxically manages to traverse space and time:

> *Closer yet I approach you,*
> ....
> *Who knows but I am enjoying this?*

> *Who knows, for all the distance, but I am as good as looking at you now, for all you cannot see me? (163)*

For that matter, the place-engaged communion that Whitman imagined extends beyond the medium of a ferry crossing to the subsequent crossings on this same site that multitudes continue to make across the Brooklyn Bridge. Completed in 1883 near the end of Whitman's life, that structure, too, came to be invested with religious symbology, in Hart Crane's lyrical paean "To Brooklyn Bridge." Crane apotheosizes this newer triumph of *techne*, successor of the ferry crossing, for its material capacity to "lend a myth to God."[31] And throughout his larger epic work titled *The Bridge*, Crane certainly reflects cognizance of Whitman's mythmaking contribution in poems such as "Crossing Brooklyn Ferry."

That "Crossing Brooklyn Ferry" dramatizes how a sacramental process of Transcendental communion can take place in a densely urban scene, rather than in the wild, is particularly noteworthy. Most remarkably, Whitman seizes gratefully rather than disdainfully on the industrial sights and sounds of New York Harbor, choosing to embrace these material agents of commerce as "glories strung like beads on my smallest sights and hearings" (160). So the poem closes with Whitman's blessing the built environment's worldly objects of trade, here esteemed as "dumb, beautiful ministers" capable of furnishing "parts toward the soul":

> *Thrive, cities—bring your freight, brings your shows, ample and*
> *sufficient rivers,*
> *Expand, than which none else is perhaps more spiritual,*
> *Keep your places, objects than which none else is more lasting.*

You have waited, you always wait, you dumb, beautiful ministers,

....

....

You furnish your parts toward eternity,
Great or small, you furnish your parts toward the soul. (165)

Given Whitman's curiosity about those who would inhabit America in future generations, I suspect he would be pleased to learn how prominently place-directed meditation also figures in the poetry of some contemporary writers. Marilyn Nelson, for example, has sustained mindful reflection on the existential and ancestral meaning of manifold sites throughout her writing career. For some years she has also practiced contemplative prayer, approached largely but not exclusively in the context of her Christian faith. Nelson has, in addition, taught collegiate courses on "Poetry and Meditation" in which students were expected, within class sessions and otherwise, to set aside time for practicing silent meditation and for developing contemplative awareness.[32] Remarkably, she has even ventured to offer this course to cadets enrolled in the US Military Academy at West Point. And in her poetry collection titled *Magnificat* (1994) she devotes a fair share of attention to ruminations on the art and spirituality of meditation. This volume highlights her inspiring and affectionate yet problematic interactions with a Roman Catholic priest and former Benedictine who lives in Mauritius and who assumes in many of her poems the title of "Abba Jacob."

Born in Cleveland, Nelson moved as a child with her family from one military base to another, later spending time in California, Pennsylvania, and Minnesota, among other places, though she has ended up residing in Connecticut for most of her adult life. In her third book of poems, however, she settles her imagination in Kentucky, to dwell at length in a home place and era of ancestral memory antedating her own birth. A house once inhabited by Nelson's African American forebears on Moscow Street in Hickman, Kentucky, serves from the outset as a material ground of inspiration, a "ragged source of memory," for the book's multigenerational course of introspection. This dwelling, a modest structure, looks like "nothing special"—"a tarpaper-shingled bungalow / whose floors tilt toward the porch, / whose back yard ends abruptly / in a weeded ravine." Yet it concretizes for the poet a genealogical identity—a home place in spirit—whose substance is otherwise recoverable only through archival fragments, through stories imperfectly recollected and gleaned from relatives, combined with the exercise of sympathetic imagination. The tale thus unfolded includes episodes of sorrow, cruelty, injustice, and loss but also tokens of perseverance, humor, compassion, and love—extending even to devout praise:

> As much as love,
> as much as a visit
> to the grave of a known ancestor
> the homeplace moves me not to silence
> but to righteous, praise Jesus song.[33]

The narrative thread of Nelson's aptly titled volume *The Home Place* begins in antebellum Kentucky. This earliest phase of this family history centers on Diverne, the poet's great-great-grandmother. A spirited woman, Diverne is portrayed as resilient, attractive, and mostly self-possessed despite her condition of enslavement prior to emancipation. As a young woman she had been dragged to a Kentucky plantation in a nightmarish journey "all the long way from Jamaica." Yet she managed to maintain a certain reserve of dignity and equipoise: amazingly through it all, it seems, "she balanced life" (8, 12).

Diverne bore in her body all the contradictions intrinsic to her place in a thoroughly patriarchal, racially stratified society. The poem "Diverne's House" describes how she had been exploited not only by Val Matson, the second of her two black husbands, who left her an inheritance "of five / measly dollars," but also by a white man, identified in another poem as "Mister Tyler" (6–7, 10). The poem "Diverne's Waltz" imagines how Henry Ashburne Tyler must have been smitten by the charms of this lively slave woman: "Taking her hands, Henry Tyler gives her a twirl /and off they waltz" (10). And as the plantation owner's son and Diverne's social superior in every respect, this well-placed white attorney—soon to leave home to fight with the Confederate Army—would be hard to resist. Probably for her, under the circumstances, impossible. Mister Tyler did leave her a house. Yet despite Tyler's later promises, some sign of affection, and the tease of romance, a man like him could offer her no enduring place in his world other than one marked by shame and denial:

> *The house of myth;*
> *the house that shame built;*
> *the house given to Diverne.*
> *The myth of a slave woman*
> *who had to be broken, but bore*
> *two children, neither Negro*
> *nor white. The myth*
> *of their father*
>
> *The myth of She Loved Him,*
> *She Loved Herself Not.* (6)

For all the shame Diverne assumed from her sexual involvement with Tyler, she and her successors nonetheless took pride in that union's progenitive outcome: the birth of a son, Rufus Atwood (otherwise known as "Pomp"), the poet's great-grandfather. "Pomp was their / share of the future," Nelson acknowledges, "And it wasn't rape. / In spite of her raw terror. And his whip" (14). Nelson's project to discover her own place in ancestral history thus becomes tangled in knots of moral ambiguity. Henry James once opined that "It's a complex fate, being an American."[34] But to be an African American means assuming a yet more complex fate and cultural heritage. One's genealogical legacy is apt to be irretrievable, effectively erased along with ancestral names by the dominant history, or else enmeshed in painful contradictions such as those Marilyn Nelson confronts in her verse. Nelson's extended narrative in *The Homeplace* does sound a note of "black pride," as in the homage it gives to latter-day family members, including the poet's storytelling mother, Johnnie Mitchell Nelson, whose photo adorns the book's cover, and her father, Melvin Nelson, a member of the illustrious Tuskegee Airmen in World War II. But it is a story in which the pride of forebears such as Diverne Atwood not only had to resist the demeaning force of white dominance but also and impossibly ended up wedding it, in the person of Henry Ashburne Tyler. Scarcely an exercise in nostalgia, *The Homeplace* thus contains within its larger flow a sad story about sleeping with the enemy—collaboration with a vengeance, so to speak.

Moreover, as in the case of another poem that Nelson published years later, the very name of Henry Ashburne Tyler carries a subsurface yet explosive irony in this context beyond the man's obvious identification with slaveholding interests and the Confederacy. For Captain Henry Tyler not only held officer rank in the Confederate Army but served, as Nelson writes, in "the ranks / of General Forrest's / ferocious raiders." Tyler fought, in other words, under Lieutenant General Nathan Bedford Forrest, the fiercely combative officer and former slave-trader who today bears a notorious reputation for his treatment of African Americans. Suspected of having ordered, or at least condoned or ignored, the slaughter of black Union soldiers who were trying to surrender during the battle of Fort Pillow in April of 1864, Forrest has often been deemed a war criminal.[35] In any case, Forrest's proslavery zeal and racism, even if moderated late in life, was pronounced even by Confederate standards. This commander of Henry Ashburne Tyler also assumed a new role, following the war, as first Grand Wizard of the nascent Ku Klux Klan.[36]

And yet, consistent with the complex fate that Nelson traces throughout her ancestral saga, she discerns, even amid these swirling undercurrents of history, signs of redemptive grace. Nelson attributes to "Aunt Annie," for example, one of her maternal ancestors, a bold and prayerful invocation that reverberates against the "white-splashed red brick walls" of a church in that same state of Kentucky where the Atwood family had endured several scenes of degradation. Literary imagination, we recall, can not only describe a place but also act to create one. Accordingly, it is through language itself that Aunt Annie's devoutly feminine yet "magnified" voice creates in this brick-enclosed space something of a restorative holy place:

> *Father in heaven,*
> *I thank You this morning.*
> *I thank You that You have given us*
> *this hallowed day.*
> *I thank You that You have made us*
> *into this nation of fellowship,*
> *conceived in slavery's deceit*
> *but raised on the breast-milk of truth.*
> *. . . . .*
> *As You shared our enslavement, Lord,*
> *through your son, Jesus:*
> *when we were heartdead;*
> *when we were woe-begotten, bleeding and whipped:*
> *Be with us again. (29)*

Perhaps surprisingly, the homeplace with which Nelson most closely identifies by the close of her book is not, in geographic terms, either her later residence in Connecticut or the story's opening scene in Hickman, Kentucky. She chooses instead as her primary setting for poems that begin the volume's final sequence, titled "Wings," a military base in Alabama. There at Tuskegee Airfield her father had trained as a combat aviator, one of the "proud black men" who were first of their race "to touch / their fingers to the sky" (41). Nelson perceives a kind of inspirational transcendence in the way these men, starting from Tuskegee, managed to soar above the limitations of their time and place. So ultimately, yet perhaps suitably in accord with the forcibly uprooted and diasporic culture she shares, she identifies as her home place a somewhere fixed nowhere on earth:

> *Suddenly*
> *when I hear airplanes overhead—*
> *big, silver ones*
> *whose muscles fill the sky—*
> *I listen: That sounds like*
> *someone I know.*
> *And the sky*
> *looks much closer.*
> . . . .
> *This is my other heritage:*
> *I have roots in the sky.*
> *The Tuskegee Airmen*
> *are my second family.*
> *This new, brave,*
> *decorated tribe.*
>
> *My family.*
> *My homeplace, at last.*
> *It was there*

> all through time.
> I only had
> to raise my eyes. (52)

NUMINOUS LAYERINGS OF PLACE AS PALIMPSEST

That place is mutable, multilayered, constantly being overwritten and altered by the changes and chances of life is a familiar theme in literature, perhaps especially so in the context of American civilization, still relatively new and susceptible to rapid change.[37] Several American writers—including John Muir, Barry Lopez, and Wendell Berry—have invoked the term "palimpsest" as a metaphorically apt shorthand to describe the multilayered, ever-changing essence of place within space and time. The term itself derives from the ancient practice of writing one text over another on parchment, leaving the prior script either effaced or obscured. Likewise from the perspective of earth science as well as human cultural history, every place on earth is always becoming another place,[38] inevitably modifying or replacing over time whatever preceded it. Every site, in a given moment, can also be construed as a multitude of interlayered if not disparate places, with the sense of each dependent on the subjectivity, personality, and immediate disposition of the human being who imagines it.

John Muir stated that just as a script when repeatedly overwritten becomes unreadable, so also we find our powers "perplexed and overtaxed in reading the inexhaustible pages of nature, for they are written over and over uncountable times" and in "characters of every size and color." It is nonetheless marvelous to imagine how "all together form the one grand palimpsest of the world." And in our own day Wendell Berry, writing of his own "Native Hill" in Kentucky, witnesses to his familiarity with the many interwoven textures, both natural and cultivated, of the land before him:

> I think of the country as a kind of palimpsest scrawled over with the comings and goings of people, the erasure of time already in process even as the marks of passage are put down. There are the ritual marks of neighborhood—roads, paths between houses. There are the domestic paths from house to barns and outbuildings and gardens, farm roads threading the pasture gates. There are the wanderings of hunters and searchers after lost stock, and the speculative or meditative or inquisitive "walking around" of farmers on wet days and Sundays. There is the spiraling geometry of the rounds of implements in fields, and the passing and returning scratches of plows across croplands.[39]

This interlayering over space and across time may be imbued with an elusive, enigmatic character that hints at something ineffable, an opening toward the numinous. Thus one finds famous Christian shrines such as Chartres Cathedral in France and the Basilica of Our Lady of Guadalupe in Mexico City, both of which honor Mary of Nazareth as the Mother of God, constructed literally upon sites where pagan goddess worship once took place. Or consider how clearly Jerusalem and Rome, two of the world's great cities esteemed for centuries as holy places, retain physical signs of their richly layered, palimpsestic histories. As Hawthorne recognized in *The Marble Faun*, the scenes observable in modern Rome reflect at once a displacement of past civilizations as well as shades of their ghostly presence and persistence. And in Jerusalem, because of the complex and problematic overlayering of religious traditions that converge there, that city continues to enfold not only numerous place-identities but also some highly contested ones.[40]

For a telling literary illustration of how place can be imaginatively construed as palimpsest, we might return for now to

Marilyn Nelson's Tuskegee, home base of the Tuskegee Airmen. Another of Tuskegee's claims to fame has been the long-term presence there of George Washington Carver, otherwise known as "the peanut man." Born into slavery, this eminent proponent of scientific agriculture taught and conducted research at the Tuskegee Institute for almost five decades prior to his death there in 1943. Through the many agricultural products he created and the methods of land management he championed, he also labored to improve the lot of impoverished black farmers across the South. So it is noteworthy that in a subsequent volume of poetry titled *Carver: A Life in Poems* (2001), Marilyn Nelson again centers her imagination on that site in Macon County, Alabama, that holds a revered and almost-sacred status in black history. Tuskegee is where Nelson's father had trained to fly—but also where Booker T. Washington, who first invited George Washington Carver to join the teaching faculty, had founded a pioneering institution dedicated to education by and for African Americans.

Nelson's poetic exploration of the scientist's life story in *Carver* leads toward a crucial epiphany in the volume's final poem, "Moton Field." Pondering the place and the memories gathered at Tuskegee, she is intrigued to find her father's career intersecting imaginatively with that of black America's iconic scientist—both of them present, though each without knowledge of the other, on the same site around the same time. As Carver departed this life at Tuskegee in January of 1943, within the shadow of a world war antithetical to his own pacifist beliefs, Lieutenant Melvin Nelson was there training to depart for military service abroad. But this place meant something different to each of them and had to mean something else again for the poet, who never resided there except in imagination. Yet by virtue of imagination, subsequently embodied in literary art, Tuskegee became indeed a meaningful place for Nelson—even, it seems, a holy place—with ties of personal feeling forming in her through sustained study and reflection on the life of George Washington Carver.

Carver: A Life in Poems explores in some depth how the life of this noted scientist, reformer, and mentor of youth came to be rooted in his Christian faith and centered at Tuskegee. Predictably, Carver sometimes found his faith sorely tried. He faced his share of adversity in the form of doubts, setbacks, and the trials of discrimination he endured—as indicated in poems such as "How a Dream Dies," "Goliath," and "House Ways and Means." In his youth, Carver suffered the privations of dire poverty and orphanhood. Throughout his life he persevered in the face of racist indignities, loneliness, and scandalous disregard for his work and welfare even on the part of Booker T. Washington and other Tuskegee colleagues. Yet through it all, the overall impression of the man that *Carver* conveys is unapologetically hagiographic.[41] Nelson's volume qualifies, in fact, as a contemporary poetic reinscription of the classic saint's life, unfolding as it does a story deemed worthy of emulation as well as admiration. That Carver understood himself to be living and acting in response to a divine calling is confirmed, for instance, through Nelson's representation of testimony from a beloved female friend of his:

> *He told me of the vision*
> *He'd had on his first day here:*
> *That the school would flourish,*
> *That Tuskegee was the place for him*
> *To be God's instrument.*[42]

Among the saintly virtues Nelson highlights in various of the poems are Carver's perseverance, charity, compassion, and tireless service to others. The services he renders, particularly through his inventive genius in botany and agriculture, are shown in "From an Alabama Farmer" to extend well beyond the students he instructs at Tuskegee. And in poems such as "My Dear Spiritual Boy," "My Beloved Friend," and "Last Talk With Jim Hardwick," Nelson shows how Carver's tutelage and long-term friendship or amorous tie with a young white man reach well beyond usual racial bounds. Carver believed that his scientific investigations, too, including his fascination with the world's material luminescence, confirmed his involvement in the great mystery of God's Creation—as dramatized in poems such as "Clay" and "The Dimensions of the Milky Way."

"Professor Carver's Bible Class" indicates the significance of Carver's larger presence at Tuskegee not only through his instruction in botany, chemistry, and agricultural science but also through the evangelical leadership he exercised within that community. For a student who had hitherto been "living in fear of a Great Master's wrath," Carver's teaching

> *Gave me the means*
> *To liberation from that slavish faith.*
> *He taught us that our Creator lives within,*
> *yearning to speak to us through silent prayer. (75)*

Steeped in biblical narratives and language, Carver sought personal guidance and wisdom not only from the Book of Nature but also from scriptural passages such as the Genesis account of Isaac's rescue from deathly sacrifice. The poem "Bedside Reading" shows Carver struggling to reconcile his reading of one text from Scripture with another scrap of writing, the Bill of Sale "for a thirteen-year-old girl named Mary." This last document represents "his only link with his mother" and the era of bondage. In every other way, he finds himself in his current place and time sadly dislocated from family members, all of them now lost and "buried out there" somewhere. But in a world that is often threatening or brutal, he clings the more steadfastly to some key elements of faith:

> When the ram bleats from the thicket,
>   Isaac ... like me ... understands
> the only things you can ever
>   really ... trust ...
> are ...
>   the natural order ...
>   ... and the Creator's love ...
>   spiraling ...
> out of chaos .... (42)

In Nelson's closing poem, "Moton Field," the volume's palimpsestic imaging of Tuskegee comes to fullest realization through its interlayered representation of this place from the divergent perspectives of George Washington Carver, Melvin Nelson, and the poet herself. The poet imagines a scene in which Carver, nearing death, signs his name shakily to some letters with a "palsied right hand" at the same time that airman Melvin Nelson ascends with a flourish and "makes a sky-roaring victory roll."

Set in the 1950s and 1960s, *La Maravilla* by Alfredo Véa, Jr. is a lesser-known, autobiographically inspired novel that captures the palimpsestic character of an Arizona squatter's community in colorfully ethnographic terms. The locale in question, known as Buckeye Road, is an impoverished, culturally heterogeneous, intensely volatile settlement situated in desert country on the outer margins of Phoenix. In this forgotten place crammed with displaced souls [the *desplazada*] there are "no street names or street signs,"[43] no cabs or streetlights or civic services of any kind.

Like Véa himself, the novel's central character, a boy named Beto, bears a mixed lineage. Having been abandoned by a mother who only later reappears to claim him, he lives in Buckeye with his grandmother Josephina, a resilient Spanish woman graced with special power as a traditional healer or *curandera*, and his grandfather Manuel, a Yaqui Indian. Josephina's inherited disposition as a generally observant Roman Catholic sets her in conflict with Manuel, who continues to honor the governing myths, beliefs, and rituals of his cultural heritage. Scorning what she takes to be the pagan recalcitrance of this husband who "does not await the Resurrection" (5), Josephina aims to instill in her grandson beliefs comparable to her own. Out of desperation she baptizes Beto repeatedly. Beto's two grandparents thus wage an ongoing "war for the child's soul" (261).

Yet despite this agonistic strain of Josephina's relation to Manuel, the two remain deeply bonded while alive, and even somehow beyond the grave, by a fierce yet often-unspoken love. Moreover, Josephina finds herself inadvertently sympathizing with much of what Manuel, despite his nominal Catholicism, has retained of traditional, Native American customs and beliefs. "'I call him a heathen,' she admits, 'and then I find myself turning to his ways.'" As Manuel recognizes, Josephina is a *bruja*—that is, a kind of "curing witch" or healer who casts out evil spirits, a "*curandera* but with a special understanding of signs and spirits" that is "definitely not Catholic, and that makes her feel very guilty" (161, 34). Her medicine bag contains esoteric herbs and powders, a brew with dead scorpions, and an oddly configured, other-than-Christian cross given her by a mystery woman—but shelters there as well a proper Catholic crucifix. Josephina proves tough enough to have once spat and stuck out her crucifix at Satan himself, while having "said the name of the Christ almighty at the same moment" (149). Even when exercising healing powers derived from pagan magic and folkways she believes she "must include Christ in these things" (161). And at the story's close, as Josephina gives up her grandson, she shouts out these final words to the daughter who is taking him away: "'If they ever ask you about me ... tell them I was a saint'" (305). Josephina has reason indeed to trust she has found favor with God, even if the sainthood she claims mainly concerns her fidelity to a lowercase "catholic" version of faith and ethics.

Beyond these basic elements of plot and characterization, though, the real essence of *La Maravilla* lies in its evocation of Buckeye's distinctive character as a place set apart from middle-class America. By extension, Véa's account of this multilayered, carnivalesque[44] community dramatizes as well the conceptual variability and permeability of place in general, above all with reference to a diversely populated built environment.

What does Véa's Buckeye Road actually look like? On several fronts, it appears to be a desolate, god-forsaken place. It is full of dust, grime, and seedy castoffs from mainstream culture including a Cadillac junkyard, cars with rotting tires, an unsightly yellow house trailer, and adobe dwellings set among tar-paper and cardboard shacks. It is the scene of prostitution, squabbles, flash floods, knifings, and other outbreaks of violence. The inhabitants of this "junk heap of a town" (22) constitute an often-contentious *omnium gatherum* of Mexicans, mestizos, "Okies" and "Arkies," Chinese, lesbian *maricones*, African Americans, prostitutes, alcoholics, pushers and gamblers, migrants, destitute vagrants, and putative spiritualists. One could even say that Buckeye Road "wasn't much of a town" at all, "just a place where a pocked and pitted road met an invisible street" (64, Figure 3.1).

Yet while god-forsaken in all these ways, Buckeye also bristles with numinous energy and presence—including, beneath the grim surface of things, some surprising incursions of divine grace. Swirling within rather than despite the array of ethnocultures concentrated in this shanty town one finds all manner of ghosts, rituals, dreamers, sacred stories and memories, receptivity to magic and mythology, and spirits both godly and ungodly. The *genius loci* sustains a vibrantly protean presence in Buckeye. Josephina rightly concludes that "For all the desolation of this place, there was a lot of life here" (98).

THE PLACE OF IMAGINATION | 135

FIGURE 3.1 Camp for cotton pickers in Buckeye, Maricopa County, Arizona. US National Archives and Records.

If at times the thick interlayering of ethnicities and human types gathered in Buckeye promotes strife, it also contributes to the fullness of life that Josephina perceives there. And as Beto's grandfather reminds the boy, his mixed but traditionally grounded heritage offers him all the more reason to claim a solidly emplaced religious identity:

"Abuelo," the boy interrupted, "is it true I am an American? Vernetta says I'm a Mexican but also an American."
"Yes, you are American, but not in the gringo sense . . . . You are Spanish and Yaqui, you are a mestizo from Aztlán, this land, right here where the Nahua people began . . . . That is what a Mexican is. But you were born here in America, *también*, and

that's what a Chicano is. You don't become nothing. It's only the gringos that become! They are Xipe," he said, referring to the ancient god of new growth beneath the old, the god the Aztecs distorted into the God of the Flayed Skin. It was Manuel's word for those people on earth who do not know where they belong.

"They become other religions like choosing a hat and become other names and have no connection to places they live. They become the things they own or the cars they drive . . . . They have no stories. They have no tribe. Their camp fire is the goddamn television." (35)

Beneath its face of impoverished desolation, Buckeye thus offers several veins of access to a sacramental grace quite unlike the disenchanted materialism that dominates America's majority culture. Josephina's love of music emerges as one such medium of sacramental encounter. Manuel, too, declares that '"All sounds are a *ventriloquia de Dios*'" (188). Entranced by the music of Duke Ellington and other black artists, Josephina once played the piano for silent movies. She even believes that, thanks to counsel received directly from the Holy Mother, she was able to capture the heart of her future husband by sounding the right notes on her keyboard. She also relishes the animated, joyous spirit of African American choral singing, which she takes to be inspiring and revelatory when she occasionally shows up at Mighty Clouds of Joy, Buckeye's black evangelical congregation. And she makes a point of attending religiously to that church choir even while remaining at home:

> "All that beauty comes from suffering," Abuela would say. She would open the window every Sunday morning and again when the congregation choir practiced on Wednesday evenings. She would stop the gramophone or the piano to listen.
> "Audacity, *mijo. Audacia*. The audacity to speak to God in their own way and no one else's. God can't help but listen to that. Do you hear it? He can't help but listen." (71)

Another sacramental dimension of life in Buckeye can be discerned in the rituals of preparing and consuming food on special occasions, especially during the town's celebration of Mexican fiesta. Véa describes in fond detail how the sights, aromas, and tastes arising from the preparation and sharing of enchiladas, tamales, each "anointed tortilla," and other foodstuffs constitute what one character recognizes as nothing less than "another translation of life" (108, 109). "You think it's just food, boy," one of the novel's old Indios says to Beto, but "Shit, it's history you can eat. The *tamal* is history you can eat" (108–109). To partake of food in this setting becomes indeed Eucharistic—that is, cause for thanksgiving. One of the fiesta guests crowded into the adobe house of Josephina, and Manuel takes it upon himself to announce that "the food you had tonight and the *música Mexicana* that you heard . . . there will never be better." Véa's narrator recalls further that the domestic space where this meal has been shared should also be revered as a hallowed place: "The old Yaquis stayed outside all right, and at dawn they formally blessed the house. Not this house, specifically, but the one that had always been there" (112). That one such place might assume a plural cultural and religious identity becomes evident, too, in the narrator's earlier report that "the spot for Josephina's new *ramada* had been roughly leveled out, then blessed by the Indians before being counterblessed" in a Christian manner by Josephina herself (51).

Within the novel's larger religious vision, food offerings and other forms of ritual expression complement several of Josephina's Christian practices—including her devotion to the Blessed Mother, her rosary, her practice of intercessory prayer, and her partly tactile involvement with statues, candles, and crucifixes. They harmonize as well with the mythical objects and practices favored by the novel's Indios. These First Nation ritual elements include the *chapayeka*, or shamanistic mask, that Beto wants to bury with his grandfather; the *pascola*, dances performed during the Easter season; the use of peyote;

and references to the mythical dog, named *Maravilla*, who by Aztec belief leads souls beyond mortal life to the spirit-world of the dead.

A kind of syncretism thus defines the novel's prevailing religious outlook. But it is a syncretism in which differing religious traditions coexist, sometimes within the same person, instead of becoming thoroughly amalgamated or necessarily diluted. The spirituality in question involves ecumenical as well as interreligious forms of personal engagement because Josephina, a confirmed Roman Catholic, also delights to share in the worship of Buckeye's black Protestant evangelicals. She apparently perceives between the two a certain continuity of soul-stirring ritual, invocation, and aesthetic practice.

Starting with its Prologue, *La Maravilla* envisions, in fact, more continuity than is ordinarily imagined between life and death, between waking reality and the realm of spirits, between bounded space and the endless permeability of place. Informed by Aztec notions of mythological rather than sequential time, and colored by techniques of magic realism, Véa's novel also reflects through dislocations of narrative sequence the elastic, liminal nature of temporality. Thus the novel begins with Josephina's disclosure that "I died some time ago" (1) and concludes with her still alive.

Even the novel's title is multivalent in a way that blurs all boundaries between life and death, here and there. One sense of *la maravilla* is the mythical dog, an ominous harbinger of death. *La maravilla* also names those "bright orange marigolds, what the *Indios* call *cempazuchiles* or *maravillas*" that tradition recognizes as "the flowers of the dead" laid upon Mexican graves (278). But yet another signification, closer to the literal sense, leads us to identify *la maravilla* with the "marvel" of ongoing life in the midst of death. So toward the novel's close, when Alberto returns from the horrors of military service in Vietnam and approaches the burial site of Manuel and Josephina, he scarcely knows where he is in geographic terms. By this time the Buckeye Road he once knew "no longer existed," with its desert having been "scabbed over with asphalt" and its identity "swallowed up by Phoenix" (280). Yet he feels at the gravesite a palpable, enduring communion in spirit with his deceased family members. After adorning their graves with marigolds, he lights candles and

> Between the candles he placed styrofoam cups of steaming *café con canela* and a plate of *pan dulce* for Josephina. There were *canitas y frijoles* for Manuel and an identical plate for himself.
> "Only you," he said softly as he ate a meal with them. (284)

One of the marvels related in this novel, albeit one clearly consonant with the Christian gospel, is the closeness to God displayed by Véa's erring, sometimes desperate, impoverished *desplazada*. Remarkably enough, too, the novel attributes to Manuel, the aged Yaqui shaman, in consort with Harold, an intellectual and scientifically minded door-to-door salesman of cleaning supplies (a Fuller Brush vendor), some telling theological insights into the continued viability of faith. At one point Manuel urges Beto to realize that, even in a dispirited age of rationalistic materialism, the scope of divine presence is all-encompassing:

> "You know how Harold talks about the god of the gaps.... You know, people putting God in the cracks where science can't see, where science hasn't been ... yet? These people believe that every scientific discovery makes God weaker, less important. And people keep thinking the gaps are getting smaller and smaller and science is getting larger. They think their world of modern kitchen appliances is outgrowing God.... We are people of the gaps, *mijo*. Only we know that the gaps are where life really is. We know that science doesn't make God smaller, it makes God bigger." (220–221)

In *La Maravilla*, the leading symbolic action by which Véa represents the imaginative capacity to live into a place without becoming dispiritedly possessed or enchained by it is airborne flight. So early in the novel we see Manuel, an old man rocking in his chair in Buckeye Road, suddenly and marvelously uplifted high into the desert sky. On such occasions Josephina cautions Beto, "Ay, *mijo*, don't get too close to him when he's flying around like that. The fool is with his witch again, *la puta*" (11). Through his memories and musings, Manuel manages to be at once a resident of Buckeye Road yet connected to a nobler Yaquis place and time and people. And eventually, in the course of undertaking his own spirit-quest under Manuel's tutelage in the desert, Beto too learns to fly:

> He climbed, tacking in the darkness, enraptured by his own swiftness and the perfect clarity of his vision. He saw the small fire flash by somewhere far below, to his right.... All at once he found himself above himself, the tremulous retching of his small human body below completely immaterial, yet vaguely important. (224)

Like Toni Morrison in her novel *Song of Solomon*, Véa exploits such figures of flight to symbolize the creative force of imagination—and, I think, the human aspiration toward transcendence. What *La Maravilla* underscores, above all, is the need of present-day Americans to become receptive once again to marvels and enchantment, to the prospect of self-transcendence and communion with God or the gods. Yet the spirituality in question is not to be equated with dislocated or other-worldly escapism. For in this narrative the imaginative core of *la maravilla* resides instead around the frayed edges, and within the gaps, of common life in Véa's ethnically interlayered barrio.

4

SACRED SITES AND GEOGRAPHIES

ORIENTATIONS OF THE *GENIUS LOCI*

Sites situated either in natural or in built, well-settled environments may claim to be invested with some form of the *genius loci*. Yet America, by virtue of its history and cultural mythology as "nature's nation,"[1] has been more inclined than Europe to identify spirit-permeated places with comparatively wild features of one sort or another. Places that attracted most attention for nineteenth-century tourists in search of sacred ground thus tended to be natural wonders such as Niagara Falls, Mammoth Cave, Yosemite, and Yellowstone.[2] Expectations for spiritual renewal at these destinations swiftly became intertwined with profane motives and consumer interests.

One may fairly conclude, in any case, that the sacred standing of all such places depends not so much on their naturally inherent sanctity as on the meanings and stories conferred on them. As theologian Belden Lane suggests, "sacred place is very often *ordinary* place, ritually set apart to become extraordinary."[3] Fiction writer Marilynne Robinson, in her trio of novels set in one of unglamorous Iowa's small towns, offers a richly elaborated illustration of this point. The first of Robinson's Iowa volumes, *Gilead* (2004), preceded *Home* (2008), and finally *Lila* (2014).

Aside from its biblically resonant name, Gilead is an ordinary, even prosaic settlement hidden away on the American Plains. Lila, the beleaguered main character and namesake of the last novel, ends up in Gilead purely by chance. She stops there only because she finds herself weary of walking, alone and homeless, along a country road, "probably hoping to get to Sioux City." And the Reverend John Ames, Lila's husband and the narrator of *Gilead*, recognizes that this all-too-ordinary town might be dismissed as a "sad old place." Yet Ames learns at length that such a place could shelter peace, that "a harmless life could be lived here unmolested." Here, too, he has learned to see and respond to "a kind of incandescence" in common humanity, to appreciate that "this is an interesting planet," deserving "all the attention you can give to it,"[4] and to gaze steadily into the divine mystery of mortality. In sum, largely by virtue of Robinson's luminescent prose, we find commonplace Gilead becoming indeed a holy place.

For individuals as well as for entire cultures, discovery of an extraordinary presence in ordinary places is apt to draw upon memory. What sort of memory? Perhaps the recollection of returning to a place previously known but apprehended now differently, more intensely. Wordsworth's "Lines Composed a Few Miles Above Tintern Abbey" supplies a familiar example. Or perhaps a collective memory of rituals and stories, conducted or accumulated over time, that help to confer sacred meaning on the space in question. Evidently, in any case, the character of whatever presence is perceived in a given place varies according to the perceiver's cultural identity and circumstance. And a multiplicity of sacred senses, even fiercely contesting faiths, may cling to a single site as has been true for millennia in Jerusalem.

In America, that singular outcropping of igneous rock in northeastern Wyoming known as Bear's Lodge, or Devils Tower, offers a striking illustration of how conflicting sacralizations can converge upon a relatively limited space of terrain. What to call it? Even the place's name is contested, with the majority culture's commitment to multiuse management of this National Monument by the US Park Service pitted against the reverence of Native Americans for a prominence where Sun Dance rituals and other observances have been conducted for centuries. Even from the largely secular standpoint of the majority culture, Devils Tower is a spectacular geological feature warranting special attention, if not veneration. Its iconic outline has permeated the general culture, having appeared on any number of book covers and featured in the 1977 science fiction movie *Close Encounters of the Third Kind*. What is more, the Tower's fame and challenging crack surface has made it a prime destination—a Mecca, so to speak—for rock climbers. The zeal of some summer climbers to pursue their sport on the tower has led to controversy, and even litigation, with Lakota and other Plains Indians who regard such intrusion on their rituals, particularly during the summer solstice in June, to be a desecration.

Whose rights and desires should therefore have primacy in the management of Bear's Lodge? Shouldn't the need of First Nation citizens to conduct their sacred rites at this site in particular take precedence over the recreational claims of rock climbers, at least to the extent of outlawing climbs throughout June? I would myself be inclined to say so, but the constitutional and other issues in dispute here are admittedly complex. Lakota interests and attitudes may not, for example, always align with those of the twenty or so other US tribes the National Park Service has identified as having interests in the matter. And some aspects of the larger dispute challenge our usual image of a secularly defined majority culture that fails to acknowledge the religious disposition of Native Americans. As reported by a law professor who has written about past efforts to negotiate a mutually acceptable Climbing Management Plan for the Tower, "recreational climbing group representatives articulated the view that for many of them, there can sometimes be a spiritual dimension to rock climbing as well: the personally transforming, even transcendent, effect of being in such focused contact with so majestic a natural formation."[5] So current management policy includes a provision requesting that rock climbers refrain voluntarily, rather than under legal compulsion, from Tower ascents in June. This odd but reasonably successful compromise demonstrates, I think, the ambiguity inherent in bids to sacralise certain spaces in the context of our pluralistic society.

One broad, not so contentious locus of spirited presence that has figured prominently in American literary tradition concerns watercourses of one sort or another—rivers, ponds, cascades, and oceans. Thoreau, Whitman, Melville, Muir, Carson, and Dillard rank among the many writers whose imaginative work draws inspiration from water. As historian John Sears has observed, Niagara Falls gained early favor not only as a "prodigy of nature" and a prime tourist destination but as a sublime occasion of "pleasurable terror" that visitors expected could "bring them closer to God." Although the United States lacked denominationally recognized shrines capable of motivating traditional forms of religious pilgrimage, natural wonders such as Niagara offered souls of any faith commitment or none certain opportunities for spiritual renewal that seemed in accord with America's pluralistic society.[6]

These points are aptly illustrated by Nathaniel Hawthorne's travel sketch titled "My Visit to Niagara." By 1832, when Hawthorne visited the falls, the place had already become a tourist mecca. Expectations ran so high that his first sight of the great cataract leaves him disappointed, even mildly depressed. And yet, as Sears points out, the author approaches this encounter as a prolonged spiritual process equivalent to a conversion experience.[7] Having purchased at the Goat Island tollhouse a walking stick he calls his "pilgrim's staff," he perseveres in his own interior pilgrimage while prolonging his bodily stay at a site he knows—but cannot initially feel—to be of unsurpassed magnificence.

Only "gradually, and after much contemplation" does the author come to feel that Niagara is indeed a unique "wonder of the world." He comes at last to envision, in the light of a rainbow shining over the American cascade, "Heaven's own beauty crowning earth's sublimity." But to reach this point of apprehension he first needs to work beyond his inflated expectations, to examine the Falls from multiple angles, to meditate at length on his experience, and to allow the roar of the endless rapids to mingle with his nighttime dreams. Although at this crowded site his "contemplations were often interrupted by strangers," his writerly imagination takes a certain satisfaction in looking upon the odd assortment of onlookers. Recollecting in tranquility all he has seen and felt, Hawthorne finds himself incorporating the presence of these others into his own appreciative response: "I spent some hours, watching the varied impression, made by the cataract, on those who disturbed me, and returning to unwearied contemplation, when left alone."[8] He understands thereby how this one spot of presumably sacred geography comes to be apprehended as many different places, depending on the identity and current mood of the observer. Finally, by recalling what he has seen and felt in written form, he creates a singular testimony of what otherwise looks to be a commonly shared or commonplace experience.

Mountains are another classic locus of epiphanic encounter—not only in America, of course, but from the standpoint of ancient biblical and other faith traditions. Gazing at or from mountain peaks, where earth seems elevated to the point of blending imperceptibly with the heavens, humans have often envisioned prospects of encountering God or the gods. Jewish and Christian scriptural narratives typically suppose the apex of numinous revelation and transfiguration taking place on liminal summits of one sort or another—on the likes of Sinai,

Moriah, Pisgah, Zion, and Tabor. Still other versions of elevated aspiration and human possibility have been identified with upland sites as varied as Olympus, Athos, Fuji, Ventoux, Tacoma-Rainier, and Bear's Lodge.[9]

In writings from colonial New England, cognizance of this symbolic cultural inheritance becomes evident even before testimony is offered about sighting or ascending actual mountains. Hence the notorious locus of Thomas Morton's seventeenth-century bid to found a neopagan, spiritual rival to Puritanism's holy city soon became known as Mount Wollaston or Merry Mount—though its current topographical standing in Norfolk County, Massachusetts, at a mere 121 feet above sea level, scarcely qualifies as mountainous, even by English standards. Likewise in William Bradford's account of Plymouth Plantation, an appeal to the Separatist community's metaphorically lofty prospect of the future ends up displacing the literal lowlands of Cape Cod first visible upon their landing. What the pilgrims immediately saw before them looked desolate, with "all things" around them standing in November "with a weather-beaten face" and the "whole country, full of woods and thickets," representing "a wild and savage hue." Neither could they, unlike the migrating Hebrew saints of old, expect to "go up to the top of Pisgah to view from this wilderness a more goodly country to feed their hopes."[10] Provincetown's topography offered no such prospect. Even so, Bradford believed they could, like Moses, look from the heights of grace and with visionary eyes toward the new Promised Land God destined for his people.

By the Romantic era, though, writers and painters of the Hudson River School were widely inclined to celebrate the sublime, spiritually evocative beauty of actual mountain landscapes. Thoreau, for example, ascribed Transcendental meaning to his ascent of several peaks scattered throughout New England, including Wachusett and Greylock in his native Massachusetts, Katahdin in Maine, and Washington and Monadnock in New

Hampshire. Awed by the "Titanic, inhuman" face of Nature he felt on Katahdin, he wrote that mountain summits "are among the unfinished parts of the globe, whither it is a slight insult to the gods to climb in and pry into their secrets." No wonder archaic peoples, conceiving mountaintops to be "sacred and mysterious," rarely venture to go there.[11]

But as one who loved to stride up and around mountain peaks, sometimes also camping there, Thoreau was enchanted by highland terrain, avowing that "on the tops of mountains, as everywhere to hopeful souls, it is always morning."[12] As he confided in his journal, how better to fulfill his self-appointed vocation of finding "God in nature" than to elevate his gaze and thoughts toward mountains, which "thus seen are worthy of worship"?[13] He recommended further that after returning "to the desultory life of the plain," we might well "endeavor to import a little of that mountain grandeur into it," and recalling that potentially "there is elevation in every hour, as no part of the earth is so low that the heavens may not be seen from."[14]

Like Ralph Waldo Emerson, Thoreau reserved a special affection for Monadnock. Although modest in elevation and not nearly so imposing as Katahdin, Monadnock held his attention. He was drawn to study closely its "sublime gray mass," intent on spending enough time around the mount to taste its blackberries and cranberries and to become well acquainted with its bogs, swamps, nighthawks, and geological features. And unlike some visitors who raced to the summit while noticing little else along the way, he wanted to take in the fullness of Monadnock's presence by considering it from several angles:

> They who simply climb to the peak of Monadnock have seen little of the mountain. I came not to look *off from* it, but to look *at* it. The view of the pinnacle itself from the plateau below surpasses any view which you get from the summit. It is indispensable to see the top itself and the sierra of its outline from one side. The

great charm is not to look off from a height but to walk over this novel and wonderful surface. Moreover, if you would enjoy the prospect, it is, methinks, most interesting when you look from the edge of the plateau immediately down into the valleys, or where the edge of the lichen-clad rocks, only two or three rods from you, is seen as the lower frame of a picture of green fields, lakes, and woods, suggesting a more stupendous precipice than exists.[15]

Even in Thoreau's day, Monadnock attracted many visitors. So it was not a site particularly conducive to solitude. On each of the four occasions when Thoreau set out to climb it, he did so accompanied by a walking partner. While seeking less frequented byways for times of contemplation during his ascents, he also shows himself pleased to survey the ample company of visitors who assembled themselves, with festive abandon, on Monadnock's summit. During his final ascent of the mountain, together with Ellery Channing, he reports seeing some forty visitors on the summit:

> When you got within thirty rods you saw them seated in a row along the gray parapets, like the inhabitants of a castle on a gala-day; and when you beheld Monadnock's blue summit fifty miles off in the horizon, you may imagine it covered with men, women, and children in dresses of all colors . . . . Children were running about and playing as usual. Indeed, this peak in pleasant weather is the most trivial place in New England. (67–68)

Monadnock continues to rank among the most frequently climbed peaks in the world. Several years ago, on the brink of my own departure from Connecticut, I too climbed Monadnock—in the company of essayist Sam Pickering, a long-time friend and professorial colleague who subsequently described our excursion in one of his essays. Like Thoreau and Emerson, whose writings we had co-taught in a course offerings at UConn, we knew we would scarcely be alone on Monadnock. Although we encountered only one other person during our climb, first along the Halfway House Trail and then the White Arrow Trail, "some ninety people awaited us on the summit," where we paused for lunch and looked around. The party gathered there included schoolchildren, several families, and a few others—all of them, apparently, appreciably younger than we. That recognition we found sobering, but also quite appropriate to an excursion felt to mark a turning point in our own mortal journeying. "In choosing Monadnock," Pickering wrote, we rejected Emerson's dictum to enjoy 'an original relation to the universe.'" Although conceding that "For the young in spirit and for that necessary consort of spirit, a youthful body, Emerson's advice is healthy," we felt disinclined as elders "to break from the past but wanted instead to forge a memory."[16] And Monadnock had by this time earned its reputation as a repository of hope and memory for multitudes who had sojourned to the place.

Tokens of sacred geography can be identified not only with discrete sites—including cartographically fixed shrines and natural features—but also with the body's directional orientation in space. Liturgical forms of Christianity, as well as various pagan rituals, favor worship aligned with an eastward orientation, toward the rising sun. The traditional placement of altars within the cruciform floorplan of many churches reflects just such an "orientation," in the term's literal sense. Poet and prose writer Richard Tillinghast reminds us that "If north is the father of all directions—its initial capital letter taking pride of place on compasses and maps—east is the mother. East is that end of a church where the mysteries are kept, where the rising sun astonishes the eye with the rose, royal purple of stained glass. It is the lilies and spices and opened sepulcher of Easter. The Neolithic stone chambers of Ireland and Britain were constructed to receive the sun's rays at the winter solstice and to fend off the dying of the light." And Tillinghast, within the course of a world-wandering career, writes that recovering his own compass of being has everything to do with an orientation formed from early memory. "Wherever I am when I need to find my bearings," he reports, he calls to mind an image of himself standing "at the center of my childhood outside our family home in midtown Memphis, facing north between two trees, a magnolia and a water oak, at the midpoint of my four directions."[17]

Yet in America at large, it is the westering impulse that has long exerted most influence on our cultural bearings. So Thoreau maintained that "Eastward I go only by force; but westward I go free." "Something like this," he suggested, "is the prevailing tendency of my countrymen," for just as "I must walk toward Oregon, and not toward Europe," so also "that way the nation is moving, and I may say that mankind progresses from east to west."[18] Jack Burden, narrator of Robert Penn Warren's *All the King's Men*, likewise confesses how in desperation he once headed west in his car "because when you don't like it where you are you always go west." And so far as Burden recollects his nation's history, "We have always gone west."[19]

True, some noteworthy exceptions to this cultural tropism come to mind. Annie Dillard's writing shows a fascination with thoughts about remote Arctic landscapes—her yearning for an inward "shedding" and "sloughing off," for a prospect of spiritual renewal she associates with "northing."[20] Twain, in *The Adventures of Huckleberry Finn*, also throws askew our usual suppositions about the moral valence of directionality. He leads us to construe the raft journey of Huck and Jim on the Mississippi as a bid for liberation, for escape from bondage. That aspiration should logically draw them toward Canada and the north, though their actual course, ironically, takes them due south, thus ever deeper into slave territory. Such a course makes sense only insofar as we come to identify the primary locus of freedom quite narrowly with the raft itself, apart from its destination, or insofar as Twain's thematic demands end up trumping geography altogether. And today, more than a century after the US Census Bureau's announced closing of the western frontier in 1890, our younger citizens tend to imagine the geographically regenerative equipoise of American life divided between settlements on the continent's east and west coastlines. But despite all this, a pull toward the West has been the prevailing orientation of America's settler culture.

Quite another sense of sacred directionality, though, has characterized the worldview of the Lakota Sioux and other Native American peoples. The reflections that John G. Neihardt and Joseph Epes Brown recorded from Black Elk, a prominent Oglala Sioux holy man who died in 1950, offer a glimpse of this visionary outlook. *The Sacred Pipe: Black Elk's Account of the Seven Rites of the Oglala Sioux* underscores the role of directionality in this tribe's ritual practices. Consistent with imaging the Sioux nation as a sacred hoop, Black Elk's account calls for a clockwise circumambulation of the ceremonial lodge and attributes a discrete religious meaning to each of the cardinal directions—"four quarters of the universe"[21]—in addition to the heavenward and earthward sight lines. Each of these six directions is associated with one of the godly powers or beings associated with *Wakan-Tanka*, the supreme being. In rituals for a worthy deceased person, the soul is kept and then released to render it one with the Spirit and thus "able to return to the 'place' where it was born—*Wakan-Tanka*" so that it "need not wander about the earth as is the case with the souls of bad people" (11). These rituals include the voicing of an invocation to the Power of each direction as relevant offerings are smoked in the sacred pipe. Because the soul's journey is thought to run southward, the prayer that Black Elk relates to the Power of the south seems particularly noteworthy:

> O You who guard that path leading to the place toward which we always face, and upon which our generations walk, we are placing

You in this sacred pipe! You control our life, and the lives of all the peoples of the universe. Everything that moves and all that is will send a voice to *Wakan-Tanka*. We have a place for You in the pipe.... (20)

Where in the world are we? And where in space might we encounter concentrations of divine presence, outposts of the beyond where time melds with timelessness? The process of ritualized orientation specified in Black Elk's religious practice leads its participants toward some fairly definite answers. Throughout most of Melville's *Moby-Dick*, however, the resolution of such questions remains tantalizingly elusive. And the entire crew of the *Pequod*, named for a displaced and nearly extinct people, consists of landless men who are all likewise displaced in one way or another from shore life and family. All find themselves ranging unmoored, on a small and precarious vessel, amid the "everlasting terra incognita"[22] of the ocean's immensity. It may be that "in landlessness alone resides the highest truth, shoreless, indefinite as God" (97), but reaching toward this supernal revelation can also be perilous, as evidenced by the early demise of Melville's Bulkington and later defeat of Ahab.

The striking liminality of place dramatized in *Moby-Dick* is, I believe, inseparable from the novel's interrogation of the word's potentially sacred character.[23] Originally conceived as an adventure tale focused on physical pursuit of a great white whale, this novel also developed for Melville into a metaphysical quest narrative. In fact, several dimensions of search come into variable play for Ahab, Ishmael, other crew members, and the author himself within the expanse of this novel's 135 chapters. One quest, propelled exclusively by Ahab, seeks personal as well as metaphysical revenge—first for his loss of a leg, finally for humankind's loss of most everything else. Another pursuit, largely attributable to Ishmael, involves the search for ways of belonging in the world and in communion with others despite the implacable savagery of mortal existence. But what engages us most powerfully, I think, is Melville's search for practical wisdom about how best to confront life's ultimate questions about meaning and reality, the character of evil, and humanity's relation to whatever God or gods there may be. Admittedly, the religious import of *Moby-Dick* defies ready summation. A brilliant chapter such as "The Whiteness of the Whale," which ends on an interrogative note, compels more attention for the questions it raises than for the answers it supplies. Yet I have long shared Lawrence Buell's verdict that "this particular fish story becomes ultimately in some sense an encounter with the divine," that "the sense of the sacred with which the world of the book and particularly the figure of the white whale are infused never evaporates, but on the contrary continues to be resuggested even as it is questioned."[24]

Remarkably, too, Melville shows how this narrative's quest for meaning throughout a vast ocean and amid "the heartless voids and immensities of the universe" (165) finally converges upon one discrete though fluidly situated place in space. That site, the endpoint of Ahab's apocalyptic rendezvous with destiny, lies somewhere in Pacific waters off the coast of Japan but is finally no larger than the white hump of a single animal. It may be that "God is everywhere" (53), as Father Mapple reminded his seagoing congregation while preaching in the Whaleman's Chapel at New Bedford. Yet neither God nor God's purposes are everywhere revealed to humankind. So one might well wonder, with Melville, "Where lies the final harbor, whence we unmoor no more" (373)? Only at certain privileged places and moments of theophany, it seems, might human beings glimpse something of ultimate truth—as the cabin boy Pip apparently does, through his near-drowning experience, when he sees "the multitudinous, God-omnipresent, coral insects, that out of the firmament of waters heaved the colossal orbs" (321). Yet because "man's insanity is heaven's sense" (322), Pip can never integrate this vision of transcendent being beyond ordinary time and space with waking reality in the world, and thus is considered mad. In "The Quarter-Deck" chapter, though, undaunted Ahab declares his intent to strike behind the mask shrouding the sacred mystery of affliction and evil. "That inscrutable thing is chiefly what I hate" (140), he intones, and he perceives the white whale above all—not unlike God, especially John Calvin's God—to be thus far inscrutable in essence.

That is not to say, given the multilayered and ever-shifting symbology at play throughout Melville's novel, that the white whale *is* a figure of God in any simple or univocal sense. Moby Dick represents a multitude of disparate things to diverse characters at successive stages of the action. He signifies not least that monumental and deranged projection about how best to respond to cosmic woe that Ahab piles on the animal's hump. Yet Melville, by way of dramatizing in this work the *mysterium tremendum* of encounter with the divine, introduces several teasing suggestions about Moby Dick's mythic and even godly proportions. In its godly bearing this whale is not only elusive, highly intelligent, and inscrutable but reputed to be immortal and ubiquitous. Melville relates how some persons, albeit those "superstitiously inclined," have entertained "the unearthly conceit that Moby Dick was ubiquitous; that he had actually been encountered in opposite latitudes at one and the same instant of time" (154).

So how, after all, could it ever prove possible for Ahab and his crew to locate this single lone animal amid the endless expanse of oceanic space where he might roam? This marvelous feat is achieved in part through Melville's subtly fictive techniques and the license of symbolic romance, which lead us to suspend disbelief about a plot resolution wherein our protagonists succeed in finding and chasing Moby Dick not only once but three times in as many days. We may scarcely even notice the submerged, tall-tale dimension of this fish tale.[25] In other terms, though,

Melville shows us how Ahab achieves his overarching aim of plotting a "zig-zag world-circle" course toward encounter with his prey through a combination of reasoned deliberation and heightened intuition.

In support of realism and reasoned science, chapters such as "The Chart" establish the point that Ahab has undertaken a scrupulous study of sea charts, log books, and other sources to learn about currents, favored whaling grounds, seasonal paths of migration, and the feeding patterns of whales. For much of the voyage he makes use of customary navigational instruments. Eric Bulson points out that "Ishmael faithfully charts the Pequod's course, and on more than eleven occasions we are given cardinal points, the accurate location of well-known cruising grounds, and changes in the ship's direction."[26] The novel abounds in place-names and map references, including those associated at the outset with Ishmael's movement across land sites such as New York, New Bedford, and Nantucket.

These applications of deliberative science offer Ahab "reasonable surmises" about where and when the white whale might be found. They are surmises supposedly "approaching to certainties" (167), according to one passage, but that fall well short of certitude by other accounts. For maps and recognizably realistic place-identifications, despite their aura of infallibility, can also err, as shown by the novel's contradictory disclosures about whether Pip hails from Alabama or from Tolland County, Connecticut. What empirical data, mapping, and scientific reason provide simply cannot take Ahab all the way to his goal. Finding the true way to Moby Dick requires in addition, and perhaps above all, a measure of intuitive faith. Thus Melville reminds us that the island from which Queequeg hails is "not down in any map: true places never are" (59). And as is arguably true of religious belief in general: The imaginative faith that finds Moby Dick must reach beyond scientific reasoning to draw as well on trust, reasons of will and heart, and the testimony of others.

Aptly enough in relation to the dynamics of faith, some of the seafarers whom the *Pequod* crewmembers meet in their several gams across open ocean doubt that Moby Dick exists. All three of the *Pequod*'s harpooners claim to have previously sighted him, however, while still others, including those aboard the *Rachel* and the *Delight*, testify graphically to having already experienced deathly encounters with him. Several signs—not proofs—of what is to come also appear. These omens conveyed prior to the climactic moment in chapter 133 when "the grand god revealed himself" (409) rising from the water suggest, without displaying outright, the proximity of his presence.

Because Moby Dick is a moving target, finding him calls for a precise placement of the ship in time as well as space. In strictly technical terms, reckoning one's position at sea ordinarily requires not only a measurement of latitude, for which purpose a quadrant would suffice, but also a longitudinal reading. Discovering such placement longitudinally, in relation to the global meridians, requires definite temporal as well as spatial data. Yet even by the nineteenth century, to say nothing of previous eras, attaining a reliable longitudinal determination at sea was problematic unless navigators had access to a proper marine chronometer.[27] In *Pierre*, published a year after *Moby-Dick*, Melville in the person of pamphleteer Plotinus Plinlimmon goes so far as to find "chronometricals," unlike the more terrestrial measurement of "horologicals," indicative of heavenly truth: "Christ was a chronometer; and the most exquisitely adjusted and exact one" by virtue of his ability to carry "Heaven's time in Jerusalem."[28]

Yet we never learn for sure whether Ahab has access to a chronometer on board the *Pequod*. He does make use of a quadrant, an "astrological-looking instrument" adorned with "numerous cabalistical contrivances" (378), until such time as he decides to smash it on the deck, but never a chronometer. Addressing the sun, he finds this great orb "tellest me truly where I *am*—but canst thou cast the least hint where I shall be? Or canst thou tell where some other thing besides me is this moment living? Where is Moby Dick?" (378). Aside from the limited technical data available to him therefore, especially if he lacks the chronometric ability to plot precise longitude,[29] Ahab relies heavily on a sort of "cabalistical" or esoteric intuition, on faith conjoined with sheer force of will, to find his way to Moby Dick. That meeting he has long fancied a consummation devoutly to be wished.

It happens otherwise, of course. To encounter the whale once again turns out to be a terrifying, catastrophic turn of events for Ahab and all but one of the *Pequod*'s crew. Yet as Moby Dick finally swims away in triumph, departing the scene into an unspecified nowhere,[30] we become aware that this story's outcome also bears a saving dimension for Ishmael, perhaps even a numinous and revelatory sense for the reader. Back in the work's opening chapter, Melville–Ishmael posed some provocative questions that resonate further by the story's close: "Why did the old Persians hold the sea holy? Why did the Greeks give it a separate deity, and make him the own brother of Jove? Surely all this is not without meaning" (20). Surely yes, because "some certain significance lurks in all things" (331). And I take it that at least part of Melville's meaning here lies in the mythopoeic artistry by which he conceives of Moby Dick, more than of Poseidon or Neptune of old, as all-surpassing *genius loci* of the entire oceanic realm. Having finally defeated Ahab's ambition, this white whale remains the presiding spirit of a vastness constituting the "dark side of this earth, and which is two thirds of this earth" (328). But as befits our own age of ecological consciousness, it is a place he would guard not so much *for* humans as *from* them.

HALLOWED BATTLEGROUNDS AND BURIAL GROUNDS

Whereas churches, synagogues, mosques, temples, and sweat lodges are commonly recognized as sacred sites within the built environment, battlegrounds may look like the profane antithesis of these sanctuaries insofar as they invariably recall scenes of hostility, strife, and slaughter. Cemeteries, too, began to assume a more secular if not profane identity than the churchyard burial plots they replaced, once the rural cemetery movement gained favor in America by the early nineteenth century.

In both cases, though, these sites often acquired hallowed meaning of one sort or another, a cultural process that literary tradition not only reflects but has also helped to sustain.[31] Even as American burial grounds, for example, became less patterned after English-style churchyard plots and more governed by private, secular associations, they amplified the benefits of providing sanctified enclaves from the grim, frenetic, often-unhealthy atmosphere of an increasingly urbanized world. These newly redesigned grounds, equivalent to the nation's first public parks, were conceived to be not only repositories for the dead but sanctuaries of psychic and spiritual restoration for the living. Their picturesque beauty within what David Sloane has called a "landscape of hope" aimed to counter earlier, Calvinist-tainted impressions of morbidity. And their freshly coined title of "cemetery" envisioned the deceased not as awaiting dread judgment but as sheltered in peaceful slumber[32]—an ideal comparable to what William Cullen Bryant had proposed in his well-known poem "Thanatopsis" (1817). The most celebrated new burial grounds emergent in suburbs of America's great cities—including Mount Auburn in Cambridge, Laurel Hill in Philadelphia, and Greenwood in Brooklyn—all featured pleasantly winding paths and artfully landscaped gardens. Yet despite the comparatively liberal, pluralistic theology represented in such sites, they continued to demonstrate, as John Sears contends, that "No place . . . could be more obviously sacred ground than a cemetery."[33]

Perhaps the foremost destination in America where literary reputation becomes ideally conjoined with mortuary space is Sleepy Hollow Cemetery in Concord, Massachusetts. The cemetery sector known as Authors' Ridge serves as a common resting place for the remains of New England's leading nineteenth-century authors including Channing, Emerson, Thoreau, the Alcotts, and Hawthorne. Given the celebrity status of this company, one might suppose the place to have inspired a purely secular spirit of homage. And it is true that William Ellery Channing, in the poetic address he delivered in connection with Emerson's "Address to the Inhabitants of Concord at the Consecration of Sleepy Hollow, September 29, 1855," underscored the site's restorative tranquility, its Edenic beauty, and its benefit not so much for the dead as for those pilgrims in life still able to "Learn from the loved one's rest serenity."

That the Concord community meant to attribute a religiously hallowed identity to its hollow becomes apparent, however, in its willingness to describe the 1855 proceedings as a "consecration." Moreover, the opening stanza of Channing's poem confirms the presence of decidedly sacral though nonecclesial specters of grace throughout this verdant grove, where "No abbey's gloom, nor dark cathedral stoops" intrude. Channing avers that Sleepy Hollow, unlike such sinks of melancholy, is a bright spot illumining "God's mercy." It affords glimpses of that eternal order where "the incessant watch-fires burn / Of unspent holiness and goodness clear."

Emerson's prose contribution to what he calls the occasion's "religious rites" extends the *memento mori* theme sounded in Channing's poem. In his address Concord's sage applauds the way "defects of our old theology" have been replaced by impressions of "divine hope and love" that pervade this garden park by virtue of the "vast circulations of Nature." Sleepy Hollow, he suggests, had already for some twenty years been aptly named because, while close to hand, it remained a place set apart that offered "seclusion from the village in its immediate neighborhood." For "in this quiet valley," he reminded auditors, "as in the palm of Nature's hand, we shall sleep well when we have finished our day . . . . Nay, when I think of the mystery of life, its round of illusions, our ignorance of its beginning or its end . . . . I think sometimes that the vault of the sky arching there upward, under which our busy being is whirled, is only a Sleepy Hollow, with path of Suns, instead of foot-paths." And within this hallowed hollow he identifies the soul's reach toward eternity not with toweringly crafted monuments but with arboreal growth:

> A grove of trees,—what benefit or ornament is so fair and great? They make the landscape; they keep the earth habitable; their roots run down, like cattle, to the water-courses; their heads expand to feed the atmosphere. The life of a tree is a hundred and a thousand years; its decays ornamental; its repairs self-made: they grow when we sleep, they grew when we were unborn. Man is a moth among these longevities. He plants for the next millennium. Shadows haunt them; all that ever lived about them cling to them. You can almost see behind these pines the Indian with bow and arrow lurking yet exploring the traces of the old trail.[34]

Battlefields, of course, bear a history quite unlike that of Sleepy Hollow Cemetery, with its reputation for pastoral serenity. Battlefields and cemeteries may nonetheless occupy common ground. In fact, domestically situated battlegrounds holding the most sanctified meaning—in terms of American civil religion, if not otherwise—tend to be Civil War landmarks that also serve as burial grounds for combatants. Gettysburg National Military Park in Pennsylvania is the prime example. Indeed this place had been established, in response to the unprecedented challenge of safely and reverentially handling the remains of thousands of Union dead hailing from eighteen different Northern states, as the first-ever nationally centralized soldiers' cemetery.[35] And of course the indispensable text that tradition has long enshrined to define the spirit of the place is the address Abraham Lincoln delivered there as part of the dedicatory ceremony on November 19, 1863, four months after the battle of Gettysburg.

Although much has already been said and written about the president's Gettysburg Address, I think it worth dwelling here on its particular relation to the ceremonial occasion and the ground upon which it was delivered. Like the nation itself, and "the great civil war" about which Lincoln would soon be speaking, the landscaped cemetery park envisioned at Gettysburg remained a place in transition, a manifestly "unfinished work."[36] Beyond sight of the huge crowd, with the task of reinterring bodies from outlying terrain into the designated area of Cemetery Hill still underway, the scene set before Lincoln and other dignitaries revealed the disturbed soil of freshly dug graves and coffins still awaiting placement. The unsettled state of things dramatized the point that transformation of this regional village into a hallowed national landmark had yet to reach fruition, just as the "new birth of freedom" Lincoln envisioned for American democracy remained at this time in a questionable state of gestation.

What I believe warrants renewed attention to Lincoln's address, in its immediate and place-identified context, is the way it participates in the dedication ceremony's ritualization of this transformative process. The process aimed to move citizens emotionally from mourning in the face of omnipresent death toward regenerative hope, and to begin moving the nation—including its northern pockets of dissension—from dismembering animosity toward purposeful unity. Through a kind of Protestant liturgy of the word, Lincoln's invocation of religious and largely Christian language served, in conjunction with other elements of the ceremony, to turn one hallowed plot of ground into a synecdoche for the country as a whole.

Prior to Lincoln's speech, devout features of the observance included a prayer of invocation by the Rev. Thomas Stockton, a Methodist minister and chaplain of the House of Representatives; common recitation of the Lord's Prayer; and the performance of Benjamin French's "Consecration Hymn," which invited guests to venerate the "sacred blood" of those "Who fell in Freedom's holy cause."[37]

A crucial aspect of the occasion's sacralizing discourse is the way otherwise abstract references to the nation's honored dead became embodied, at this place and time, by the soldiers' real presence close at hand. Those assembled for the occasion could scarcely miss the aptness of standing on what Lincoln pointedly calls "this ground" rather than anywhere else—that is, in the physical company of countless soldiers' bodies. Orator Edward Everett's lengthy address began on a note that heightened the crowd's cognizance of the "graves of our brethren beneath our feet." French's hymn lyrics confirmed that "Tis holy ground— This spot, where, in their graves / We place our country's braves." Language intoned in the hymn's subsequent verses— "Here where they fell" and "Here let them rest"—reiterated the sentiment.[38] If, as Lincoln reminded his audience, the rites in question were performed "under God,"[39] all of them were also conducted above soil sanctified by the remains of heroic men.

So place undoubtedly mattered in connection with the conduct of Gettysburg's dedicatory rituals. And although it continues to matter across the ages largely because of "what they did here," the meaning it holds in remembrance plainly derives as well from Lincoln's own words—despite his modest prediction that "what we say here" would fall into oblivion. The speech's biblical cadences, together with its elevated yet relatively familiar and accessible vocabulary, contribute to its impact. Moreover, and despite Lincoln's avoidance of overt biblical references,[40] his pronouncement draws supreme authority from its invocation of religious language and principles. One way the Address advances this viewpoint is through its repeated use of three keywords: "dedication," "devotion" and "consecration." Lincoln speaks of dedication and its variants, for example, no fewer than five times within a total space of only 272 words. The speech's reiterated *invocation* to dedication, signifying here a call to set aside ordinary space for some higher or extraordinary purpose, therefore amounts as well to a ritual *incantation*. Several allusions to consecration, both within and beyond the text of the Address, likewise amplify the reverential sense evoked through the proceedings.

In religious terms, the sacrificial dimension of this consecration has particular relevance for the Address. Lincoln points out that ground had already been consecrated at Gettysburg not only or mainly through ceremonial, but through selfless dedication on the part of the combatants themselves, both living and fallen. What might such consecration have actually achieved, though, to justify concluding that "these dead shall not have died in vain"? Clearly part of the answer lay in the appreciable and bodily contribution these soldiers had made to a larger war effort that, though not yet completed, promised if sustained to yield not merely victory for the North but a "new birth of freedom" for a reunited nation. Part of the answer, too, came from the renewed inspiration fallen countrymen could supply to all who needed to be "here dedicated to the unfinished work which they who fought here thus far so nobly advanced."

But the efficacy attributed to that consecration of which Lincoln speaks draws on still deeper chords of feeling too,

I think, insofar as belief in the regenerative power of blood sacrifice and self-abnegating death lies at the heart of many religious systems. It plays a major role not only in Christian and Jewish teaching, but in the psychic bearing of other, more primordial faith practices. Christian tradition has long seen mystical powers of personal and collective transformation flowing from the blood of martyrs, whose gravesites inspire veneration as seedbeds of worship, cultic observance, and the life of the church.[41] Thus exploiting while extending that strand of tradition, Lincoln ends up portraying the fallen at Gettysburg—"those who here gave their lives that that nation might live"—as latter-day saints and martyrs for the nation.

Other stylistic and rhetorical features of the Address enlarge upon this theme of sacrificial, self-effacing dedication. Despite Lincoln's high office, for example, he includes nothing self-referential in this fragment of speech, which shrinks from any claim of oratorical celebrity. The president's personal voice is subsumed here into one representing common citizenry, focused on shared homage for those bodies resting in place all around. Moreover, the discourse's other-affirming, self-negating rhetoric of *meiosis* effectively draws attention to the place itself, and especially to the honored dead who will inhabit it permanently, rather than to "we" who comprise the day's visiting speakers, dignitaries, and citizenry: "But, in a larger sense, we cannot dedicate—we cannot consecrate—we cannot hallow—this ground. The brave men, living and dead, who struggled here, have consecrated it, far above our power to add or detract." All as if to say that this solemn place, newly hallowed by the bodies it has received, has an eloquence of its own. So for Lincoln the place itself mostly, if not entirely, speaks for itself. Even the extreme brevity of the president's offering, all the more remarkable for its time, coincides with the meiotic tenor of its rhetoric.

For reasons of health and other practical considerations, David Wills (a local banker and attorney appointed by the governor of Pennsylvania) and other authorities charged with handling burial or reburial of the thousands of bodies left on the Pennsylvania battlefield wisely decided against organizing a transport of bodies that would send each soldier back to his home state. Neither did they wish to dishonor the Union dead by gathering them all into mass graves. So they planned to undertake in stages the immense project of reinterring these men individually in the newly designed plot at Cemetery Hill, identifying by name as many as they could. Although grouped by state, the deceased were equally spaced from the cemetery's chief monument and arranged without regard to rank.[42] Drawing on experience gleaned from the rural cemetery movement, architect David Saunders reinforced egalitarian principles by "arranging the graves in great curving ranks" so as to avoid any "preferential treatment of the states or inequality in the ranks of the fallen."[43] This fairly novel democratization of the burial process, as well as the unusual plan for its time to gather the deceased from regionally diverse states into a national soldiers' cemetery, matches the spirit of Lincoln's closing tribute to the ideal of a cohesive American democracy. In the process of creating the park at Cemetery Hill, a provincially situated locale in Pennsylvania was transformed into a national landmark.[44] As historian Mark S. Schantz points out, "the change that Lincoln's address ushered forward" involved a fresh perception reaching beyond state lines that "The dead at Gettysburg belonged fully to the American nation, not to their friends, and not even, in the end, to themselves."[45]

One more place-relevant feature of the Address that I find it intriguing to ponder has to do with what it does *not* say—that is, with Lincoln's tactical avoidance of references to the Confederate dead or to the presence of non-Union corpses at Gettysburg. Understandably, no Rebel soldiers could be approved for burial at Cemetery Hill, and every effort had been made to screen the bodies of all those slated for reinterment there. Understandably, too, the reverence Lincoln expressed in his remarks for "these honored dead" covered only the Union dead. With the war's outcome still uncertain, and in the wake of July's ghastly battlefield carnage, it would scarcely be appropriate for the president in November 1863 to broach themes of mercy and compassion toward the South of the sort he would eventually express in his Second Inaugural Address. And yet, as he surely recognized, neither did the solemnity of the occasion encourage him to indulge in sectional polemics, gloating triumphalism, or explicit vilification of the Confederacy, whose soldiers, likewise "brave men," had likewise "struggled here." Of course thousands of soldiers in gray were also numbered among the roughly 10,000 Americans who surrendered their lives on that ground.[46]

At the time of the ceremony, in fact, as everyone, including Lincoln, had to have known, scores of Confederate dead still lay scattered, anonymously and in improvised mass burials, throughout the fields and settlements of Gettysburg. It would take about a decade for many or most of them to be removed to their home states. In the meantime, the town's territory contained any number of sites where fallen Confederates had been shoved hastily into shallow graves. Under the circumstances, some might even have been mixed mistakenly among burials of the unknown on Cemetery Hill.[47] In any case, Lincoln's strategically phrased conclusion of the Address allowed everyone who heard it space to acknowledge, at least implicitly, that successful prosecution of the Union cause and a subsequent regeneration of American democracy would have to mean accepting southerners once again as full citizens of "this nation." If the war were to mean anything, "this nation" must mean more than a federal alliance of northern states. By 1887, in fact, by virtue of an evolving sense of national identity linked to civil religion, veterans' reunions of both Blue and Gray began to find common ground as they met together at Gettysburg.[48]

So there is, I think, an intriguing backdrop to the vision of a newly defined and unified nation that Lincoln sets forth here, given the unseen and unmentioned presence on the scene of all those dead southerners.

Gettysburg is not the only Civil War landmark to which reverential or provocatively imaginative meanings have been attributed. A famous battlefield in western Tennessee, for example, another killing field that saw huge casualties during a pivotal encounter, even plays thematically into the action of Bobbie Ann Mason's contemporary short story titled "Shiloh." The working-class protagonists of that tale, a married couple from western Kentucky, fantasize that visiting Shiloh's historic grounds will somehow help to renew their hope in life and each other. They picnic near the battlefield cemetery and buy a souvenir Confederate flag for one of their parents. Yet Mason sets the marital tension of the couple's own civil war in ironic juxtaposition to the history they brush against at Shiloh. Sorely wounded themselves in heart and spirit, they remain wrapped in touristic fantasies that render them oblivious to all the blood, agony, and death still permeating the grounds on which they walk.[49]

THE SPIRITUAL FECUNDITY OF WASTELANDS

Like battlegrounds, deserts and deserted tracts of "wilderness" have also shown surprising promise as scenes of religious revelation and regeneration. Building on familiar biblical tales recounting how Moses with other wandering Hebrews, followed by John the Baptist and Jesus, underwent identity-defining encounters in the desert, the spirituality of early Christianity developed significant affiliations with unsettled, dry, forbidding landscapes. During the patristic era, between the third and fifth centuries of the church's formation, the ascetical intensity of those Desert Fathers and Desert Mothers who retreated as solitaries or within communities of monks to isolated plots in Egypt and Syria swiftly became legendary. And they were drawn to these desert places not so much because of what the land contained as what it was presumed to lack—worldly distractions, social spurs toward ambition, and many though scarcely all of sin's allurements. In accord with Thoreau's existential motto, those who wander alone in wastelands are not only invited but virtually required to "reduce life to lowest terms." And the intensity of resolve with which these desert monks typically approached their vocation coincided remarkably well with what Belden Lane has described as the "fierce landscapes" they inhabited.[50]

Curiously, Ed Abbey's latter-day personal narrative in *Desert Solitaire: A Season in the Wilderness* (1968) ends up voicing in a new key themes once sounded in the desert spirituality of ancient Christianity, despite the author's post-Christian rejection of theism. For all of his outspoken brashness, Abbey also displays a contemplative's attention to his place in the world, an almost monkish fondness for silence and solitude. Asceticism, albeit an austerity that coalesces for Abbey with hedonistic zeal, is another of his ties with spiritual masters of the past. Abbey's service in the late 1950s as a park ranger in Arches National Monument near Moab, Utah, required his accepting a bracing austerity with respect to material comforts and human companionship, particularly during tourist lulls when he alone held sway over the territory's 33,000 acres. Not a primitive life, exactly, given the ties to civilized sustenance he gratefully enjoyed in his metallic government-issue house trailer, yet one of chastening simplicity and vulnerability before the otherwise inhospitable environment that surrounded him. "Despite the great variety of living things to be found here," he observes, "most of the surface of the land, at least three-quarters of it, is sand or sandstone, naked, monolithic, austere and unadorned as the sculpture of the moon. It is undoubtedly a desert place, clean, pure, totally useless, quite unprofitable."[51]

At first glance the "red wasteland" (4) Abbey chose to inhabit might indeed be mistaken for a moonscape—or, more aptly still, a face of Mars. Not long ago, during a hiking expedition of my own through "Abbey's country" near Moab, I found myself confirming that impression as I gazed on much the same terrain "Cactus Ed" had known and loved decades ago. Yet for Abbey, of course, the elemental, unadorned face of this landscape presented much of its appeal. In his mind the ascetical trial of residing there alone coalesced happily with the neopagan pleasure of camping in an unrecognized, rock-garden "paradise," complete with reptilian fellow creatures who vitalized the place or guarded him like "totemic deities" (23). No wonder he is moved to declare these canyon lands, viewed imaginatively in the light of creation's new dawn, as "the most beautiful place on earth" (1).

What Abbey esteems most about the desert is its stark physicality, its "thisness," its apparent unwillingness to testify to any realms or meanings beyond its own implacable presence on earth. He declares his wholesale rejection not only of theism and revealed religion, but also of Romantic anthropomorphism and all totalizing worldviews. He yearns to banish all "fantasies of the supernal" (200) in favor of a thoroughgoing materialism that favors actuality over iconography, earthiness over myths of heaven. For him the desert's chief signification is that of an empty signifier, an unadorned *ding an sich*. And while thus aspiring to embrace a solidly atheistic materialism, Abbey prefers to describe himself in affirmative terms—not as an atheist but an "earthiest," one pledged to remain "true to the earth" (208). The pronouncement Abbey makes in his opening chapter comes closest to defining the hard-core essence of a personal credo radically purged of illusions:

> I am here not only to evade for a while the clamor and filth and confusion of the cultural apparatus but also to confront, immediately and directly if it's possible, the bare bones of existence, the elemental and fundamental, the bedrock which sustains us. I want to be able to look at and into a juniper tree, a piece of quartz, a vulture, a spider, and see it as it is in itself, devoid of all humanly ascribed qualities, anti-Kantian, even the categories of scientific description. To meet God or Medusa face to face, even if it means risking everything human in myself. I dream of a hard and brutal mysticism in which the naked self merges with a non-human world and yet somehow survives still intact, individual, separate. Paradox and bedrock. (6)

Students of mine commonly report their admiration for Abbey's directness and earnestness in this passage. There is indeed something appealing and refreshing about his concentration, throughout *Desert Solitaire*, on the land's elemental features of "light, space, rock and silence," on the writer's own pleasure in savoring the palpable "surface of things" (240, xi). But there is also reason to doubt any human being's capacity to view the nonhuman world "in itself," apart from "humanly ascribed qualities." Despite Abbey's stated commitment to a rigorous and ecocentric materialism, further references to his "dream" and to an almost oxymoronic "hard and brutal mysticism" betray a forceful, subsurface resistance to that commitment. In sum, one can scarcely read the whole of *Desert Solitaire*, probing its depths as well as its surfaces, without sensing how thoroughly the country it evokes is enspirited, and how surely this land qualifies for Abbey as sacred in its singularity.

That Abbey's book reflects a robust though religiously unorthodox ecospirituality seems to me evident on several fronts. Thus in "Down the River," his powerfully elegiac account of a last "dreamlike voyage" through Glen Canyon on the Colorado River, he wonders if the canyon walls around him might shelter something numinous if not supernatural. "Is this at last the *locus Dei?*" he asks himself, and might he even glimpse there "a rainbow-colored corona of blazing light, pure spirit, pure being, pure disembodied intelligence, *about to speak my name?*" (184, 200). And Abbey's insistence on holding irreplaceable assets of the national parks in reverential esteem stands in logical opposition to the polemical passion with which he denounces their profanation by industrial tourism:

> We have agreed not to drive our automobiles into cathedrals, concert halls . . . and the other sanctums of our culture; we should treat our national parks with the same deference, for they, too are holy places. An increasingly pagan and hedonistic people (thank God!), we are learning finally that the forests and mountains and desert canyons are holier than our churches. Therefore let us behave accordingly. (60)

As historian Mark Stoll points out, Abbey's early upbringing included exposure to the Reformed heritage of the Presbyterian Church, which continued to affect his sensibility even during his anti-ecclesiastical and indubitably lapsed adult years.[52] What Abbey retained of that Reformed tradition in later life, in consonance with his personal disposition, was arguably something of a Calvinist anthropology largely divorced from Calvinist theology. Like Thoreau and Muir, in other words, Abbey often betrayed at least a touch of misanthropy—that is, a suspicion that humankind's failings marked the species as more conspicuously "fallen" than the loftier and divine beauty of the natural world. Abbey wrote with mischievous hyperbole when he confessed he would "rather kill a *man* than a snake" (20). But neither did he suffer gladly those many mortals he regarded as fools, developers, hucksters, despoilers of earth's beauty and bounty. His feisty yet often-stirring iconoclasm, the indignation he felt in the face of unreflective and exploitative humanity, is everywhere apparent in *Desert Solitaire*. Hardly the most congenial or solicitous of park rangers, Abbey evidently found the prospect of occasionally living alone at Arches less a privation than pleasurable. "Earth First!" as chanted by those radical environmentalists he inspired, rather than "up with people," serves best as this man's motto. Abbey might well have said with Thoreau that, except perhaps for his friend Ralph Newcomb, "he never found a companion so companionable as solitude."[53]

Disdaining what he takes to be the otherworldly, illusionist mindset of Christian theology, Abbey yet voices a conviction that "wilderness," recalling that "womb of earth from which we all emerged" (189) warrants not only preservation but veneration as a sacred presence. For all his professions of impiety, Abbey thus defines himself as closer than one might suppose to John Calvin's sense of the nonhuman world as a theatre of divine glory.[54] And much as Calvin's insistence on the depth of human depravity was qualified by hope in God's promise of regenerative conversion for some, so also the elegiac sadness of Abbey's voyage through Glen Canyon in his "Down the River" chapter is set against the euphoric, born-again sensation of discovering thereby "the delirious exhilaration of independence, a rebirth backward in time and into primeval liberty" (277).

The *genius loci* of Abbey's country looks to be, in effect, polymorphous rather than uniquely discernible, given the intermingled pantheistic, animistic, and polytheistic impulses in Abbey's spirituality. For Abbey, natural objects and organisms as varied as the moonflower, Spanish bayonet yucca plants, rocks, the Colorado River, side canyons, and snakes all inspire reverence. And among the many geological marvels displayed in what is now Arches National Park, no feature draws Abbey closer to primal worship than that "ring of stone" known as Delicate Arch. To gaze on the Arch's striking, mysterious yet understated beauty is, Abbey suggests, to absorb "the shock of the real" (41–42).

The only time when I, too, found occasion to sit gazing at Delicate Arch was in May of 2015 in the company of twenty-seven Sewanee undergraduates who, together with their instructors and a few others, had enrolled in a hiking tour and field course on the Geology of the Western United States. A weary calm settled over our group as we reached Delicate Arch shortly after dawn, following the exertion of our ascent to this endpoint of the park trail. Mostly silent, we sat still as light settled into the niches scattered across a rock face, every eye among us fixed intently on the Arch. For my part, sharing this experience with those better versed than I in earth science helped me recall that despite the monolith's imposing solidity, it too floated within nature's perpetual tides of change. I had to acknowledge that Delicate Arch, standing in splendid isolation upon what was once a seabed, its sandstone artistry shaped by wind and water over millions of years, was destined to erode away within only a few strokes of geologic time. Still I found it sobering to consider how vastly its scale of physical and temporal being differed from that of our own mortal bodies (Figure 4.1).

Later, after we had been sitting there for some time, all of us staring contentedly yet solemnly at the Arch, geology professor and group leader Bran Potter pointed out to me how unusual it was that on this occasion no one in our group had presumed to approach the Arch directly—to touch it, clown around it, or pose within it for photos in the style of most tourists. I, too, was struck by the untutored, reverential mood that stirred all of us at the time to keep our distance from the Arch, as though allowing it space to remain fully itself—apart from us and our normative proprietary instincts. I knew that a fair proportion of the students there had previously read *Desert Solitaire* or other works by Abbey. So I couldn't help wondering if Ed Abbey's spirit, as a kind of *genius loci pro tem*, had somehow managed to insert itself into the scene though Abbey had been dead for a quarter century.

FIGURE 4.1 Morning sunlight at Delicate Arch, Arches National Park, Utah. Charline Poher, Shutterstock Photo.

That suspicion may have been fitting, even from the standpoint of literary analysis, because in *Desert Solitaire* what had impressed Abbey most about the iconic minimalism he attributed to Delicate Arch and other desert spaces was a spirituality of presence-in-absence. The apparent desolation of these canyon lands only underscored for him the strangeness and otherness of nature's inhumanism.[55] Even though or still more *because* it was ill fitted for human habitation, arid country embodied for Abbey "a realm beyond the human." "There is something about the desert," he concluded, "that the human sensibility cannot assimilate, or has not so far been able to assimilate." In its absolute indifference toward the likes of us "The desert says nothing . . . . [It] lies there like the bare skeleton of Being, spare, sparse, austere, utterly worthless, inviting not love but contemplation" (272, 270). Abbey finds "the unique spirit of desert places" not only consonant with silence, but also comparable to the post-Romantic, bleakly experimental music of composers such as Alban Berg, Arnold Schoenberg, and Elliott Carter. "Their music," he writes "comes closer than any other I know to representing the apartness, the otherness, the strangeness of the desert. Like certain aspects of this music, the desert is also a-tonal, cruel, clear, inhuman, neither romantic nor classical, motionless and emotionless, at one and the same time—another paradox—both agonized and deeply still" (286). Likewise paradoxically, it is by virtue of the desert's obvious indifference to all human projections and comforts that it becomes for Abbey gifted land—an arena of regenerative encounter with more-than-human holiness.

From the standpoint of a familial lineage steeped in Mormon piety across five generations, Terry Tempest Williams sets forth a rather different version of personal witness to the spiritual fecundity of Utah's fierce desert terrain in essayistic volumes such as *Refuge: An Unnatural History of Family and Place* (1991). Abbey and Williams, both of them confirmed naturalists and activists, also shared a zeal to honor putative wastelands, ecosystems thought to be hostile or bleak. Yet the northwest corner of Utah that Williams writes about in *Refuge* is closer to home—indeed at the time for her *is* home—than the terrain in eastern Utah that Abbey memorialized during his two-year stint. "I remember the country I come from and how it informs my life," she attests, having been "marked by the desert"[56] through her personal and family history.

And despite Williams's strained relation to the Church of Latter-Day Saints, her account in *Refuge* honors as well the community of life and love that that body of faith has preserved across time. "I was raised to believe in a spirit world," she writes; and in contrast to Abbey's vehement anticlericalism, she thankfully blends her own form of what Wordsworth termed "natural piety" with a spirituality realized through participation in traditional Christian practices of prayer and ritualized worship, including distinctively Mormon rites of blessing and anointing.

The physical face of Utah that Williams draws us to contemplate in *Refuge* centers on the Great Salt Lake and the basin it occupies. Given the lake's huge expanse, not all of this geography counts as arid, strictly speaking. Yet amid the salt desert "wilderness" adjacent to Utah's largest city stands an abundance of water "no one can drink" (5). Government planners and others had long regarded the region as waste land because of the severity, even the apparent hostility, of its terrain. Not far from the Great Salt Lake, in fact, stands a large municipal dump, one of those "urban wastelands" with "acres of trash heaped high" that nonetheless serves, ironically, as "wildlife's last stand" (54) for birds that Williams loves. A poignant thread of narrative throughout *Refuge* is Williams's tale of how she believes exposure to fallout from atomic bomb tests in the region during the 1950's spawned breast and ovarian cancer in her mother, herself, and several women in her family. "When the Atomic Energy Commission described the country north of the Nevada Test Site as 'virtually uninhabited desert terrain,'" she remarks acerbically, "my family and the birds at Great Salt Lake were some of the 'virtual uninhabitants'" (287).

For Williams, though, Utah's salt desert is a holy place, offering restorative grace and a sanctuary from grief and despair. It serves as "her basin of tears" as well as her "refuge" from life's changes and chances (280). The serenity of the Great Basin, with its gulls soaring overhead, eases the pain of witnessing her mother's decline and eventual death from cancer, among other woes. Williams grieves as well over the threat to birds and other wildlife posed by the salt lake's floodwaters, which for a time engulf the Bear Migratory Bird Refuge. Throughout her reflections this last hope for "refuge," a resonant word whose literal sense here applies to endangered animals, plays against her own yearning for human solace and sanctuary. Yet all the while, consciously inspired by the example of Christ's sojourning in the desert, she pays homage to the land's severe, piercing beauty:

> If the desert is holy, it is because it is a forgotten place that allows us to remember the sacred. Perhaps that is why every pilgrimage to the desert is a pilgrimage to the self. There is no place to hide, and so we are found.
>
> In the severity of a salt desert, I am brought down to my knees by its beauty. My imagination is fired. My heart opens and my skin burns in the passion of these moments. I will have no other gods before me. (148)

In her personal response to this environment, Williams centers her attention on birds, the desert creatures she finds most congenial, comforting, and potentially numinous. In fact, she structures most of her book's chapter headings around the manifold species of aviary life this region supports. Ranging from burrowing owls to avocets and stilts, thirty-six different species supply titles for these short chapters, thereby dramatizing the region's surprising abundance of animal life. Williams displays a true naturalist's fund of ornithological knowledge while elaborating on the distinctive character, habits, and links to humanity of each species. And she is scarcely the first to attribute to birds a kind of magic, an outward imaging of spirituality. Such creatures manage, after all, to "bridge cultures and continents with their wings" and to stir faith in the prospect of transcendence as they "mediate between heaven and earth" (18).

Fowl of the Great Basin even become, for Williams, her own sacramental medium of divine worship. "I pray to the birds," she confesses—and, we must presume, likewise prays *for* the birds as they face destruction of their habitats through human incursions and rising flood waters. As much as anything, the sight of wings upholds her hope of maintaining faith and love amid the desolation, loss, and death that surrounds her. Within the discrete setting of this essayistic paean to place, birds serve as visible counterparts of the land's unseen *genius loci*. And for Williams, cultivating a spirit of inward identification with birds becomes an essential feature of her contemplative practice:

> I pray to the birds because I believe they will carry the messages of my heart upward. I pray to them because I believe in their existence, the way their songs begin and end each day—the invocations and benedictions of Earth. I pray to the birds because they remind me of what I love rather than what I fear. And at the end of my prayers, they teach me how to listen. (149)

The author of *Refuge* finds such angelic "invocations and benedictions" supplementing rather than displacing more traditional forms of collective worship practiced over the course of Mormon and broadly Christian history. In this respect Williams's eclectic spirituality differs from that of other proponents and practitioners of so-called "nature religion." Moreover, in one section of *Refuge* she ends up overtly recognizing her sympathetic kinship with that desert spirituality of ancient Christian monks and anchorites we began recalling in connection with Abbey. Participating with her mother in a Vespers service at the Abbey of the Holy Trinity in Huntsville, Utah, she finds the "light translucent, the music transcendent" (191). Williams betrays no scruple about sharing in the peace and sense of release she feels suffused among all these Trappist, Roman Catholic men.

A comparable breath of denominational religiosity can be seen in writings by the renowned poet and essayist Kathleen Norris, who calls herself "a complete Protestant with a decidedly ecumenical bent."[57] Raised as a Methodist before shifting as an adult from unchurched skepticism to membership in a Presbyterian Church, Norris, too, has found spiritual nurture in Roman Catholic monasteries. Her existential convictions about life in community have been shaped decisively, in fact, through encounter with the *Rule of St. Benedict*, together with the practice of *lectio divina* and immersion in contemplative silence. And like Williams, Norris aims in her best-known work of creative nonfiction to capture the sense of a land with ancestral ties that she had made her home but that many dismiss as unappealing. In *Dakota: A Spiritual Geography* (1993), she concedes that the vast prairie country she came to know and love near Lemon, South Dakota, may look from afar like a cultural wasteland, an apparently empty region that "no one wants" (10) and where nothing ever happens.

Norris moved with her husband into the same house in Lemon she had known as a child during summer visits that her grandparents had built decades earlier. Yet she began her new life on the Plains as something of an outsider. Inevitably, the open, semiarid prairieland of western Dakota placed her in a different world from the one she inhabited at her previous home in New York City. Comparing herself to those desert monastics in the ancient Mediterranean who removed themselves from settled centers of their civilization, she saw herself making a "counter-cultural choice to live in what the rest of the world considers a barren waste." So "I'm in a marginal place," she muses, albeit one situated "at the very center of North America" (3, 107).

Above all, what Dakota's terrain and communities offered Norris was a home place where she could feel her family history, beauty, and holiness all starting to converge. Here where her maternal grandparents had lived out their faith she, too, hoped to regain "a sense of being at home on this planet" (41). Moving to South Dakota in 1974 thus constituted her own "search for inheritance, for place," as well as "a religious pilgrimage" that presumed she might "find both the means and the end" of her search quite literally "on the ground of my grandmother's faith" (93). And the Plains offered still other grounds of faith. It is a setting, for example, long imbued with Native American spirituality and earth reverence. "It was in moving back to the Plains," Norris goes on to say, "that I found my old ones, my flesh and blood ancestors as well as the desert monks and mystics of the Christian church," so that for her "Dakota is where it all comes together, and that is one definition of the sacred" (131).

Largely forgotten by mainstream America, the region Norris portrays nonetheless qualifies as storied and richly enspirited. "The spirit of land is not an abstraction in western Dakota," she asserts, "but a real presence," offering any mindful soul "access to the spirits of land and of place" (128, 169). From her opening page, she is eager to report that "Nature, in Dakota, can indeed be an experience of the holy" (1). And Norris finds the monasteries scattered across the Plains, which she often visits to receive the grace of Benedictine hospitality, surprisingly compatible with the towns and Protestant churches that also appear on the rural scene. "Living with people at close range over many years, as both monastics and small-town people do," she observes, "is much more difficult than wearing a hair shirt" (120). Is it absurd, she wonders, that she should find "a Benedictine monastery and a tiny Presbyterian church in the middle of nowhere to be so absolutely and perfectly complementary" (175)? No matter. She welcomes the chance to share as fully as possible in both.

But although Norris does apprehend a holiness surrounding life on the Plains, in the land's soil and small towns alike, she also wants to avoid romanticizing what such a place represents. "The beauty of the Plains," she explains, "is like that of an icon; it does not give an inch to sentiment or romance," though it affords "a door into some simple and holy state" (157). Her extended exposure to small-town Dakotans convinces her that they can be endearing but also stubborn, petty, insular, unadaptable—even, at times, deficient in their sense of community. Their houses of worship, including one she identifies by name as Hope Presbyterian Church, are in decline. Few of these rural faith communities, now sadly diminished in membership, show signs of enduring. The landscape's austerity, too, provides few opportunities for employment or inducements for young people to remain. Norris herself has since moved elsewhere. In worldly terms, the country in question looks indeed like a dying land. But even as *Dakota* ends on a note of resignation, it sustains belief in the giftedness of this otherwise obscure corner of North America:

> Maybe the desert wisdom of the Dakotas can teach us to love anyway, to love what is dying, in the face of death, and not pretend that things are other than they are. The irony and wonder of all this is that it is the desert's grimness, its stillness and isolation, that bring us back to love. Here we discover the paradox of the contemplative life, that the desert of solitude can be the school where we learn to love others. (121)

CITY SCENES OF GRACE

Most celebrated works of American environmental literature, including those noted for vividly evoking the spirits of place, devote primary attention to First Nature as reflected in unsettled or less-settled landscapes. Ecocriticism, too, remains largely, though not exclusively, governed by assumptions linked to a wilderness aesthetic. Aside from houses of worship, features of the built environment are rarely seen as sites of spiritual regeneration or numinous encounter. American culture has been even less inclined to regard large urban centers as spirit-nurturing environments. Ranging from Jefferson's pastoral mythology, which associates high-density settlements and manufactures with European decadence, to fictional images such as those found in Theodore Dreiser's *Sister Carrie*, American cities have commonly been figured as scenes of degradation equivalent to "sin city."

Particularly after 1900, though, some noteworthy migrant sectors of the population looked to American cities not only as home ground, but as enclosing the only sites likely to be apprehended as holy within their current, New World *Sitz in Leben*. Three such groups concentrated in a city like New York include Roman Catholics resettling from Europe, African Americans of mostly Methodist or Baptist upbringing displaced from the rural South, and Jewish immigrants from several quarters of Eurasia. I have chosen here for brief consideration three texts, each associated with one of these groups, to suggest how various culturally inflected engagements with a spirituality of place have all been conducted in the same metropolis—that is, in greater New York. My trio of works comprises James Baldwin's early novel, *Go Tell It on the Mountain*, together with two cases of personal narrative: Dorothy Day's *The Long Loneliness* and Alfred Kazin's *A Walker in the City*.

Although Day came to identify herself thoroughly with America's twentieth-century Roman Catholic subculture and still more with the mass of impoverished urban dwellers and immigrants among whom she lived and worked for decades, this identity was one she came to by adoption rather than by birth. Day was born in Brooklyn and later became widely known for her activist lay ministry in Manhattan as founder of the Catholic Worker Movement. She also resided at various times in California, Chicago, Mexico, and elsewhere. But the desperate poor occupying Manhattan's streets, tenements, and Catholic Worker houses of hospitality are the lead characters in Day's story, which she relates with a gritty artfulness shaped by the same journalistic training that enabled her to produce the Catholic Worker's legendary, socially transformative newspaper.

Day begins her essayistic memoir on an explicit note of what she calls "confession." She candidly recalls an early adulthood spent in profane wandering, Bohemian experimentation, and bold participation in radical social causes that she never fully disavowed. Yet all the while, despite her "godless spirit" (44) and her prevailing pattern of life as a "sybaritic anchorite," she felt "haunted by God."[58] She admired that honest passion for social betterment she perceived in many of the Communists, Socialists, and anarchists with whom she found common cause. But she remained uncertain about her own core beliefs. "I wanted life and I wanted the abundant life," she admits, and "wanted it for others too" but hadn't "the slightest idea how to find it" (39). Moved to pray on occasion, she scarcely knew why or to whom such impulses were directed.

A turning point in this unlikely saint's quest for a life grounded in faith came with her pregnancy, her giving birth to a beloved daughter, and her subsequent decision to have this child baptized over the objection of her atheistic partner in parenthood. At first she found her passage toward conversion difficult, often joyless. It meant severing relations with her lover, denying other familiar habits of her being. Moreover, given her disposition, she would always be finding fault with the public witness of the church, whose leadership she typically saw standing on the wrong side of social reform movements to which she was devoted. "I love the Church for Christ made visible," she explains, but "Not for itself, because it was so often a scandal to me" (149–150).

Yet in the course of conversion, by the time of her baptism in 1927, she found herself ineluctably drawn to embrace the Church's communitarian identity, its embodiment of a divine fellowship-in-communion. She admired its promotion of spiritual discipline and its insistence that all faithful members participate in collective and sacramental rather than purely individualistic modes of worship.

Above all, she appreciated how the poor and dispossessed found in the church a natural place of welcome. She noticed how the Roman Catholic Church at this time "held the allegiance of the masses of people in all the cities where I had lived," and she relished seeing them pour "in and out of her doors on Sundays and holy days, for novenas and missions." All of this witnessed, she felt, to our common "need to worship, to adore" in solidarity with others. So she resolved to find her own place within this godly yet conspicuously proletarian fellowship: "I had heard many say that they wanted to worship God in their own way and did not need a Church in which to praise Him, nor a body of people with whom to associate themselves. But I did not agree to this. My very experience as a radical, my whole make-up, led me to associate myself with others, with the masses, in loving and praising God" (139). In sum, Day's conversion led her to conclude that only such a corporate faith could henceforth sustain her heart and spirit, combining as it did both Mass and the masses. And for her a predictable locus of encounter with Christ in both Mass and the masses was a place like Manhattan.

What Day discerned as the city's holiness, intermingled by incarnation with its sordidness, was plainly a function of its inhabitants rather than of its physical structures or natural features. The grace and joy of her mature working life in New York owed nothing to the city's aesthetic or cultural riches, everything to the satisfaction she derived from working with and among the poor. And her discovery of that vocation owed much, in turn, to the decisive event of her encounter with Peter Maurin in 1932.

Prior to that meeting, Day had met and sometimes formed ties with an impressive array of literary celebrities. That roster includes Eugene O'Neill, Hart Crane, John Dos Passos, Allen Tate, Caroline Gordon, Kenneth Burke, and Malcolm Cowley. Comparatively speaking, Peter Maurin was nobody—in worldly terms, just an unkempt, eccentric, penniless French peasant. Yet before long Day recognized him as a saintly visionary, a man with a mission, someone uniquely gifted to see and love others—particularly the dispossessed—as living members of Christ's Mystical Body. She was drawn to participate in that mission so far as to make it her own. Peter Maurin, more than anyone else, inspired her to invent and pursue a vocation that included launching an unprecedented publication (the well-known newspaper likewise titled *The Catholic Worker*, still distributed for just a penny), leading a national movement, and founding numerous regional houses of hospitality—all of this achieved without visible means of support. And honoring the *alter Christus* manifested in God's poor lay at the heart of the enterprise she shared with Peter:

> We felt a respect for the poor and destitute as those nearest to God, as those chosen by Christ for His compassion. Christ lived among men. The great mystery of the Incarnation, which meant that God became man that man might become God, was a joy that made us want to kiss the earth in worship, because His feet once trod that same earth . . . . He was familiar with the migrant worker and the proletariat, and some of His parables dealt with them . . . . And He directed His sublime words to the poorest of the poor. (204–205)

The chastened joy to which Day alludes here must be distinguished, though, from the sort of buoyant ecstasy that Emerson, Thoreau, and Muir often attributed to their interactions with unsettled landscapes and features of the natural world. For Day, the destitute sector of Manhattan was indeed a place where God lived and grace happened—but where they often revealed themselves in the shape of Christ on the Cross. So the spirituality of place reflected in her account reflects a corresponding deep-seated participation in affliction. The saving grace of densely ordered community that Day, even more than Maurin,[59] associated with urban settings counteracts but never erases the specters of loss, illness, death, and existential loneliness that pervade her narrative. Along the way she records how the Catholic Worker Movement extended its reach not only to many cities across the country but also to certain farming retreat sites where, thanks to Maurin's influence, it showed a surprising kinship with principles advanced by the southern agrarians. Yet the defining locus of the Catholic Worker Movement has always been New York City—and, more pointedly still, the two houses at 115 Mott Street, on the Lower East Side of Manhattan, that became the Movement's headquarters for some fourteen years, beginning in 1936 (Figure 4.2).

From north of Mott Street, in the Harlem sector of Manhattan, a hard-won holiness yoked to pain and affliction

FIGURE 4.2 Breadline outside the Catholic Worker Office, 115 Mott Street, ca. 1938, New York City. Photo courtesy of Thomas Merton Center at Bellarmine University, Louisville, Kentucky.

likewise came to define the spirituality of place informing much of modern African American literature, including James Baldwin's *Go Tell It on the Mountain*. Like the author, the largely self-modeled protagonist of Baldwin's first novel, John Grimes, undergoes a decisive yet enigmatically portrayed spiritual crisis in Harlem the day after his birthday in 1935 at age fourteen, only a year or so before Day and her cohorts moved to Mott Street. Moreover, the neighborhood in which Grimes lives and moves reflects the formative environment of Baldwin's early life in Harlem. Baldwin knew the "turf" of his world to lie almost exclusively within bounds of "Lenox Avenue on the west, the Harlem River on the east, 135th Street on the north, and 130th Street on the south."[60]

Baldwin's recollections of this home place in Harlem are largely grim, even horrific. The atmosphere within which young Grimes–Baldwin struggles to flourish in *Go Tell It on the Mountain* is one rife with poverty, crime, violence, squalid tenements, racism, familial strife, sexual tensions, and the loveless intrusions of a tyrannical stepfather. Alienated from mainstream American culture, Baldwin's compatriots experience in Harlem a demeaning captivity. Baldwin saw the turf imprisoning its inhabitants within their one assigned place in the world. Or as he remarks in his "Fifth Avenue, Uptown" essay, "the people in Harlem know they are living there because white people do not think they are good enough to live anywhere else."[61] These desperate ghetto dwellers are continually made to *know their place* in patronizing terms, even as they feel themselves denied any real place of dignity and esteem in a country defined apart from their interests.[62]

Yet some features of the metropolitan landscape, at a time before "hideous" housing projects replaced older Harlem structures,[63] retained for Baldwin a comparatively satisfying familiarity. Grimes, like Baldwin, shows an almost-visceral identification with the texture of his surroundings in upper

Manhattan. Among the landmarks shaping the moral geography of young, impressionable Grimes–Baldwin are a favorite hill in Central Park, scenes along Lenox and Fifth Avenues, the stone lions fronting New York's great public library on 42nd Street and, above all, storefront Pentecostal churches that played a decisive role in his rite of passage during these years.

Such places of ecstatic worship became focal points of adolescent awakening for Grimes as well as for Baldwin, both of whom also chafed under the influence of stepfathers who served as preachers. The site where John Grimes's second birth in the spirit takes place, and where Grimes's father occupies the post of head deacon, is called the Temple of the Fire Baptized. Baldwin had attended and undergone *his* transformative faith crisis not in his stepfather's Baptist church but in Mount Calvary Pentecostal Faith Church on Lenox Avenue, overseen by a charismatic female pastor named Mother Rosa Horn.[64] Yet for Baldwin, too, who for some three years preached from pulpits after believing himself "saved," it could fairly be said that the tabernacle where he worshipped was "more completely real to him than the several precarious homes in which he and his family had lived."[65] Throughout his adult life Baldwin could scarcely forget how decisively Christian faith communities in Harlem and elsewhere had shaped the collective identity of African Americans, galvanizing their support for the Civil Rights Movement.

Yet already by the age of seventeen he had disavowed his evangelistic vocation and commitment. He found the Christian church as a whole to be deficient in love, untrustworthy and racially compromised; and the Pentecostal-Holiness movement stifling. Other artistic leaders active in the Harlem Renaissance held similar views. Baldwin, in autobiographical accounts such as "Down at the Cross: Letter From a Region in My Mind," collected in *The Fire Next Time*, rather cynically describes his former evangelistic career as the paradoxically fortunate "gimmick" by which he escaped the hopelessness and poverty of life in the ghetto.[66]

Baldwin nonetheless retained in adulthood a sensibility steeped in biblical language and imagery. He retained as well a potent spiritual impulse, an ambiguously defined and passionately agonistic faith in something larger than the self that finds expression in the culminating chapter of *Go Tell It on the Mountain*. There he writes of how John Grimes felt himself thrown onto the threshing floor of his Pentecostal church, where he lay writhing in crisis for hours on the evening of his fourteenth birthday. The episode plainly recreates the author's own youthful epiphany, one night in church, in which he felt "everything came roaring, screaming, crying out," as he "fell to the ground before the altar." Baldwin adds the telling disclosure that "It was the strangest sensation I have ever had in my life—up to that time, or since."[67]

It is likewise telling that the physical setting of John Grimes's epiphanic encounter is a dusty church floor, beside an altar with a golden cross bearing the legend "Jesus Saves." Floor, altar, and a cross—emblems in this context not of uplifting grace and divine consolation but of agony and affliction. Baldwin underscores the point that Grimes, amid a wordless darkness, "remembered only the cross; he had turned again to kneel at the altar, and had faced the golden cross." For a time, staring at the cross, he believes "the Spirit spoke, and spoke in him" (229). But the episode as a whole confirms that if Grimes experiences here in a dusty Harlem storefront something of genuine encounter with the spirits of place, as we have reason to affirm, the spirits in question are far from uniformly benign or comforting. Moreover, that this epiphany turns out to be not an occasion of uplifting transcendence, so much as a crisis event in which Grimes feels at the first oppressed, overwhelmed, struck down:

> And something moved in John's body which was not John. He was invaded, set at naught, possessed. This power had struck John, in the head or in the heart; and, in a moment, wholly, filling him with an anguish that he could never in his life have imagined . . . had opened him up; had cracked him open . . . so that John had not felt the wound, but only the agony, had not felt the fall, but only the fear; and lay here, now, helpless, screaming, at the very bottom of darkness. (227–228)

As articulated in Baldwin's retrospective narrative, what Grimes comes to see and know through his visionary encounter enfolds the whole painful history of his family and racial community. It encompasses his deathly fear and guilt, his agonistic relation to his stepfather, and his disillusionment with faith itself. It requires of him a terrifying descent into darkness and affliction—his own, as well as the whole company of earth's "despised and rejected." Yet he is sustained along the way by those "saints" and family members who stand "above him, waiting, watching" (237, 229), and especially by Elisha, the beloved soul-friend who prays him through his torment.

Together with critic Albert J. Raboteau, I believe that *Go Tell It on the Mountain*, despite its author's adult rejection of Christian doctrine, gives eloquent voice to spirit-truths Baldwin could express only in terms of imaginative literature. Raboteau astutely observes how key passages in this novel cast the whole "meaning of African American history within the biblical story of salvation in language that echoes the idiom of black religious culture."[68] Baldwin recalls that church members had assured him, on the morning following his own threshing-floor ordeal, that he had been "saved," in response to which he later notes that "well, indeed I was, in a way," insofar as he had thereby been "released, for the first time, from all my guilty torment"[69] (47).

Above all Baldwin's novel reveals, through language aptly enough inspired by the biblical Book of Revelation, how tokens of saving grace might be seized from an affliction known in solidarity with the saints—Christian saints of old, as well as saintly brethren and forebears of the author's own race. Like John of Patmos, putative author of the Book of Revelation, John Grimes testifies to having witnessed and heard the Spirit through rather than despite his painful ordeal. And sounds of the spirit, resonant in the soulful music that made churches like the Temple of the Fire Baptized "to *rock*" (246), had always "filled John's life, so it now seemed":

> And now in his moaning, and so far from any help, he heard it in himself—it rose from his bleeding, his cracked-open heart. It was a sound of rage and weeping which filled the grave, rage and weeping from time set free, but bound now in eternity; rage that had no language, weeping with no voice—which yet spoke now, to John's startled soul . . . of the deepest water, the strongest chains, the most cruel lash . . . . Yes the darkness hummed with murder: the body in the water, the body in the fire, the body on the tree.
> . . . .
> . . . .
> *I, John, saw the future, way up in the middle of the air.*
> . . . .
> . . . .
> Who are these? Who are they? They were the despised and rejected, the wretched and the spat upon, the earth's offscouring; and he was in their company, and they would swallow up his soul. The stripes they had endured would scar his back, their punishment would be his . . . . *Thrice was I beaten with rods, once I was stoned, thrice I suffered shipwreck, a night and a day I have been in the deep.*
> . . . .
> . . . .
> and the room was filled with a multitude of people, all in long, white robes

....
....
Then John saw the river, and the multitude was there.
....
....
They endured the cross, and they despised the shame. (236–242)

Is "the body on the tree" envisioned here that of Christ or of a lynching victim? Arguably for Baldwin it is both. He likewise identifies horrors his forebears once endured under the lash of slavery with abuses St. Paul writes of having suffered in 2 Corinthians 11:25. Nor does Baldwin's disenchantment with the Christian church prevent him from claiming writerly access to the power of the divine Word, his own evangelistic vocation to tell widely—as on a mountain—all he had learned growing up black in 1930s Harlem about the soul's struggles and life on the streets.

Alfred Kazin, the distinguished literary critic and writer, also recalled growing up in a poor, sometimes bleak, minority enclave of New York in the 1930s. Yet Kazin's natal "turf" in East Brooklyn's neighborhood of Brownsville, today populated largely by African Americans, otherwise differed markedly from the New York Baldwin knew. Most of the Brownsville neighbors Kazin recalls in his vividly evocative and ambulatory memoir, *A Walker in the City*, belonged to working-class Jewish immigrant families, like his own, hailing from Eastern Europe. Kazin writes of growing up "with the belief that the natural condition of a Jew was to be a propertyless worker like my painter father and my dressmaker mother."[70] He understood, too, that densely settled yet provincial Brownsville, situated on "the margin of the city," scarcely qualified as New York at all in relation to Manhattan or even to greater Brooklyn. "We were in the city but somehow not of it" (10, 11), he notes. So although he relished the chance to walk in summers to Brooklyn's Highland Park or to stroll around sites of interest in Manhattan, he acknowledged Brownsville to be his home place—at least until such time, around his sixteenth year, when he felt moved to defy and escape it.

The Brownsville of his youth could be, Kazin admits, a place of "damp sadness," especially during those seasons of the Depression era when his parents and others were out of work. Neither does he ordinarily testify to having experienced this familiar territory as holy ground. Few of those around him, including his irreligious, freethinking father, "seemed to take God seriously" (6, 46), or to care whether he understood the meaning of Hebrew texts that were read out in synagogue and that he was called upon to profess at the time of his confirmation (a ceremony sometimes parallel with, or performed subsequently to Bar Mitzvah rites) at age thirteen.

For all that, it would be a mistake to overlook the spirituality—even, at times, the ardent religiosity—that permeates *A Walker in the City*.[71] Consistent with Judaism's traditional interfusion of sacred with secular apprehensions of the world, Kazin expresses not only appreciation but also something of reverence for the sensate stimulation that Brownsville's sounds, sights, and smells had once afforded him. He recollects hearing and learning to sing, Friday evenings at home, "Yiddish folksongs and Socialist hymns" (58); he recalls those melodies of communal sorrow he played on his violin before his family in their dining room, and "the great *Kol Nidre* sung in the first evening hours of the Day of Atonement" (99). He recalls the enchanting darkness of the neighborhood movie house and his culture's almost ritualistic, domestically centered "veneration of food"—associated with such material elements as "that deep and good odor of lox, of salami, of herrings and half-sour pickles, that told me I was truly home" (32).

Beyond his family dining room, two particular sites in Brownsville offered Kazin space to express the "private orthodoxy" of his uncertain, agonistic if not at times agnostic religious faith. One of these was the small, worn, undistinguished wooden synagogue where he joined in prayer with others, learned to read Hebrew text aloud, and sat amid that "stale air of snuff, of old men and old books." Watching his elders, "wrapped in their black-striped prayer shawls, their eyes turned to Jerusalem, mumbling and singing in their threadbare voices" (100, 45, 42), he was never sure how much he shared the beliefs professed in his synagogue, or even whether there was much he liked about its atmosphere. No matter. It was enough to realize that it was indeed *his* synagogue, that "I belonged there before the Ark, with the men, sitting next to an uncle," such that "I felt a loveless intimacy with the place." There he could feel confident that

> Whether I assented to its right over me or not, I belonged ... no matter how far I might drift from that place, I belonged. This was understood in the very nature of things; I was a Jew. It did not matter how little I knew or understood of the faith, or that I was always reading alien books; I belonged, I had been expected, I was now to take my place in the great tradition. (44, 45)

Moreover, despite the doubts and uncertainties he entertained about the Deity venerated in that tradition, Kazin confesses that "I never really wanted to give Him up," because "in some way it would have been hopeless to justify to myself—I had feared Him so long—He fascinated me"; He "seemed to hold the solitary place I most often went back to" (47). That same contemplative impulse, it seems, led Kazin to welcome the holy darkness and emptiness of Brownsville's streets on late Friday afternoons as the Sabbath approached.

Oddly, the other local site aside from the synagogue where Kazin recalled hearing God speak was even closer to home: a perch on the fire escape of his family's tenement. Beginning one summer when he was thirteen, he climbed out alone to the morning air, prayer book in hand, and absorbed from the volume's texts in English as well as Hebrew words that had never so moved him before:

> The voice that spoke in that prayer book seemed to come out of my very bowels. There was something grand and austere in it that confirmed everything I had felt in my bones about being a Jew: the fierce awareness of life to the depths, every day and in every hour: the commitment: the hunger. (103)

In such a mood Kazin recalls taking satisfaction even in the ritual observances of Yom Kippur, especially the moment when all the faithful, bowing their heads and smiting their breasts, "went through the long catalogue in unison, finding in its enumeration, as I thought, a kind of purifying ecstasy, for they were summing up the whole earthly life of Brownsville" (102).

For Kazin and his fellows, Brownsville of the 1930s derived, in turn, much of its collective place-meaning from other places and times. This latter-day, New World settlement retained an uncommon self-awareness of its roots in the Old World, above all in the faith practices and enspirited language of those who inhabited ancient Israel.

Kazin's neighborhood synagogue, with its Ark and aged doors, offered him a perpetual reminder of Brownsville's intertopological ethos, its standing as a place perforce grounded in other places. "Old as the synagogue was," Kazin writes, and "old as it looked and smelled in its every worn and wooden corner, it seemed to me even older through its ties to that ancestral world I had never seen. Its very name,

Dugschitz, was taken from the little Polish village my mother came from." (42).

Of course no Jewish homeland had yet been established by the period Kazin describes in his memoir, and the predominantly Jewish subcity of Brownsville to which he once belonged no longer exists. For that matter, neither does, bodily, Alfred Kazin, the writer having died in 1998. Yet in one form or another, one place or another, much of the world's Jewish population continues to live out in diaspora a religious and cultural identity situated *somewhere* while at the same time maintaining a form of spiritual citizenship—much as Nathaniel Hawthorne had said of himself—"somewhere else."[72]

5

CONTEMPLATING SITE-BASED EDUCATION AND PLACE-MAKING

CURRENT CONCEPTS AND PRACTICES OF SITE-BASED EDUCATION

In the previous chapters I hope to have shown in diverse cases how literary imagination not only describes place, along with whatever *genius loci* might be perceived to dwell therein, but helps to create it. Many of us, for good or ill, can scarcely bring to mind "Nebraska" without envisioning that land, at least as it once was, in the light of Willa Cather's fiction. Much the same could be said of Sarah Orne Jewett's Maine, William Faulkner's Mississippi, John Muir's Yosemite, James Baldwin's Harlem, or the Massachusetts of Emerson, Thoreau, Dickinson, and Hawthorne. Literature can doubtless evoke for us the spirit of places we have never seen or visited, sometimes more effectually than where we *have* set foot, emplacing us in settings removed from our own in time as well as space.

These figurative versions of place-making need not express blind topophilia. As we have seen, troubled and troubling spirits also lurk along with soul-friends in localized narratives such as Baldwin's *Go Tell It on the Mountain*. Still, literary imagination can conceivably do much to inspire the art of personal or corporate place-making. But these life projects evidently require more of their practitioners than literary study alone. Those of us who serve as educators recognize the role formal schooling also plays in this process, for good or ill. Consider, for example, that familiar yet in some sense peculiar custom by which we expect many Americans in late adolescence to leave their home ground to undertake collegiate study somewhere else. What implications might this mass migration bear for place-making, individuation, and cultural identity? And what might it look like to make place-making—in its fullest intellectual, existential, and social context—a deliberate goal of higher education?

Only a few decades ago, the four-year residential model of higher education remained solidly in place throughout America. In urban areas, especially, a fair number of commuter students had for some time managed to pursue collegiate studies while remaining at home. But the idea of housing college students on campus, where the institution could presumably oversee their growth in character and civic identity as well as in scholastic learning, became something of a rite of passage toward adulthood in middle-class American culture. Following World War II and at least until the late twentieth century, this supposition became all the more firmly entrenched as an ever-greater proportion of young persons began to attend college.

Lately, though, the residential model has been called into serious question. As the overall cost of higher education—including tuition—has escalated in recent years,[1] it becomes harder to justify the further expenditure required for providing room, board, and other facilities for students living away from home. Many believe that advances in digital technology, together with the proliferation of MOOCS (Massive Open Online Courses) and other forms of distance learning, are already spurring the obsolescence of residential colleges and universities. Many wonder, too, whether enrolling at a residential institution is worth the heavy cost and debt burden it often entails, particularly in a faltering economy in which the long-term salary gain of graduates falls below previous expectations.

Skeptics press the case further still. Isn't it time to replace the nation's current premium brand, a four-year college degree, with low-cost badges of competence that any determined student might pursue online, while living anywhere? Or time at least to reduce that all-too-costly four years of retreat from normalcy to three? And if many professors themselves no longer believe that their vocation extends to shaping the character, morality, spirituality, or civic virtue of young people,[2] why should we maintain the costly, rarefied living environment once deemed essential for cultivating these educational aims? Especially when the chief reason some students today seek residential schooling in the first place may be its ready access to partying, institutionally sponsored entertainment, and a respectable means of avoiding or at least postponing their assumption of adult obligations. Surveys confirm that students today, at virtually every sort of collegiate institution, devote less time to solitary study than their counterparts once did in previous generations. Administrators, too, are often more inclined to market their institution's capacity to offer an array of presumably transformative "experiences" than its effectiveness in intellectual training and development. The college's academic identity thus becomes only one more function—not necessarily paramount, or more celebrated than intercollegiate athletics—among the several sustained by its operational structures and in the minds of undergraduates.

This emergent, all-too-familiar model of higher education surely warrants skepticism. As historian Wilfred McClay wryly observes, "Perhaps we do not need college to be what it all too often has become: an extended *Wanderjahre* of post-adolescent entertainment and experimentation, played out in the soft protected environment of idyllic, leafy campuses, less a rite of passage than a retreat to a very expensive place where one can defer the responsibilities of adult life."[3]

Large universities whose instruction depends on a preponderance of high-enrollment lecture courses are particularly vulnerable to these critiques. Students may perceive little difference, after all, between auditing someone's formal lecture in a crowded lecture hall and learning at home through newer forms of digital instruction. Yet insofar as self-conscious place-making continues to matter, or should matter all the more at a time of unsettling dislocation for young adults—both culturally and within a pivotal phase of their own life cycle—the educational mission of small, liberal arts colleges remains critical. Such institutions, or intentionally organized subcommunities of learning within larger ones, encourage the face-to-face interchange of ideas in close community. Residential campuses present a favored setting for such interchange, whose efficacy for deep learning has been acknowledged since the time of Socrates. Campus architecture, the site's exposure to discrete features of both First and Second Nature, and the character of a school's artistic décor likewise contribute substantially to the atmosphere of learning that students inhabit.

Again I find Wilfred McClay's summation of the matter compelling. In the face of claims that higher education must now be refashioned radically through technological and mass-market innovation, McClay cautions that

> we should not be too quick to discard an older model of what higher education is about, a model that the conventional four-year residential liberal-arts college, whatever its failures and its exorbitant costs, has been preeminent in championing. And that is the model of a physical community built around a great shared enterprise: the serious and careful reading and discussion of classic literary, philosophical, historical, and scientific texts[4]

By extension of these principles, several forms of place-based courses have arisen that reconceive the campus environment—including its physical expression and surrounding communities—not merely as the setting for learning but as a subject of educational inquiry in its own right. Such courses have commonly been associated with environmental studies programs or with modes of service learning. And despite the ever-diminishing proportion of Americans engaged in farming, student interest in food production and practices associated with alternative agriculture continues to mount—not merely at land-grant institutions, where there is historical precedent for such involvement, but at liberal arts colleges as well.

Whereas students in earlier generations might suppose that higher education offered a pathway of escape from lives of confinement and hard labor on the farm, students today often look to rediscover some form of hands-on involvement with growing things, an activity sometimes conjoined with academic course work, on a university farm. Among the many schools eager to advertise the availability of these experiences are such diverse institutions as Sewanee, Colorado College, Warren Wilson College, St. Olaf College, and Yale. At Sewanee, there is a curious irony in the way that campus farming, once undertaken—and subsequently abandoned—for the utilitarian purpose of supplying much of the food served to boarding students, has lately returned to favor. Along the way, our justification for sustaining a campus farm has changed. The small-scale field operation in which students now volunteer to work from time to time is not expected to contribute a major share of the dining hall's food store. Its aim is rather to offer students a practical, hands-on means of advancing their education in matters related to agriculture, food production and distribution, sustainability, and soil science.

The University of the South's extensive landholdings, across its 13,000 acres of contiguous campus terrain known as the

Domain, include woodlands, fields, caves, and watercourses that constitute a natural laboratory for field science courses in geology, forestry, archaeology, and biology. One of the institution's legendary instructors, Professor Bran Potter, regularly teaches a three-week, walking and "study away" course on the Geology of the Western United States. Complementing these fairly traditional models of place-grounded education are newer curricular offering such as Potter's own localized, interdisciplinary course on "Walking the Land," courses linked to studio art or psychology, and a span of courses under the common rubric of "Southern Appalachian and Place-Based Studies." In 2014 a grant from the Andrew W. Mellon Foundation enabled the University of the South and Yale University to launch a partnership, known today as "The Collaborative for Southern Appalachian Studies," to develop curricular and cocurricular programs involving faculty and students from both institutions.

Place-based educational programs may also reflect a sociopolitical or ethical dimension, along with some activist intention. At Sewanee, for example, a roster of designated Community Engaged Learning courses enable students both to acquire understanding of various local institutions—including health clinics and elementary schools—and to contribute something to these ventures. And the national Bonner Foundation, which currently numbers more than sixty campuses as network members, orchestrates a community-engaged Bonner Leaders Program with representation at Sewanee. As described by our campus office, the program "aims to educate students for lives of achievement and service while collaborating with community partners in and around Sewanee." Selected students are expected to "complete the Bonner Path to service, which starts with establishing a connection to community partners and ends with your taking full leadership responsibility."

Yet programs of place-based learning rarely identify, among their stated aims, cultivation of a student's spirituality or religious awareness. That is true even at faith-related colleges and universities. Indirectly, of course, various study away courses and programs end up addressing some dimension of religious culture and experience. Sewanee's "Road to Santiago" course, offered in summer through the Spanish Department and inviting students to walk a classic European way of pilgrimage, is one such offering. A number of colleges and universities have also come to affirm the educational relevance of "contemplative pedagogy"—as a useful technique for learning and knowing if not one allied perforce to religious practice. So I think it worth considering just how a contemplative approach to learning might bear upon the advancement of place-making and site-based education.

THE RATIONALE FOR CONTEMPLATIVE LEARNING IN PLACE

On its face, the notion of contemplative learning stands well outside the mainstream of consensus—such as it is—on the ideals of higher education. In truth, however, educators across the nation currently express little agreement about how those ideals should be defined or ranked, and still less accord about what, if anything, every college graduate should be expected to know by way of subject matter. Conviction about the worth and theoretical identity of a liberal arts education is still strong on the part of those working at institutions committed to that model, but liberal arts colleges like my own continue to enroll an ever-diminishing share of America's collegiate population. Meanwhile, throughout all halls of higher education, "interdisciplinary" remains a hallowed buzzword, thematically defined general education requirements have become ever more popular and idiosyncratic in place of specifically mandated courses, and broadly curricular concern with instruction in skills rather than content is the order of the day. As faculty members and administrators differ more and more on virtually everything else pertaining to formation of a core curriculum, skill in critical thinking is the one attribute aside from problem-solving that educators agree students must learn to master in college. Ironically, though, the gains in critical thinking and complex reasoning skills that students seem to have registered over the course of their years in college look to be modest at best.[5] As one prominent educator, Derek Bok, contends in his appraisal of *Our Underachieving Colleges,*

> Despite the favorable opinions of undergraduates and alumni, a closer look at the record in the chapters that follow shows that colleges and universities, for all the benefits they bring, accomplish far less for their students than they should. Many seniors graduate without being able to write well enough to satisfy their employers. Many cannot reason clearly or perform competently in analyzing complex, nontechnical problems, even though faculties rank critical thinking as the primary goal of a college education.[6]

Although American higher education continues to garner praise in many quarters as the envy of the world, other analysts have, to varying degrees, echoed Bok's pessimistic view of the current system. Louis Menand in his book *The Marketplace of Ideas* argues, for example, that the model now in play is essentially outdated, "still a late nineteenth-century system, put in place for late nineteenth-century reasons" (17). A major defect, he believes, is the mismatch between the specialized doctoral training professors receive and the breadth of training and vision their pedagogical vocation presumes. Reform of higher education in America must therefore include revamping "the way that the producers of knowledge are produced."[7]

Such assessments nonetheless come across as clearer, more compelling, in their diagnosis than in their prescription. Menand proposes that "academic inquiry, at least in some fields, may need to become less exclusionary and more holistic" (158), but it is hard to know just what such a shift would entail or look like. And while I endorse Bok's contention, shared in turn with journalist David Brooks, that higher education should indeed concern itself with character building and moral reasoning,[8] it remains doubtful just how—aside from ensuring students' exposure to courses in applied ethics—this aim can best be pursued.

What I take to be one promising way toward realizing more holistic ideals in higher education highlights for students the value of cultivating greater mindfulness and imaginative resourcefulness. Rarely, after all, are such traits named as educational priorities in mission statements or strategic plans. Yet it is surely possible to overvalue the essentially deconstructive *telos* of critical thinking, set apart from the creative, reconstructive dynamic of imagination. And I think it arguable that genuine contemplative learning, fostered in tandem with analytic reasoning, has less to do with fuzzy sentiment than with a disposition linked to classic virtues of a liberal arts education. This left-brained disposition includes a sustained, deliberate focus on the inherent beauty of ideas, a capacity to apprehend and affirm the otherwise unseen communion among disparate things. The latter attribute is expressed in the exercise of creative imagination, as elaborated in Chapter 3. It corresponds as well to what has lately been described as "placed education"— a mode of learning more concerned with "health and homecoming" than with yearning to locate an ever-elusive "better place." As authors Jack R. Baker and Jeffrey Bilbro point out, "An education for health begins by forming the imaginations and affections of students so that rather than desiring upward mobility, they can imagine healthy, placed lives."[9]

Such instruction enables students to appreciate not only the storied coloration of whatever place they inhabit or visit, but also the spirituality of a "contemplative ecology"—as Douglas E. Christie terms it—that leads them to apprehend how the particularities of a place participate in "the larger whole of the living world." As Christie explains, contemplative ecology is best understood as "a spiritual practice bound to a particular place and arising from it." He finds an instructive embodiment of it in the monastic and anchoritic traditions of ancient Christianity, above all in the sixth-century Rule of St. Benedict and the desert wisdom preserved from figures such as Antony, Evagrius, and Cassian. The monastic vow of *stabilitas*, for example, undergirds the principle that a monk's crucial, lifelong journey toward full conversion of heart "entails a steady but gradual reorientation of one's entire being to the presence of God in a particular monastic community, that is in a particular place." What these ancient traditions taught about deep receptivity to the otherness of the natural world and God, about single-minded concentration, about learning to center one's whole being in silence—all of this, Christie proposes, can still today "help us reimagine our place in the world."[10]

No less than physical projects such as forest trailblazing, urban beautification, or earth-friendly farming, the practice of meditating in and upon one's setting in the material world constitutes a mode of place-making.[11] One vein of this earth-grounded spirituality, traceable in Jewish and Christian tradition from ancient and medieval times to the present, was commonly described in seventeenth-century England as meditation on or from the creatures. Together with two other modes of interior concentration—meditation on the self and meditation on the biblical Word—it had by then become an established practice in both Catholic and Protestant devotionalism. It is reflected in writings by seventeenth-century poets and clergy ranging from George Herbert, Joseph Hall, and Thomas Traherne in England to Edward Taylor and Anne Bradstreet in North America. And its integrative ideal was at once to unify the self—drawing together a soul's inward faculties of memory, understanding, and will—while reconstituting that self's harmonious connection with the whole of God's Creation.[12]

Some age-old versions of meditation on the creatures are still practiced today and retain a potential attraction for college students. One of these, likewise a favored discipline among devotees of Asian religion, is walking meditation. In another common form of the meditative exercise, practitioners simply fix their gaze on some discrete natural object, sustaining their attention on the object long enough for its gifted presence to penetrate their being. Any reasonably stationary object such as a stone, waterfall, stream, feather, or tree might serve the purpose. A series of late poetic meditations by Denise Levertov, for example, centers its attention on Mount Rainier, viewed at a distance from the poet's home in Seattle.[13] The whole of Whitman's "Song of Myself" amounts to a richly elaborated meditation on a single blade of grass. The bodily aspect of such meditation may be supported as well by mindful breathing, as seems to have been the case for Whitman.

Of course, the main challenge one faces in introducing students to centering exercises of this sort, within a curricular context or otherwise, are all the cultural allergies to silence and stillness they will have absorbed by the time they reach college. Sitting still in place does not come easily to most of us or to them. Many will nonetheless prove receptive if they are tactfully initiated to contemplative practices, first in a corporate setting and by means of brief exposure, and particularly if persuaded of the exercise's relevance to the proposed course of learning. Some will be predisposed to cooperate by virtue of their experience with Hatha yoga or similar practices; still others, troubled by stress, welcome most any prospect of relief compatible with their generation's craving for ways toward "wellness."

One of several modes of curricular access to contemplative learning available to students at Sewanee is a course offered regularly by Jennifer Michael, a professorial colleague of mine in the English Department. Titled "Poetry, Nature, and Contemplation," it approaches poetic composition, and above all the mindful reading of poems, as contemplative practices. Students enrolled in this course are expected to engage in periods of daily meditation, both in and outside of class sessions. So far as I have had a chance to observe, they do so willingly and often fruitfully. And as Professor Michael explains, such practice offers heuristic benefits in a class such as hers:

> Meditation helps us to slow down, both as readers and as observers of the world around us. It's countercultural for students to be asked to bring their whole selves into the classroom, and for that matter, it's countercultural for professors to do the same. I find that a 5-minute meditation at the beginning of class helps us all to arrive here and to clear the decks for the work ahead. I have less control over the meditation they do outside class—they're on their honor to record it—but in their journals I ask them to reflect both on their meditation practice and on the readings. The ones who are most faithful in meditation often develop deeper insight into the readings, even if they were not the most accomplished readers of poetry beforehand.

Professor Michael has shared with me, too, this revealing comment that one student recorded in her class journal: "Nature doesn't ask me a million questions or demand to know the moral reasoning behind my life decisions. It just asks the question 'who do you want to be?' and then is silent while it actually lets me answer for myself

... I feel that nature calls to me, wanting me to be a part of it, regardless of who I am. And that's the kind of person I want to be to other people."

"Frankly, if a student gets that out of my class," Michael concludes, "I'm less concerned about whether she knows what iambic pentameter is" because she has shown herself to be "someone engaged in real growth, real learning." That judgment seems to be sound. For if we suppose real or deep learning to be thoroughly integrative, so as to contribute discernibly to students' moral and spiritual development as well as their intellectual growth, contemplative education looks like a promising means toward that end. But it is indeed countercultural—not only in relation to American society at large, but also vis-à-vis those within higher education who insist that colleges must intensify their sponsorship of entrepreneurial ambition and technological innovation. That industrially colored imperative finds little use for contemplative pedagogy. Nonetheless, signs of interest in contemplative learning, as at least an experimental curricular option, continue to surface across the nation. Granted, this approach presumes the sometimes doubtful willingness of instructors to teach in ways beyond the scope of their professional training. Still, contemplative learning offers even practical benefits for institutions concerned about student retention and welfare because it shows potential to enhance student wellness yet requires no special expenditures for equipment or facilities.

A CASE STUDY IN LOCALIZED LEARNING

A curricular offering at Sewanee I think it worth describing more fully here by way of lending concreteness to these issues is a distinctive, place-based course for first-year students originally titled "Discovering a Sense of Place." In 2015 and again in 2017 I served as one of the instructors assigned to this team-taught enterprise. And though altered over the years, with the single-course concept later evolving into a program comprising several distinct but interlinked courses, the course as I knew it in 2015 is mostly how I aim to represent it here.

The course in question was formally launched in 2013. Often tagged since then with the familiar title of "Finding Your Place" (under the acronym of FYP, likewise indicative of "First-Year Program"), it has centered attention on local settlements and natural features, including those represented on the University's own extensive, 13,000-acre land base otherwise known as "the Domain." One impulse behind creating such a course was, in fact, the chance to draw fully on the unique educational resources available in the Domain's wealth of woodlands, fields, geological features, and community settlements. Another aim was to expose first-year students at the outset to a stimulating course of intellectual inquiry with existential resonance, pursued through an intensive schedule of discussion and field study prior to their involvement in additional courses or other campus activities.

The distracting and often-corrosive influence of Greek social organizations is pervasive at Sewanee, seizing the attention of first-year students as soon as they encounter older students on campus. So the FYP course, with its early start date at a time when first-year students mostly have the campus to themselves, allows us to initiate students from the start to an atmosphere of serious learning defined by probing discussion, close bonding among students and faculty instructors, and manifold site visits. Although course instructors have been drawn from departments spanning the full range of arts and sciences disciplines, they are challenged to pursue forms of inquiry well beyond their fields of academic training and specialization. The course was thus conceived to be *sui generis* rather than moored to any single department, discipline, or category of general education. Students, too, have been encouraged to appreciate the value of compound and complementary ways of knowing, particularly in an opening two-week period of intensive, all-day instruction known as "interdisciplinary immersion." The course aims to provide not only an effectively transdisciplinary mode of intellectual training, but also a practical means by which students might advance discovery of their own place on campus and in the wider world.

As originally approved, the official catalog description of First-Year Program 100 read as follows:

> *Discovering a Sense of Place—Upon and Beyond the Domain*
> *This interdisciplinary course invites first-year students to reflect upon several dimensions of their new living environment, both within and beyond the University's extensive land base of the Domain—and thereby to enlarge their intellectual and existential understanding of what a "sense of place" might mean in several diverse and ever-widening contexts. Touching eventually on global issues, the inquiry begins with study of the Domain's natural features in conjunction with its built environment—including its associations with surrounding communities, its stories of settlement past and present, and its agricultural and resource assets. Much though not all of this field and community-linked exploration takes place in concentrated form during a special curricular session, set aside for first-years only, scheduled for two weeks prior to the start of the regular academic term. Further class sessions within the regular term will conclude before Thanksgiving. Some instruction takes place in plenary group sessions, linked to a common core of reading assignments. There is also a variable thematic coloring to each small-group section of the course. Individual instructors define the angle of emphasis relevant to their section, and students have some option to enroll in a section whose subtitle accords with their interests.*

As academic dean of the College of Arts and Sciences from 2007 to 2014, I had a role in developing and initiating presentation of the course. But it was not until the fall semester of

2015 that I first served as one of its instructors. At that time ten sections were offered, each with its own flavor and schedule of field excursions, though all sections shared a body of core principles, procedures, expectations, and lecture sessions. Around fifteen students were enrolled in each section. Biology professor Deborah McGrath ably directed the logistics of the enterprise, as she had done the previous two years since its inception and continued to do through the summer of 2017. Faculty members of the instructional team in 2015 represented eight different primary disciplines: archaeology, art history, studio art, biology, chemistry, English, geology, and religion. Beyond the course's emphasis on interdisciplinary approaches to learning, especially in the opening immersion phase, secondary modes of attention and subject matter in each section varied according to the instructor's disciplinary outlook. In my own section, I wanted to involve students in contemplative and experiential as well traditionally academic modes of reflecting on placement. Along the way, I also wanted to encourage students' receptivity to religious implications of our inquiry. And given my departmental affiliation, I thought it appropriate to underscore literary imagination as the leading term in the notice shared with prospective students:

> *FYP100, Section B Making a Place for Literary Imagination*
> In this section we'll reflect on forms of literary expression—stories, poems, and nonfictional accounts—that most vividly color and capture humanity's sense of place. How we imagine and write about sites that matter to us not only records them but truly helps to create them—as storied places, not just spaces on the map. Our reading will focus on American texts, those evocative of scenes close to home in Sewanee as well as farther away.

Common reading assignments for students in all sections of the course included selections addressing more theoretical aspects of place as well as more discretely localized commentaries and narratives from an array of disciplinary perspectives. Among the assigned readings in the latter category were David Haskell's reflections on *The Forest Unseen* (discussed in Chapter 2), faculty colleague Bran Potter's account of the region's geological and historical foundations, and a historically layered personal narrative by Ely Green, a young inhabitant of Sewanee village, about the challenges of approaching maturation as a biracial youth in the late nineteenth and earlier twentieth century. Several site visits were scheduled for each section, with two of the sections combining forces for some excursions. Site visits for my section included walks in tracts of relatively unsettled forest as well as encounters with historic campus structures, cave outcrops, cemeteries, and nearby civil war sites such as Stones River National Battlefield in Murfreesboro, Tennessee. I looked to pair each site visit with a reading assignment in one or more texts. A rare feature of the 2015 offering was a two-day plenary schedule of events with Wendell Berry and members of the Berry Center. In light of that opportunity, I thought it fitting to frame the syllabus for my course section with an opening motto drawn from one of Berry's Sabbath Poems, which speaks of belonging "to your place" and caring for it "by your own knowledge / of what it is that no other place is."[14]

Although survey evidence confirms the course's effectiveness in several respects, it remains a work-in-progress. Some of its faults may derive from the scale of its ambitions, given its combined role as a broadly conceived overture to student life in a particular residential community as well as a suitably demanding course of academic study. Its opening phase takes place around the same time each year as the campus launch of another program offering for new students—this last program having been clearly identified as an optional, pre-academic phase of orientation focused on outdoor group activities, rather than as a credit-bearing course. It may be no wonder, then, that students registering for the FYP offering have sometimes failed at the outset to grasp its character as an authentic academic course, complete with reading assignments and graded assessments of their work. Even after the start of this course, given its intensive sequence of field trips, some begin to think of it as chiefly an exercise in localized tourism and fellowship building, thus amounting to one more feature of that nonacademic process of student orientation they already know to be conducted these days at most American colleges and universities. Although those of us serving as team instructors have tried to uphold expectations of intellectual rigor by defining standards of student work that include more-or-less common reading assignments, copious amounts of reflective writing, and a substantial capstone project, entering students may also question the academic seriousness of a course lacking exposure to traditional quizzes and exams.

The informal title this course acquired early in its history, "Finding Your Place," also seems to carry certain liabilities as well as assets. On the favorable side, such a title encapsulates the worthy ideal of a personal, existential outcome to the course's approach and subject matter.

It rightly suggests that students may derive from academic study findings pertinent to personal meaning and values that surpass purely objective or analytic knowledge. Surely one such benefit of the FYP course in particular is its demonstrated capacity to ease students' transition to a new home and way of life, enabling them from the start to find their place socially, spiritually, and geographically in a singular rural community unlike any other place they had known or inhabited. In fact, many students report that their involvement in FYP proved invaluable to them in forming friendships within the first week of their arrival on campus. All this is to the good. Yet our "Finding Your Place" nomenclature does reinforce the faulty impression that this course is simply a nonacademic extension of orientation lacking in serious curricular demands. It also risks reinforcing the already self-absorbed inclination of many students in late adolescence. Educators may at times need to challenge rather than endorse that inclination. If FYP is supposed to be all about *me* after all, and about how to find *my* place in the world, why waste so much time reflecting on how other people from other eras have interacted with *their* environments, either in this place or elsewhere? One student of mine expressed puzzlement, in fact, about why a program presumably devoted to "finding your place" should concern itself at all with studying how others had lived in the past.

Another problem we have faced in configuring this course is a diminishment of student engagement and effort following the opening immersion period, a time when the course's subject matter and interaction with fellow students and FYP faculty had absorbed their full attention. The course's subsequent phase—characterized by a higher proportion of classroom instruction and a narrowing of our pedagogical approach toward discipline-linked subject matter in place of plenary sessions—requires both students and faculty to adapt accordingly. This transition can be especially trying for students, as they find their attention suddenly divided by involvement in three new courses beyond the FYP as well as by their freshly encountering a multitude of non-FYP students. Unfortunately, too, the upper-division student mentors and peer guides assigned to each section during the immersion phase loosen ties with their group once the regular term begins, adding to the strain of transition. Neither have we always found it easy to extend the course's affective involvement in notions of place beyond local scenes, which students can experience directly in the field, toward more distant horizons of place and time beyond our region.

Despite these failings that we still hope to overcome, it becomes evident that students feel an intense, unmistakable enthusiasm about this course of inquiry from the start of plenary sessions and field expeditions in August. All of us begin thematically with reflection on "Concepts of Place," linked to formulations by writers such as Yi-Fu Tuan, Wilfred McClay, Wendell Berry, and Barry Lopez. From there we proceed to common consideration of "Elements of Place," "Foundations of Place," and "Peoples of Place," incorporating along the way references to sites both near to hand and distant.

How, though, might this course have managed to consider or honor notions of reverence for the spirits of place? To what extent have religious or theological issues figured in its presentation? To be sure, a religious perspective on *topos* studies has rarely gained prominence in our course curriculum, either in plenary sessions or in class meetings of individual sections aside from mine or that of Professor Sid Brown from the Department of Religious Studies. Professor Brown's class has included visits to Buddhist and Hindu ritual sites in the region.

Yet the course has from its inception encouraged students to develop a mindset and practices consistent with contemplative learning. And a contemplative bearing qualifies as at least congruent with a religious worldview, if not a strict corollary. Religion, after all, in its root sense of *religare*, involves a binding together of disparate realms and epistemologies. A religious outlook characteristically acknowledges, yet presumes to surpass and to incorporate, strictly analytic ways of knowing. During plenary sessions several of our team instructors— including Deborah McGrath, as program director—stressed the relevance for our inquiry of combining contemplative ways of knowing with more traditionally academic, investigative approaches to learning. More than once, in fact, our sequence of joint sessions has culminated in a panel presentation devoted expressly to "Contemplative Learning." Throughout other plenaries, this call for imaginative synthesis has found elaboration through testimony of several sorts from course instructors trained in disciplines ranging from natural sciences to visual arts. In 2015, it was reinforced by closing panel sessions with exchanges involving Wendell Berry, Mary Berry, Leah Bayens from St. Catharine College in Kentucky, and Norman Wirzba from Duke University.

As all of us realized, contemplative habits of being and learning do not come naturally to most people, including today's college-age students whose attention spans have been shortened through constant exposure to digital forms of kinetic stimuli. But while flickering screens and smart phones have by now become an inescapable if not essential fact of daily life for most of us, I have found first-year students willing enough to observe short-term, experimental periods of withdrawal from digital devices if rightly drawn to do so. During brief intervals of ten minutes or so, they have on several occasions demonstrated a capacity to practice silent, mindful attentiveness to the sights, sounds, and tactile presence of their physical surroundings—first in the dramatic, comparatively wild setting of stream and cascade vistas in regional enclaves bearing colorful titles such as Fiery Gizzard and Buggytop Cave, then within a sheltered portion of the Domain's old-growth forest known as "Shakerag Hollow." These interludes, understood as forays into a kind of temporary nonelectronic sabbath time, offer students at least a taste of meditative consciousness. Meditative exercises of this sort also seem a fitting complement to our group and individual reflections on literary texts. Such is especially true in the case of lyric verse—including Wendell Berry's Sabbath Poems, which by their very nature invite readers to practice the same sort of emplaced, meditative mindfulness that inspired their creation.[15]

Throughout the course I have also tried introducing students, with varying success, to other place-centered meditative techniques. So I have asked them, for example, first to ponder individually and then to share in discussion what they take to be the evocative import of some familiar place-names near campus they have chosen to ponder at length. What might they make of names such as Abbo's Alley, Sewanee, Shakerag Hollow, Rebel's Rest, Morgan's Steep, or Monteagle? What interlaying of languages, cultures, personalities, or historical sensibilities does each label reflect? For as George R. Stewart once observed in his classic study touching on nomenclatures across time for the entire nation, "names lay thickly over the land," beginning with "the naming that was before history" and extending to successive eras with "the nature of the land itself" often prefiguring "something of what was to be."[16]

It helps, of course, for students approaching the matter to inquire first into the historical background of each local name they are pondering in relation to its physical address, with benefit of an excellent resource work they can consult for the purpose.[17] Once they move beyond this analytic preparation, though, I encourage them to dig deeper, reflecting on the name's sound and sense while taking account of its personal and intuitive resonances, both past and present. What the name comes to signify for them, consciously and otherwise, clearly depends as well on what they can glean from visiting the relevant site.

Yet another technique of mindful engagement I believe can be fruitful begins with asking students to select and to adopt for sustained attention a particular tree they have encountered somewhere on the Domain. A few trees around campus have even won a kind of iconic standing within the community. These include several odoriferous ginkgo trees planted in the central campus as well as a large, majestic sycamore grown from seed carried to the moon and back on the 1971 Apollo 14 mission. Human beings have long cherished the kinship they perceive between many different arboreal species—and, in many cases, with individual trees. Solidly rooted in earth, they also draw our attention heavenward with intimations of transcendence. The contemplative prose commentary titled *The Songs of Trees*, by my faculty colleague David George Haskell, effectively dramatizes the ways in which trees claim a distinctive presence in our consciousness of the larger world, figuring as they do the manifold ways in which both they and we participate in nature's networks.[18] Given the emotive connection humans commonly form with trees, and all the elemental and mythic associations these organisms call to mind, it is scarcely surprising that Henry Thoreau and others should be described—albeit at times disdainfully—as "tree huggers."

For students looking to appreciate just what it might look like to meditate and visit for some time by way of developing personal ties to some local tree, I recommend that they consult an article published a few years back in the *Sewanee Magazine*. There they can read about why eight different faculty members have each formed a memorable attachment to specific trees. One, a professor of classical languages, tells of his pleasure in learning that a linden and white oak planted beside the University Chapel happened to square with a favorite classical myth of his, related by Ovid, concerning the arboreal transformation of Baucis and Philemon. Another tells of how a dogwood tree, first planted in honor of a noted clergyman and civil rights leader, continues to hold that person in beloved memory as it grows. Still another, an alumna of the College, writes about how she came to revere a grand tulip poplar, planted along one of Sewanee's woodland trails, which struck her once during a visit to campus while she was living elsewhere but then became a material harbinger of her return as professor to the community.[19]

Robert Frost's "A Tree Outside My Window," "Birches," and countless poems by others likewise illustrate how human interaction with trees can mirror a panoply of moods, aspirations, crises, and memories. So I expect students, as a concluding stage of this meditative exercise, to identify and to respond in writing to some related literary text, preferably one evocative of the same species of tree they will already have pondered and visited repeatedly.

My aim more broadly, throughout the course's reading assignments, has been to highlight the complex interplay between some written work and its localized context, whether or not we can together visit the sites in question. In the case of Ely Green's memoir, one of the common course readings, several scene settings and landmarks—including Morgan's Steep, Green's View, Natural Bridge, and Shakerag—lie conveniently near to hand for students to recognize because most of this author's narrative unfolds within the village of Sewanee. In fact Ely's Lane, where the author's mother once lived, happens to run beside my own home.

Yet students swiftly learn from their reading how drastically the world Ely Green faced in Sewanee, as an adolescent of mixed race in the early twentieth century, differed from theirs. Green's life story looks to be essentially one of staunch perseverance in the face of adversity and alienation. The academic village in which Green struggled to define his identity was a highly structured community, steeped in traditions that he found by turns inspiring and dehumanizing. It remained a decidedly segregated settlement, divided with respect to social class as well as race.

Yet for Green, at least during his childhood years, the place did offer certain satisfactions and solace. At times it could even strike him as idyllic. With some encouragement from local Episcopal clergy, one of whom served as his godfather, he aspired to love everyone while recognizing his own self-worth as another child of God. He reports having at one time "loved every thing about Sewanee, even if I could not go to school like the white people."[20] Although barred from attending the local military academy, he especially relished the chance to gaze upon its young cadets processing to worship. But given the triple stigma he bore as biracial, illegitimate, and orphaned from an early age, he never quite managed to find his place in a community where neither blacks nor whites were consistently disposed to accept him. His unnamed father had belonged to the town's white gentry. And he was still a child when his mother, an African American housemaid, died from consumption, leaving him homeless with occasion to interact only rarely with his eccentric and unstable yet resourceful grandfather, a former slave.

Green's sense of belonging was shattered most grievously at the age of nine when he was refused service at a drugstore in town. Following this rude awakening, he gradually became more self-reliant, defiant toward any who might harm him, and confident in his resolve that "I am going to be a man" (137). Eventually when he turned eighteen, fearing for his life at the hands of brutal "sagers" (poorer white men) who held him in contempt, he skipped town and fled to Texas after a hair-raising descent on a flatcar down the Sewanee plateau.

Prior to that move, Green could only believe himself to be free, at home, and "never alone" while dwelling somewhere in the region's mountainous wilds. "I had felt adopted by the mountains," he recalls (142). Determined to make his own way in the world, he had become a jack of all trades—a resourceful and entrepreneurial worker in town but above all an expert hunter, trapper, formidable marksman, and gatherer of nuts, berries, roots, and herbs while roaming the woods. As a confirmed mountaineer, he had learned how to shoot or to trap effectively many specimens of wildlife ranging from skunks, raccoons, and possums to birds and wild boar.

Yet even as Green became tougher, more steeped in the archaic knowledge of a woodland hunter–gatherer and more disposed to confront adversaries with force, he seemed to have retained a deeply spiritual outlook on the world. True, he voices along the way some confusion about how best to claim his religious identity, denominationally, amid the divergent Episcopal, Methodist, Baptist, or Pentecostal influences to which he has been exposed. Yet for the most part he understands himself to be an Episcopalian and a Christian, albeit never "the shouting kind" (121). He reports attending Sunday school faithfully throughout his youth.

Most notably, though, Green witnesses to discovering within the region's wilder world of nature a revelatory, contemplative spirituality that speaks most eloquently to his soul and inspires inward change at crisis periods of his life. The rocky lookout and waterfall at Morgan's Steep mark the chief site of these epiphanies. At one point, when he is close to seventeen, he describes experiencing there a visionary episode in which he hears his deceased mother telling him to "Be brave, my son, be patient. Go up and look at the beauty in God's mountains" (134). He receives this insight after confiding that "I sat at the waterfall for a long time, thinking for the first time about life—what is to be done with life.... I thought of everything I felt that had been done to me." He goes on to describe how "I began to pray asking to be shown what to do and how. I lay back on the rock, looking into the sky. It was pleasant and warm on this rock." And he concludes with a measure of confidence and resolve:

> I could almost hear the mountains say "This is where you belong." ... I had found the answer to what I wanted to know. These mountains were my home. They belonged to God. I rose and started home in soft twilight. Something had happened that day that I did not try to tell anybody about. (134–135)

Closer to the time of his abrupt departure for Texas, Green once again has a kind of numinous encounter at the falls below Morgan Steep—in this case, at a frightening moment when he narrowly escapes disaster following a dam break that sends huge cascades of water and debris in his direction. He recalls that

> The water rose up twenty feet during the churning. I clung to the boulder as water rushed around me waist-deep.... This was the first time I became [sic] to know God had his arms around me.

CONTEMPLATING SITE-BASED EDUCATION | 223

> I stood by the boulder which I had sat on many times meditating my troubles, and where one time I had believed my mother had come from heaven and talked to me. (176–177)

Despite the changes and chances that human involvement over the years must have brought, those boulders and the waterfall at Morgan's Steep are still there. And they still expose a vital face of nature comparable to what Ely Green once saw. Understandably, then, I make a point of leading students in my class to walk and sit at Morgan's Steep sometime after they have absorbed Ely's narrative. Once they have taken in the stirring view available from the summit and scampered down the steep incline to perch on the boulders below, they too seem content to sit and center themselves at least for a time—if not, following Ely, for "a long time"—by the waterfall. In the meantime I, who occasionally like to retreat to this spot alone, am content to allow them space to entertain their own thoughts together with whatever water spirits may speak to them. I realize that their sense of the place today can scarcely be identical to Ely's. Neither should it be. But I do think it fair to imagine their experience enlarged as they read and reflect on how Ely had once responded to the site.

To draw students toward reflection on places beyond those they may know personally, I also assign readings meant to transport us all elsewhere. For example, back to the prairie terrain of late nineteenth-century and early twentieth-century Nebraska, through the medium of Willa Cather's *My Ántonia*. That novel rewards sustained attention to the meaning and influence of place-grounded identity in several spheres. Of course its primary locus of interest is the Great Plains terrain of Nebraska, the agrarian way of life that Cather once knew and still admired in that land, and the hardy pioneers, newly transplanted from across Europe, who had struggled to survive there. But as the story unfolds Cather dramatizes the inevitable interplay between this setting, which claims center stage, and still other lands and cultures. These other places include Virginia, birthplace of the story's narrator, Jim Burden, and of Cather herself; Bohemia and several regions of the "Old Country," points of origin for the many hopeful and often desperate souls who found their way to America; and New York, that quintessentially modern metropolis and antithesis of rural Nebraska, vantage point of the larger story, and the author's physical locus of being at the time she composed it. Much of our discussion in the FYP class thus tries to address the intertopological dynamics of Cather's presentation. How does the cultural identity of a place like fictional Black Hawk, Nebraska, come to be interfused with that of other sites across and beyond America? What comparable melding or interaction might we discern in the case of real-life settings closer to home?

Another place-grounded feature of this novel one can scarcely ignore is the numinous aura of the landscape it evokes. Although apparently stark and forbidding, Nebraska's treeless expanses of windswept red grass reveal for Cather a kinetic vitality that transcends human understanding and expectations. That impression of the land, recollecting in turn earth's landless ecospheres, is conveyed through an expressive lyricism:

> As I looked about me I felt that the grass was the country, as the water is the sea. The red of the grass made all the great prairie the color of wine-stains, or of certain seaweeds when they are first washed up. And there was so much motion in it; the whole country seemed, somehow, to be running.[21]

For Cather the original unfenced face of the Great Plains presented a landscape of absence, which threatened to blot out the whole of one's identity and "spirits" of the past while exposing the "complete dome of heaven, all there was of it" (718). In one famed visionary passage, part of her chapter titled

"The Hired Girls," she describes the "heroic" image of a forgotten plow magnified against the sun toward nightfall, a virtual apotheosis of agrarian ways that modern life and global strife had already begun to eclipse by the time of publication in 1918. A highly if not overly romanticized and elegiac outlook, to be sure. Yet FYP students also notice the earthy, elemental aspects of this visionary sense—as when Jim Burden relates early on how the "earth was warm under me, and warm as I crumbled it through my fingers." For Cather a moment like this offers ordinary mortals at least a touch of heaven on earth, something equivalent to that self-transcending felicity of finding oneself "dissolved into something complete and great" (724).

Yet another way to stimulate fresh recognition on the part of students in a place-based course of this sort is to couple, in comparative perspective, site visits of a similar but distinct character. One such pairing I have tried involves our heading first to a gathering place of ceremonial ritual favored by pre-Columbian indigenous peoples, located some thirty miles northwest of campus. With that spot still in mind, we then spend some time examining afresh a structure on home ground with which they are already familiar: the University's central gathering place and chief worship space in All Saints' Chapel.

Located near Manchester, Tennessee, on a peninsular confluence of the Duck River and Little Duck River, the prehistoric sacred site we visit belongs now to a state archaeological park. Its most striking features are the extensive mounds or walls that surround a prominent, fifty-acre plot amounting to a hilltop enclosure. Because white settlers supposed these mounds to have been constructed for defensive purposes, the place came to be known as "Old Stone Fort," though it is no fort at all. Later investigation revealed that the mounds never served either a military or mortuary purpose. Neither, given the dearth of relevant artifacts, do they signal the presence of any long-term settlement. Instead they were likely constructed to define a place of sacred assembly, perhaps for the sake of gathering there on occasion several ancient Indian cultures. The walled enclosure dates originally from some 1,500 to 2,000 years ago, placing it within Tennessee's Middle Woodland period. Setting these mounds in place evidently required enormous labor and engineering, applied over the course of centuries.[22]

Once students circle the entire enclosure site on foot trails and are prompted to learn what it would take to build these mounds without benefit of modern machinery, they can marvel not only at the sheer antiquity of human presence on the spot, but also at the scale of labor and resolve invested in such a project. But the site's most intriguing feature lies at a narrow stretch of the enclosure, poised between the two rivers at an entrance passageway from the east. Researchers have discovered that the complex of parallel mound walls placed at this point is aligned to within one degree of sunrise at the summer solstice (Figure 5.1).

Even though our FYP meetings in August come too late beyond June for students to witness that turn of earth directly in the course of our visit, cognizance of the alignment does provoke further thoughts and questions as we stand together, discussing the matter, at the enclosure's entryway. How and why, we're led to wonder, were ancient cultures in American and elsewhere impelled to mark the solstice in such a manner? How did they gain the astronomical knowledge needed for this physical construction and alignment? And what ritual actions might they have performed on the occasion to express their participation in the sacred geometry and creation myths the solstice must have inspired? Was their solstice observance accompanied by dancing and other ceremonial actions? Or as trench firepits and practices elsewhere suggest, were ritual blazes set at the enclosure's entryway?

Though it is fair to speculate, I understand that answers to these questions remain elusive even for professional archaeologists. Neither do we know why those who built the

CONTEMPLATING SITE-BASED EDUCATION | 227

FIGURE 5.1 Sunrise on Summer Solstice at Old Stone Fort, Tennessee.
Tennessee State Parks photo.

mounds, whoever they were, finally met their demise. But it is reasonable to surmise that some sort of symbolic meaning, allied with fertility rites and nature religion, derived from the enclosure's larger topographical setting, given the way prehistoric Indians and other ancient peoples appreciated the spiritual import of watercourses, plunge pools, and cascades as portals to another world.[23] For that matter, the beauty of this site's waterfalls and river flows continues to entrance visitors.

Even the absence of artifacts from within the enclosure, enforcing an emptiness reminiscent of that preserved within the ancient Hebrews' Holy of Holies, suggests the presence here of a religious principle and practice. As one archaeologist authority on the site has proposed, "Although it is evident that a large force of laborers built the structure and presumably used it at least periodically, thus far it seems they left few prosaic objects within the walls. It is almost as though an effort was made not to profane this sacred place with mundane things."[24] The enclosure's topographically elevated setting could likewise express a people's aspiration to raise their quotidian life on earth toward engagement with those celestial mysteries, enacted in perpetuity, they were so zealous to study.

As we return in our vans to campus from Old Stone Fort, I encourage students to recall that Sewanee, too, occupies a hilltop preserve encircled by forest. Often, in fact, devotees of the place and its unique mythos speak of this locale as "the holy mountain," though the mount in question is technically a plateau. A portrayal of this promontory community that has endured across generations images it poetically as "A towered city set within a wood, far from the world, upon a mountain's crest."[25] And not surprisingly for a faith-related institution, the structure that most visibly marks this mountain's center and focal point, both geographically and symbolically, is All Saints' Chapel, an imposing neo-Gothic edifice built of sandstone largely quarried from the University's own Domain.[26]

Although groundbreaking for the current structure took place in 1904, the project with its ambitious program of stained-glass windows was not substantially completed until 1959, under the personal supervision of University Vice Chancellor Edward McCrady. As it stands today, All Saints' is a place interfused with still other places, most of them distant from rural Tennessee. Predictably, much of its iconography harkens back to lands of the ancient Middle East, for example, whereas the architectural design of its rose window and sanctuary links it to medieval France.[27] Above all, in accord with other specimens of campus architecture, this building together with interior points of design brings to mind sundry houses of venerable learning and worship found in England. It epitomizes what could be described as an oxymoronic remnant of Oxford in rural Tennessee.

Even unchurched incoming students, during their first few weeks on campus, recognize the Chapel as a familiar landmark. They will already have visited it in the course of our standard tour for prospective students. They will have assembled there, too, for initiation and orientation events scheduled soon after their arrival as first-year students. They know it is where their commencement ceremony will take place once they conclude their studies. But regardless of their own religious background or beliefs, they have not usually found cause to reflect seriously on the building's character as sacred space. So an FYP session wherein we probe that dimension in relation to selected features of Old Stone Fort can be instructive. The exercise serves, among other things, to defamiliarize a place—and, for that matter, a long-standing faith tradition—whose meaning students may suppose they have already absorbed from their nominally Christian culture.

Embodying as it does Sewanee's Christian and Episcopal heritage, though a site commonly shared today with those of all faiths or none through corporate events, All Saints' Chapel is plainly a different sort of sacred space from Old Stone Fort. Among the revealing parallels between them, though, is a common deliberateness in geophysical orientation. At Old Stone Fort, aligning the plot's entry mounds with morning light from the east seems to have played a crucial role in ritualizing the solstice, not unlike the spiritual principle conveyed by an east-facing orientation of worship in liturgically configured spaces such as All Saints' Chapel.

An elemental symbology associated with stones and water—perhaps fire as well—[28]also figures notably in the layout of both sites. Although the chapel contains no plunge pools or rivers, for example, worshippers entering from the west are traditionally invited to pass by, even to touch, holy water preserved in the stone baptismal font while moving forward toward the light breaking each morning through sanctuary windows in the east. Neither is this font the only touchstone of holy water relevant to the site. Natural water springs, too, had much to do with patterns of settlement on the Mountain, and their fluid presence—as for Thoreau at Walden Pond or for indigenous peoples who gathered near the stream conjunction at Old Stone Fort—has long carried spiritual as well as practical meaning. It is therefore telling that one of the Domain's most revered springs of pure water, originally named "Otey Spring" after the first bishop of Tennessee and a University founder, continues to flow beneath a rock overhang and through a ravine located just a stone's throw from All Saints' Chapel. The sacred and even liturgical standing of this site, currently undergoing some devoted work of restoration, derives in part from its history because it is where Bishop James Hervey Otey chose in 1861 to baptize the first child born into the Mountain's newly settled Euro-American community.

Besides water, the primordial presence of stones and stonework suggests yet another conceptual linkage between Old Stone Fort and the Chapel. A meaningful feature of the construction at Old Stone, for example, is the way stones and earth, unadorned materializations of nature, constitute the enclosure walls that define sacred space. In the case of All Saints' Chapel, beyond the obvious stonework framing the entire structure, innumerable "sermons in stones" are conveyed through discrete specimens set within the nave and sanctuary areas.

Within the nave's south wall, for instance, a plaque signals the presence of stone taken from St. Augustine's Abbey in Canterbury, England, thus effecting a linkage to the genesis and central locus of Anglican tradition in pre-Reformation Britain. Another reliquary stone, fused with a silver cross and set into marble on the chapel's high altar, comes from another sector of Britain—the high altar of a medieval cathedral that once stood on the windswept island of Iona off the coast of Scotland. It thus embodies another form of sacramental communion across space and time—communion with a Celtic Christian tradition, anchored in St. Columba's sixth-century evangelism, still more ancient than that of Canterbury.

Likewise relevant to the poetics of place dramatized both at the Chapel and at Old Stone Fort is the consecrated import of an elevated enclosure. The Chapel qualifies as an elevated enclosure, to begin with, by virtue of its standing atop the holy mountain. But a further rise appears in the steps leading to its sanctuary area, from there to the high altar, and finally up to the three clerestory windows of the apse with their visualizations keyed to the fourth-century hymn *Te Deum Laudamus* (We praise you, God).

Students are taken aback when I point out to them how the centrally positioned pane of these windows dares to picture Sewanee Mountain, crowned by the Chapel itself, as yet another sacred promontory and "thin place"—in the familial lineage, presumably, of biblical summits such as Zion in Jerusalem, Sinai, and Tabor. It seems an oddly postmodern irony that artists have ventured in this very place to picture that same place, including a community processional of its members, in light of an end-time redemption. I tell students, too, of how Sewanee's most eminent theologian, William Porcher DuBose, had identified this same highland with the summit in Galilee upon which Jesus had once been visibly transformed in glory. In a 1911 sermon preached on August 6, the liturgical Feast of the Transfiguration, DuBose reminded his hearers that "We stand indeed today together upon an exceeding high mountain— upon this mountain, not only as itself transfigured, but as itself no less a Mount of Transfiguration."[29] For DuBose this vision of divine transformation extended ultimately to human nature and the entire cosmos. By the same token, that sanctuary window in the chapel opens awareness toward a cosmic perspective through its evocation of God's Creation in blue swirls of color (Figure 5.2).

FIGURE 5.2 Detail from eastern window, *Te Deum Laudamus* triptych in All Saints' Chapel, Sewanee. Buck Butler photo.

Remarkably, then, this window sets forth a vision of place that is at once cosmic and almost whimsically self-referential and localized. So it strikes me that perhaps sitting still together in silence, gazing together at what is imaged here, is not a bad way for our company to conclude a class session devoted to sense of place. Could a session like this help students over the long term to discern a new, compelling strangeness amid scenes they had thought to be familiar? How might they, or for that matter any of us, hope to learn more deeply how, in T. S. Eliot's language, "To arrive where we started / And know the place for the first time"?[30] I can't yet claim to know but want to remember to ask some of these students, sometime before they graduate, just what of this place has for them either endured or changed along the way.

AFTERWORD

"THE HISTORY OF OUR FRIENDSHIP with God is always linked to particular places which take on an intensely personal meaning; we all remember places, and revisiting those memories does us much good. Anyone who has grown up in the hills or used to sit by the spring to drink, or played outdoors in the neighborhood square; going back to those places is a chance to recover something of their true selves."

>Pope Francis, *Laudato Si': Encyclical Letter on Care for Our Common Home*

"I am going home, to the home where I have never been in this body."
>Thomas Merton, *Asian Journal*

Marilynne Robinson, partway through the second of three luminous novels situated in the fictional town of Gilead, Iowa, sets her character of Glory Boughton to pondering this question: "What does it mean to come home?" Moreover, Robinson's work takes, as its all-pervasive biblical subtext, the Parable of the Prodigal Son. A story all about homecoming, both human and divine. Not coincidentally, the novel itself bears the elemental title: *Home*. Resonating in manifold ways throughout the work, this question of what homecoming means, as a token of our insatiable longing for things enduring and ultimate, qualifies as pivotal not only for Robinson's characters but for the whole of humankind. Literature as well as life testifies abundantly to this. Throughout the whole of place-engaged discourse, I would argue, no single word in English is more pervasively evocative than "home."

Home signifies in the first instance, of course, a person's birthplace and point of origin. "Home is where one starts from," as Eliot recalls in his poem "East Coker." A primary locus for ancient veneration of the *genius loci* was, after all, the personal domicile. Such *domus*-honoring conviction supposes in turn that where we live, especially in our primal dwelling, is a place enveloped in something like a palpable force field of spiritual energy.

"Home is where one starts from," but it also defines one's final destination and destiny. So, at least, it has traditionally been conceived from the standpoint of Christian and other forms of Abrahamic faith. Or as Eliot in "East Coker" likewise confirms, "In my beginning is my end." William Bradford, too, in his *History of Plymouth Plantation*, describes saintly members of his covenanted community as *perpetual* pilgrims—not only or mainly with reference to their oceanic crossing, but throughout a life journey that afforded them no enduring home on earth. In the spirit of St. Augustine, he believed that humanity's only place of rest that could fulfill its deep-seated longing lay with and in God, beyond the bounds of mortal time. Only an eternal, transcendent Presence could satisfy that "repining restlessness" which poet George Herbert had clearly felt and named as such. Harriet Beecher Stowe believed the same. Consider, for example, how she dramatizes the death of Augustine St. Clare, an aptly named character of hers in *Uncle Tom's Cabin*. To be sure, she suffuses the scene with all the sentimental flourishes familiar in nineteenth-century deathbed stories. Yet there is a penetrating note of earnestness in the way her slaveholding antihero Augustine, sorely conflicted and self-estranged, ends up countering at the point of death a doctor's judgment that "'His mind is wandering.' 'No!' he insists, 'It is coming HOME, at last! . . . At last! At last!'"

That is not to say that idealizing or sacralizing the notion of home—and, by extension, of place-mindedness as such—is always warranted, even from the standpoint of religious orthodoxy. Partly because places and those who inhabit them are constantly changing, the identity of home remains ambiguous, inherently elusive. A fair share of writing in America's literary canon, to say nothing of other literatures as timeworn as Homer's *Odyssey*, portrays the prospect of returning home again as problematic and disheartening, if not simply impossible. Stories of homecoming, even for Robinson, typically reveal more irony and pain than they do solace and blessing. Even when homecoming happens for real, it is rarely apt to fulfill our fondest expectations. Thus, in Robert Frost's poetic narrative of "The Death of the Hired Man," the male half of a rural couple mocks the idea of home for their friendless, former employee as simply a last-ditch endpoint of life, nothing more than that "place where, when you go there, / They have to take you in."

How much credence, then, can still be invested today in notions of sacred space, of enspirited places, of home places bearing intimations of immortality? Is it not, for example, at best an idle fantasy or mystification—at worst, a destructive fallacy—to conceive of wilderness tracts as in any sense sacred or sublime, charged with supernatural presence, given our present-day knowledge of ecological science? Don't such attitudes end up fostering disregard for other dimensions of the thoroughly material world we inhabit? Surely some would say so—and have, despite my own verdict to the contrary. In any case, from the standpoint of most theistic apprehensions of the world, one must acknowledge the paradoxical principle that place matters but *not* absolutely, and never permanently in its particularity. No place in Creation can or does wholly contain the Creator's essence.

Moreover, even as seen in a more secular light, the concept of home retains something of a transcendent aura insofar as its emotive connotations plainly surpass the geophysical coordinates of its address in space. Mary, the wifely speaker in Frost's dialogical poem, captures this sense pointedly when she remarks, by way of revising her husband's characterization of home, that "I should have called it / Something you somehow haven't to deserve." Something simply given, if experienced at all, rather than earned or deserved. For Christians, home viewed in this light carries unmistakable overtones of giftedness, of sacramental grace. Potentially, at least, home or another version of hallowed place qualifies as an incarnational sign of the numinous, though our mortal experience always falls short of that promise. In less orthodox terms as well, literary tradition manifests an enduring yet variegated fascination with spirits of place, often identified with those unfathomable, unmappable tokens of mysterious presence that we either discover within, or attribute to, certain sites more than others.

My main intent in this book has been to explore how, across the span of American literary history, writing that extends to later-day authors such as N. Scott Momaday, Terry Tempest Williams, Wendell Berry, and Barry Lopez can inspire reverence for particular places, especially those we have come to know and love. For without some such exercise of *reverence*, in Paul Woodruff's sense of the term, it is hard to see how humanity's *care* for places wild or otherwise, and for the planet that constitutes our larger home, can ever be sustained.

NOTES

Introduction

1. Yi-Fu Tuan, *Space and Place: The Perspective of Experience*. For a range of social science perspectives on the topic, see *Key Thinkers on Space and Place*, ed. Phil Hubbard, Rob Kitchin, and Gill Valentine. Works beside Yi-Fu Tuan's that have also proved to be seminal in the shaping of place-identified discourse include Martin Heidegger's "Building Dwelling Thinking" and Mircea Eliade's formulations (esp. chapter 1, "Sacred Space and Making the World Sacred") in *The Sacred and the Profane*. For reference to some later conceptualizations of place and its potential sacrality, see David Landis Barnhill's "The Spiritual Dimension of Nature Writing." A revisionist view of these matters, arguing that place-identified discourse has thus far exaggerated the significance of localized attachments and should recognize the primacy of our current need for a "globalist consciousness" or "eco-cosmopolitanism," is set forth by Ursula K. Heise in *Sense of Place and Sense of Planet: The Environmental Imagination of the Global*.
2. From US Census Bureau Statistics, available at http://www.census.gov/prod/2012pubs/p20-567.pdf
3. *Why Place Matters: Geography, Identity, and Civic Life in Modern America*, ed. Wilfred M. McClay and Ted V. McAllister,

4. My previous publications in this vein include *Making Nature Sacred: Literature, Religion, and Environment in American From the Puritans to the Present*; "Rediscovering the Earth"; and "Meditation on the Creatures: Ecoliterary Uses of an Ancient Tradition."
5. *A Place on Earth: An Anthology of Nature Writing From Australia and North America*, ed. Mark Tredinnick, 31.
6. One may nonetheless identify some noteworthy exceptions to this rule. Among them is Lawrence Buell's *Writing for an Endangered World: Literature, Culture, and Environment in the U.S. and Beyond*. The book's third chapter, devoted to "Reinhabiting the City," addresses texts and cultural ideas associated with what might be called urban environmentalism, whereas its second chapter, on "The Place of Place" (55–83), engages broader issues of place-studies in a manner consonant with the inquiry I am pursuing here.
7. My phrasing here suggests a familiar understanding that place is in some sense created from or within space—i.e., that space exists prior to place. But I also see reason to appreciate the seemingly contrary argument advanced by philosopher Edward E. Casey that, from another perspective linked to comparative valuation and the history of ideas, place should rightly be viewed as "prior to space" (319). See Casey's *Getting Back Into Place*, 317–324; and John Inge on "The Eclipse of Place" in *A Christian Theology of Place*, 5–13.
8. David Brown, *God and Enchantment of Place: Reclaiming Human Experience*, esp. 5, 16–18, 21. Brown points out (17, n 40) that Weber's most prominent reference to "the disenchantment of the world," a phrase first articulated by Schiller, can be found in Weber's essay on "Science as a Vocation."
9. Such is, in essence, the argument advanced by Gary Eberle in *The Geography of Nowhere*. It also corresponds to the vision articulated in many works, particularly works of creative nonfiction, by contemporary writers such as Wendell Berry, Gary Snyder, and Barry Lopez.
10. Gary Snyder, interview in Bill Moyers, *The Language of Life*, 366–367.
11. Gary Snyder, "The Place, the Region, and the Commons," 193.

12. By now there is an extensive body of commentary available on ecospirituality and matters related to religion and ecology. Among the works most useful in gaining an overview of this scholarship are *The Oxford Handbook of Religion and Ecology*, ed. Roger S. Gottlieb; and *The Encyclopedia of Religion and Nature*, ed. Bron Taylor et al.
13. Jane Chance Nitzsche, *The Genius Figure in Antiquity and the Middle Ages*, 4.
14. Nitzsche, *The Genius Figure*, 9.
15. The most relevant biblical texts giving rise to these three constructions would include Genesis 3:1–19, Numbers 21:4–9, and John 3:14.
16. Nathaniel Hawthorne, "The Ambitious Guest," in *Twice-Told Tales*, 326.
17. See, for example, Matt Hokom's essay on "Cather's Use of Genius in O Pioneers!" in *The Willa Cather Archive*, http://cather.unl.edu/mt.spr04.05.html. Traces of the *genius loci* tradition might also be found in Washington Irving's framing of tales situated in the Catskill Mountains and around the Hudson River, or in Mark Twain's evocation of haunted woodland toward the close of his opening chapter in *The Adventures of Huckleberry Finn*.
18. Saints that have by tradition acquired a place-identified status include, for example, Saint George for England or Saint Geneviève for Paris. Neither has the impulse to develop and preserve such identifications been restricted to Roman Catholic or Eastern Orthodox cultures. I am grateful to my colleague Ross Macdonald for reminding me of how Milton in "Lycidas" thus describes the elevation in spirit of Edward King-Lycidas, following his death by drowning, into something of an honored patron saint: "the genius of the shore."
19. David Brown, *God and Enchantment of Place*, 159.
20. Belden Lane, *Landscapes of the Sacred*, 15.
21. David Brown, *God and Enchantment of Place*, 162, 189; Thoreau, *Walden*, 213.
22. Emerson, *Nature*, 29.
23. "Lines Composed a Few Miles Above Tintern Abbey," *William Wordsworth*, 110.

24. Eudora Welty, "Place in Fiction," in *The Eye of the Story*, 116. See also H. L. Weatherby and George Core, *Place in American Fiction*.
25. Craig Bartholomew, *Where Mortals Dwell*; Douglas Christie, *The Blue Sapphire of the Mind*; Michael Northcott, *Place, Ecology and the Sacred*.
26. Barry Lopez, "The Language of Animals," in *A Place on Earth*, 162.

Chapter 1

1. Gaston Bachelard, *The Poetics of Space*, 4, xxxiii.
2. Michael S. Northcott, *Place, Ecology and the Sacred*, 164. Northcott credits, in turn, Margaret Barker's book *The Gate of Heaven* for enlarging his appreciation of what the Jerusalem Temple signified.
3. Emerson, *Nature*, in *Ralph Waldo Emerson: Essays & Lectures*, 48.
4. See James Dougherty's revealing essay on "House-Building and House-Holding at Walden." Dougherty's commentary takes account of details in the house's construction, as well as the Transcendental poetics of its architecture, its relation to the artistry of Thoreau's writing, and the history of its use and removal following Thoreau's stay at Walden.
5. Dougherty, "House-Building and House-Holding at Walden," 231.
6. Dougherty, "House-Building and House-Holding at Walden," 226–227. I comment further on the sacramentality of Thoreau's vision in *Making Nature Sacred*, 130–132 and 264, n 11.
7. *The Writings of Henry D. Thoreau: Journal*, 2:156.
8. *Walden*, 60.
9. Marilyn R. Chandler, *Dwelling in the Text*, 31–32.
10. At the same time, Emerson himself readily acknowledged—as in his poem "Hamatreya," with its allusion to several early settlers of Concord—the contingency of all claims to owning anything on earth. For his part, Thoreau betrays ambivalence about the value of owning one's own dwelling. On the one hand, he censures the vanity and unreality of purporting to own any form of real estate; on the other, he boasts of his ability to own his house outright, without incurring either mortgage debt or rental obligations, by building it simply and with his own hands. He therefore in one respect undercuts but in another reinforces what Marilyn Chandler

has called the American penchant for defining home ownership as "the essential symbol of an independent life" (*Dwelling in the Text*, 13).

11. Lawrence Buell comments on the enduring appeal of Walden for secular pilgrims in *The Environmental Imagination*, 311–338. On the complex fate of the house following Thoreau's departure, see Dougherty's "House-Building and House-Holding at Walden," 225, 232, 234–236, 246.
12. Nathaniel Hawthorne, "Fire-Worship," in *Mosses from an Old Manse, Centenary Edition*, 10:146.
13. Hawthorne, "Mosses," in *Mosses*, 10:5; I comment further on the implications of this feminized imagery in my *American Madonna*, 10–15.
14. Emerson, *Nature*, 7. That Emerson had written most of *Nature* while living in the Manse, as Hawthorne reminds his readers, also complements the way Hawthorne describes the beauty of this dwelling's natural setting.
15. "The Old Manse," in *Mosses*, 10:13, 14, 8, 27, 19.
16. *The Scarlet Letter*, 10, 35.
17. *The House of the Seven Gables*, 168.
18. The double sense of "house," as pertaining both to a physical dwelling and family lineage, is thus operative in *Gables*, as it is in Edgar Allan Poe's famous tale, "The Fall of the House of Usher."
19. To be sure, Hawthorne himself was ill disposed to recognize the extent to which America's nineteenth-century economy rested on the "original sin" of slavery. But elsewhere, as in his "Main-Street" sketch, he shows at least some cognizance that New England's settlement by Europeans—allied to the novel's fantasy, with its parallel recollection in Hawthorne's family history, of obtaining vast possessions in Waldo County, Maine—depended on the seizure of Indian lands and the destruction of native culture. Even Matthew Maule's original homestead, though presumably "hewn out of the primeval forest" (7), lay within generally inhabited territory. On Hawthorne's overall portrayal of Native Americans, see also Margaret B. Moore, *The Salem World of Nathaniel Hawthorne*, 128–131.
20. I have previously elaborated on this point and on other issues linked to Hawthorne's religious attitudes in "Progress and Providence in *The House of the Seven Gables*."

21. Hawthorne's remarks to various correspondents indicate that he considered *The House of the Seven Gables* to be not only a better work than *The Scarlet Letter*, but also one "more characteristic of my mind, more proper and natural for me to write." See *The Letters, 1843–1858*, Centenary Edition 16: 406, 421, 461.
22. Harriet Beecher Stowe, *Poganuc People*, 178. For additional comment on Harriet's sense of the Litchfield parsonage, see Joan Hedrick's *Harriet Beecher Stowe: A Life*, 17–19, 28–29; and Nancy Koester's *Harriet Beecher Stowe: A Spiritual Life*, 1–18.
23. *Poganuc People*, 166.
24. Harriet Beecher Stowe, *Uncle Tom's Cabin*, 17.
25. Hawthorne, "Fire-Worship," in *Mosses*, 10:139, 146. One contemporary American author whose remarks on this theme coincide with those of Hawthorne is Gary Snyder, who writes that "The heart of a place is the home, and the heart of the home is the firepit, the hearth." See "The Place, the Region, and the Commons," 184.
26. See also Hedrick, *Harriet Beecher Stowe*, 18; and Reynolds, *Mightier Than the Sword*, 97.
27. See Reynolds, *Mightier Than the Sword*, 98.
28. Stowe's reminiscences as recorded in *The Autobiography of Lyman Beecher*, 1:225.
29. Harriet Beecher Stowe, *The Minister's Wooing*, 326.
30. See Reynolds, *Mightier Than the Sword*, 87, 99–101.
31. See also Karen Haltunen, "Gothic Imagination and Social Reform."
32. It seems that part of Stowe, despite the more modest architectural symbology she favors in *Uncle Tom's Cabin*, was indeed attracted to grand living quarters. In the closing chapter of *The Minister's Wooing*, for example, she writes with satisfaction of "the grand house, otherwise described as "a fair and stately mansion" (326), that James Marvyn has constructed for his bride.
33. This architectural trajectory is paralleled by the novel's larger figurative geography that David S. Reynolds traces perceptively in *Mightier Than the Sword*. Reynolds's larger analysis, which freshly illuminates many aspects of *Uncle Tom's Cabin*, shows how "Stowe imagines North America as a biblical landscape that reflects the geography of slavery" (37).

34. Eleanor Charles, "Harriet Beecher Stowe's Link to Litchfield for Sale." Other journalistic accounts of the house's uncertain fate and latter-day controversy include Rebecca Sausner, "Beecher Stowe's Birthplace: A Discarded Bit of History"; Patrick Raycraft, "History in the Unmaking: Dedicated Workers Are Dismantling Harriet Beecher Stowe's Litchfield Birthplace . . . Very Carefully"; Joel Lang, "Who is Chandler Saint, And Why Did He Hide Harriet Beecher Stowe's Birthplace?"; and Maggie Behringer, "Gone From Litchfield, Saint's Efforts Go On."
35. Willa Cather, *The Professor's House*, 116.
36. Chandler, *Dwelling in the Text*, 181. Chandler's reading is valuable for its attentiveness to physical and architectural details in Cather's story that I have not attempted to discuss here, its remarks about the author's "sensitivity to the politics and poetics of space" (185), and its comparative consideration of domiciles in other Cather writings.
37. For further remarks on possible links between this novel and Cather's life and personal disposition, see Janis Stout, *Willa Cather: The Writer and Her World*, 122, 204, 209.
38. *Selected Letters of Willa Cather*, 567.
39. For relevant comment on Cather's engagement with this larger theme of the *genius loci*, see Matt Hokom, "Cather's Use of Genius in *O Pioneers*."
40. *My Ántonia*, 876. It is perhaps telling also that Godfrey is made aware of Tom's acquaintance with Virgil's *Aeneid* upon his very first meeting with Tom.
41. See, for example, Cather's letter of 1896 to Mariel Gere, in *The Selected Letters*, 39. Critical assessments of Cather's religious attitudes continue to differ sharply, as suggested, for example, by the essays represented in *Willa Cather and the Culture of Belief*, ed. John J. Murphy.
42. Cited in Janis Stout, *Willa Cather: The Writer and Her World*, 250.
43. Marilynne Robinson, *Housekeeping*, 177. In *Making Nature Sacred* (219–224) I discuss this work more fully, in a slightly different context.
44. Bradford, *Of Plymouth Plantation*, 47. Morison points out that the biblical reference here is to Hebrews 11:13–16.

45. There is a certain irony, too, in Phillip's subsequent comment that the first time he had lost his footing—in this case, favorably and metaphorically—had been at the "moment of his conversion" when God "lifted the burden of sin from my shoulders" and "I swooned, I fell" (57). In this first instance, though, which evidently recalls the biblical precedent of St. Paul's fall on the road to Damascus, Phillip had lost his presumption of self-sufficiency. But his later sense of complacency, with his perceived standing of success in his community, suggests he is ripe for a second conversion.
46. Ernest J. Gaines, *In My Father's House*, 16.
47. In accord with its Latinate root, the "Alma" character in this novel relates to Phillip, particularly in the closing scene, more as maternal nurturer than as spousal companion.
48. Thus Sophia Hawthorne had in 1843 engraved with her diamond ring, on a pane of her husband's study window at the Old Manse, "Man's accidents are God's purposes," to which Hawthorne added a further message for the future. See James R. Mellow, *Nathaniel Hawthorne in His Times*, 228.

Chapter 2

1. For an account of how the preindustrial New England village has been described and conceptualized, see Lawrence Buell's chapter on "The Village as Icon" in his *New England Literary Culture*, 304–318.
2. Christine Rosen, "The New Meaning of Mobility," in *Why Place Matters*, ed. McClay and McAllister, 182, 183.
3. These contrasting terms, cited more than once by Wendell Berry, can be found in Wallace Stegner's *Where the Bluebird Sings to the Lemonade Springs*, xii, 4.
4. Wendell Berry's personal life story, as he relates it in "A Native Hill," is a case in point. Berry also observes there that in returning to the locale of his birth, "I had made a significant change in my relation to the place: before it had been mine by coincidence or accident; now it was mine by choice." Cited from "A Native Hill" as reprinted in *The Art of the Commonplace*, 7.

5. A useful geographic and cartographic account of Thoreau's lifetime travels can be found in Robert Stowell's *A Thoreau Gazetteer*.
6. Although I understand that anthropologists differ about the timing and mode of human migrations into the Western Hemisphere, I take it there is broad agreement that those who originally settled in North America migrated to the continent from somewhere in Asia.
7. See, for example, Gary Snyder's "The Place, The Region, and the Commons," 194. Other texts that draw heavily on this phrase include Wes Jackson's *Becoming Native to This Place*, Wendell Berry's "A Native Hill," and David Landis Barnhill's multicultural anthology titled *At Home on the Earth: Becoming Native to Our Place*.
8. Gary Snyder, in the Introductory Note first published in 1969 to his poetry volume titled *Turtle Island*, explained that he understood this "old/new name" to be "based on many creation myths of the people who have been livening here for millennia, and reapplied by some of them to 'North America' in recent years."
9. Allusions here are to Edward Johnson's "Wonder-Working Providence of Sions Saviour" (published 1654), cited in *The Puritans*, ed. Perry Miller and Thomas M. Johnson, 1: 144–145, 153, 148.
10. Bradford, *Of Plymouth Plantation*, 61.
11. Crèvecoeur, *Letters From an American Farmer*, 68–69.
12. John Sears assesses this cultural development, with reference to sites such as Niagara Falls and Yosemite, in *Sacred Places*.
13. Barry Lopez, "Learning to See," in *Vintage Lopez*, 18, 20.
14. Lopez, "The Naturalist," in *Vintage Lopez*, 117, 122.
15. Lopez, "The American Geographies," in *Vintage Lopez*, 81–97.
16. Lopez, "The American Geographies" in *Vintage Lopez*, 83; and "Landscape and Narrative," in *Crossing Open Ground*, 61–71; see also Lopez's story "The Woman Who Had Shells," in *Winter Count*, 79–86.
17. "Winter Count 1973: Geese, They Flew Over in a Storm," in *Winter Count*, 62.
18. Lopez's writing draws heavily on his experience of living in native villages and consulting with indigenous peoples, as he

acknowledges in *Arctic Dreams*, xiv. See also his essay on "The Language of Animals."
19. Paul Woodruff, *Reverence: Renewing a Forgotten Virtue*.
20. "Landscape and Narrative," in *Crossing Open Ground*, 67.
21. "The Stone Horse," in *Crossing Open Ground*, 14.
22. Carolyn Servid, *Of Landscape and Longing*, 8, 7, 15.
23. Berry, *Imagination In Place*, 15.
24. Victor Turner and Edith Turner, *Image and Pilgrimage in Christian Culture*, 1, 39, 7, 6. In "Toward a Theology of Pilgrimage," I also consider the ways in which three recent devotional works address the theology of pilgrimage.
25. Nathaniel Hawthorne, *The Marble Faun*, 3.
26. See Turner, *Image and Pilgrimage in Christian Culture*, 26, 148, 207, and 40–103. As my visits to both of these pilgrimage sites would confirm, what they share is not only a pronounced strain of folk and Marian piety, but also a distinctive affirmation of ethnic solidarity.
27. In a chapter titled "The Thoreauvian Pilgrimage," Lawrence Buell discusses the enduring, iconic attraction of visitors to Thoreau's Walden and other sites in Concord, Massachusetts. See *The Environmental Imagination*, 311–338.
28. Dillard, *Pilgrim at Tinker Creek*. Hawthorne was among the nineteenth-century authors most imaginatively drawn to Bunyan and to the use of pilgrim or pilgrimage figures, as evidenced by tales of his such as "The Celestial Railroad" and "The Canterbury Pilgrims."
29. Whitman, "Song of the Open Road," *Leaves of Grass*, 149.
30. Muir, *A Thousand-Mile Walk To the Gulf*, xxi, 211, 1. See also James B. Hunt, *Restless Fires*.
31. Abbey, *Desert Solitaire*, 220.
32. Momaday, *The Way to Rainy Mountain*, 1, 3, 7.
33. One such well-known, book-length account of a Santiago experience is Jack Hitt's *Off the Road*. "The Way," a 2010 film, has drawn still more media attention to this pilgrimage route. And the popular "Road To Santiago" course that my own college at Sewanee conducts abroad for undergraduates is one of several collegiate offerings in this vein that are available nationally.

34. Joyce Ransome supplies an informative account of Ferrar, his circle, and life in this community in *The Web of Friendship*.
35. Brochure for participants in "Little Gidding Pilgrimage: Leighton Bromswold to Little Gidding, 30 May 2015."
36. I offer a more detailed reading of Bradstreet's "Contemplations" in *Making Nature Sacred*, 40–48.
37. Henry Thoreau, "Walking," in *The Natural History Essays*, 95
38. David Brown, *God and the Enchantment of Place*, 154–163.
39. Susan Power Bratton, *The Spirit of the Appalachian Trail*, xvii, 14.
40. Cited from Christine Rosen's "The New Meaning of Mobility," in *Why Place Matters*, 183.
41. N. Scott Momaday, *The Way to Rainy Mountain*, p. 113.
42. Heise, *Sense of Place and Sense of Planet*, 10, 9.
43. Heise, *Sense of Place and Sense of Planet*, 43–45, 29–32, 37–38, 48–49, 10, 59.
44. Heise, *Sense of Place and Sense of Planet*, 13.
45. McKibben, *The End of Nature*, 216–217.
46. Heise, *Sense of Place and Sense of Planet*, 10, 41.
47. Snyder, "The Place, The Region, and the Commons," 193.
48. Snyder, "Riprap," in *The Gary Snyder Reader*, 404.
49. Snyder, "The Place, The Region, and the Commons" (184) and "Blue Mountains Constantly Walking" (210, 203, 204), both cited in *The Gary Snyder Reader*.
50. Snyder, "Blue Mountains Constantly Walking," in *The Gary Snyder Reader*, 205.
51. This interpretation is reflected in an earlier essay of mine, "Coleridge's 'Fears in Solitude' and the Prospect of Social Redemption."
52. Berry, "The Making of a Marginal Farm," in *Recollected Essays*, 330, 331, 337.
53. See also the topical grouping of Berry essays on "Agrarian Economics" (205–275) in *The Art of the Commonplace*.
54. Bilbro, *Loving God's Wildness*, 146.
55. Berry, "Two Economies," in *Home Economics*, 55, 56–57.
56. A conspicuous precedent in American environmental literature for the articulation of this notion, and for an ecologically

encompassing definition of "land" as more than material soil, is Aldo Leopold's *A Sand County Almanac*.
57. "The Gift of Good Land," cited in *The Art of the Commonplace*, 304
58. Berry, untitled poem in *A Timbered Choir*, 52.
59. From #XIV of "Sabbaths 2013," *Sewanee Review*.
60. Berry, "Christianity and the Survival of Creation," in *The Art of the Commonplace*, 308.
61. Berry, "The Wild Birds," in *That Distant Land*, 356.
62. Berry, *Remembering*, 3.
63. Berry, "A Native Hill," in *The Art of the Commonplace*, 5.
64. Berry's exposition of a broadly communitarian spirituality in this work is grounded as well in biblical allusions and imagery, as Phillip J. Donnelly recognizes in the course of his discerning "Biblical Convocation" essay.
65. "The Boundary," in *That Distant Land*, 291, 294.
66. David George Haskell, *The Forest Unseen*, xii.

Chapter 3

1. James Engell, *The Creative Imagination*, esp. 3.
2. See Michelle Karnes, *Imagination, Meditation, and Cognition in the Middle Ages*.
3. Coleridge, *Biographia Literaria*, 1:201, 202.
4. I elaborate on this point in "'Not a Tame Lion': Animal Compassion and the Ecotheology of Human Imagination in Four Anglican Thinkers."
5. Lawrence Buell, *The Environmental Imagination: Thoreau, Nature Writing, and the Formation of American Culture*.
6. In a seminal essay titled "The Reach of Imagination," Jacob Bronowski once argued that the imaginative faculty warrants recognition as "the common root from which science and literature both spring and grow and flourish together" (200).
7. See also Engell, *The Creative Imagination*, 29, 329, 338, 362.
8. Engell, *The Creative Imagination*, 341, 4, 365, 344–346.
9. Thoreau, *Walden*, 205, 204.
10. Emerson, "The Poet," in *Emerson: Essays and Lectures*, 455, 461; Denise Levertov, "A Poet's View," in *New and Selected Essays*, 246.

11. Wendell Berry, *Imagination in Place*; H. L. Weatherby and George Core, *Place in American Fiction*; Eudora Welty, "Place in Fiction." In his Introduction to *Place in American Fiction*, George Core points out (5) that sense of place is, if anything, more strongly represented in modern American writers than it is in their European counterparts. Shakespeare, *A Midsummer Night's Dream*, 116. Theseus in his entire speech actually purports to be somewhat dismissive of the Imagination. But a contrary attitude emerges in still fuller context, especially as Theseus's statement is set in dialogical juxtaposition with Hippolyta's subsequent verification of what imagination reveals in contrast to "Fancy's images."
12. Eudora Welty, "Place in Fiction," 117, 118, 122.
13. Wendell Berry, "American Imagination and the Civil War" and "Imagination in Place," both in *Imagination in Place*, 32, 30, 1. In "American Imagination and the Civil War," Berry explains his own sense of imagination with reference to the work of William Carlos Williams, an atypical literary precedent for the purpose.
14. Berry, "Imagination in Place," 15, "American Imagination and the Civil War," 32. And in using the term "consubstantial," I am recalling Coleridge's reference in *The Statesman's Manual* to symbols as "consubstantial with the truths of which they are the conductors," cited in *English Romantic Writers*, ed. Perkins, 502. Coleridge's formulation here, which relates symbology to the Imagination and recognizes "the translucence of the eternal through and in the temporal" recalls, in turn, phrasing in the Nicene Creed concerning Christ's sharing of "one being [that is, consubstantiality] with the Father," a principle that coincides in turn with Berry's religious outlook.
15. "Imagination in Place," 15, 4.
16. See Craig Bartholomew, *Where Mortals Dwell*, and Edmund Husserl in *The Essential Husserl*.
17. M. Merleau-Ponty, *Phenomenology of Perception,* esp. 243, 203. See also David Seamon; John Inge, *A Christian Theology of Place*, 13–20; Edward S. Casey, *Getting Back Into Place*, esp. xxii, 317–323; and Belden Lane, *Landscapes of the Sacred*, 19, 52–58. Lane aptly summarizes the phenomenological principle shared by relevant theorists as an insistence "that all human perception of landscape is relentlessly interactive" (53).

18. *The Essential Husserl*, 66.
19. Martin Heidegger, "Building Dwelling Thinking," 348, 362, 351–352.
20. Debate continues about the nature and degree of Heidegger's complicity with operations of the Nazi regime.
21. See, for example, David Brown's *God and Enchantment of Place*, 1–36; John Inge's *A Christian Theology of Place*, 59–90; Philip Sheldrake's *Spaces for the Sacred*, 71–89; and Craig Bartholomew's *Where Mortals Dwell*, 222–225 and 238–239.
22. John Inge, *A Christian Theology of Place*, 67.
23. Berry, *A Timbered Choir*, xvii.
24. By now an abundance of critical commentary has accumulated on American meditative poetry, writing that sustains while modifying an English literary tradition that Louis Martz effectively analyzed and brought to attention decades ago in *The Poetry of Meditation*.
25. I offer commentary on these poems in *Making Nature Sacred*, 239–243.
26. Eliot, "Dry Salvages" from *Four Quartets*, in *The Complete Poems and Plays*, 136.
27. Ignatius of Loyola, *The Spiritual Exercises*, 21.
28. *Walt Whitman's Leaves of Grass: The First (1855) Edition*, 25. Subsequent references to the 1855 poem (later "Song of Myself") and the Preface to *Leaves* are to this edition.
29. Among the modern philosophic writers who make a comparable case for the somatic significance of emplacement is Edward S. Casey. In *Getting Back Into Place* Casey proposes, for example, that "knowledge of place begins with the bodily experience of being-in-place" and that a place "gathers *in* the dimensions and directions indicated by the body's insertion into it" (74, 46).
30. Walt Whitman, "Crossing Brooklyn Ferry," in *Leaves of Grass*, 161, 159.
31. Hart Crane, "To Brooklyn Bridge," 34.
32. See, for example, Marilyn Nelson's essay on "The Fruit of Silence," posted by The Center for Contemplative Mind in Society.
33. Marilyn Nelson, *The Homeplace*, 4–5.
34. Henry James to Charles Eliot Norton on February 4, 1872, cited in *Complete Letters of Henry James*, 2:438.

35. Forrest's precise role in the Fort Pillow Massacre remains in dispute. True, General Forrest has also been admired in some quarters, particularly in the South, as a military genius and exemplar of the resolute, self-made man. See, for example, Andrew Nelson Lytle's *Nathan Bedford Forrest and His Critter Company*. Yet disdain for Forrest and what he presumably represents continues to surface in our own day, as demonstrated by the recent controversy and campaign to remove the brass statue honoring him from a park in Memphis, not far from Fort Pillow in Tennessee. See Emily Yellin, "A Confederate General's Final Stand Divides Memphis."
36. Both Forrest and Tyler figure as well in another of Nelson's poems, a powerfully resonant piece titled "To the Confederate Dead," collected in *Faster Than Light*. Titled after one of Allen Tate's signature poems, Nelson's work was inspired by her own chance visit to an obscure Confederate cemetery in Middle Tennessee. It probes the import of several artifacts and landscape features she witnessed at that site.
37. As compared with most settings in Europe, the unusually ephemeral character of built landscapes in America—perhaps especially in places like California—has long been noted. Thomas Jefferson, for instance, in a letter of 1788, presciently observed that "we build of such perishable materials that one half of our houses must be rebuilt in every space of twenty years." Cited in *The Portable Thomas Jefferson*, 433.
38. By the nineteenth century, the "new geology" of Charles Lyell and other scientific breakthroughs challenged the previously prevailing sense of natural landscapes as more-or-less fixed and permanent. In writings by Henry Thoreau and John Muir, for example, that sense is largely supplanted by recognition of the earth's perpetual fluidity and mutability. Accordingly, Muir's portrayal of Yosemite's rock-hewn majesty is far from static, emphasizing instead his perception of the land's energy and constant flow.
39. Muir, *A Thousand-Mile Walk to the Gulf*, 164; Berry, "A Native Hill," in *The Art of the Commonplace*, 13.
40. David Chidester and Edward T. Linenthal emphasize this theme, in relation to various American settings, throughout their edition of *American Sacred Place*—in their own Introduction as well as in

essays provided by other contributors. They observe that "sacred space is inevitably contested space, a site of negotiated contests over the legitimate ownership of sacred symbols" (15).
41. This impression is verified and amplified, with ample documentary evidence, in Christina Vella's splendid prose biography, *George Washington Carver: A Life*.
42. Nelson, *Carver: A Life in Poems*, 52.
43. Alfredo Véa, Jr., *La Maravilla*, 24. An actual town of Buckeye, which I gather to be quite unlike the settlement Véa describes, can still be found in Arizona on the outskirts of Phoenix.
44. John S. Christie, *Latino Fiction and the Modernist Imagination*, 141–144. Alluding to Bakhtin, Christie considers how distinctive traits of what he calls the "Latino carnivalesque" (144) reflect the "polyphonic inconclusiveness" (143) of Véa's novel, particularly as dramatized through a railway accident that spills whiskey and car parts into Buckeye Road from two boxcars toward the story's close.

Chapter 4

1. For previous generations of academicians, the phrase became familiar following publication of intellectual historian Perry Miller's book titled *Nature's Nation*.
2. These destinations and their distinctive attractions are among those discussed by John F. Sears in *Sacred Places*.
3. Belden C. Lane, *Landscapes of the Sacred*, 25.
4. Marilynne Robinson, *Lila*, 26, 242, 44, 28. Robinson's two previous novels set in this same town are *Gilead* (2004) and *Home* (2008).
5. Lloyd Burton, *Worship and Wilderness*, 5, 4, 129–134, 141–144, 297.
6. Sears, *Sacred Places*, 7.
7. Sears, *Sacred Places*, 16.
8. Hawthorne, "My Visit to Niagara," cited in *Hawthorne: Tales and Sketches*, ed. Roy Harvey Pearce, 245–250.
9. In *Landscape and Memory*, 385–513, Simon Schama offers an illuminating, wide-ranging discussion of how diverse world

cultures have imagined the sacred character of mountainous reaches. Schama considers, for example, how Taoist and other Asian attitudes toward portraying and ascending sacred peaks differ from Western attitudes and artifacts, including the sculpture project on Mount Rushmore.
10. Bradford, *Of Plymouth Plantation*, 62.
11. Thoreau, *The Maine Woods*, 58. J. Parker Huber provides a useful compilation of Thoreau's diverse climbing adventures, together with an introductory commentary, in *Elevating Ourselves: Henry David Thoreau on Mountains*.
12. Henry Thoreau, first version of *Walden*, cited in J. Lyndon Shanley's *The Making of Walden*, 138.
13. Thoreau, journal entries of September 7 and September 12, 1851, cited in *I to Myself: Annotated Selection from the Journals*, 99.
14. Thoreau, "A Walk to Wachusett," cited in Huber, *Elevating Ourselves*, 15.
15. Thoreau, journal entry from August 9, 1860, in Huber, *Elevating Ourselves*, 68.
16. Sam Pickering, *Autumn Spring*, 14.
17. Richard Tillinghast, "Four Directions," 469, 462.
18. Thoreau, "Walking," 105–106.
19. Robert Penn Warren, *All the King's Men*, 327.
20. Dillard, *Pilgrim at Tinker Creek*, 255.
21. *The Sacred Pipe*, 18.
22. Melville, *Moby-Dick*, 224.
23. I am grateful to a former undergraduate student of mine, Ansley McDurmon, for conversations related to this topic in connection with her senior honors thesis (2016) on "The Liminality of Place in Melville's *Moby-Dick*."
24. Lawrence Buell, "*Moby-Dick* as Sacred Text," 53–54.
25. This point stands out among the several disclosures offered by Eric Bulson in a discerning chapter on "Melville's Zig-Zag World-Circle," 43–64. Derek John Woods likewise considers the implications of Melville's mapping and classification references in "Knowing When You're in Terra Incognita."
26. Bulson, 50.
27. See Dava Sobel and William J. H. Andrewes, *The Illustrated Longitude*.

28. Melville, *Pierre or The Ambiguities*, 248.
29. Melville never specifies the span of years when this novel's action presumably takes place. If the story is situated as early as 1820 or thereabouts, consonant with timing of the *Essex* sinking, the *Pequod*'s possession of a marine chronometer becomes doubtful because "chronometers at this time were expensive and not yet widely used on Nantucket whaleships," as Nathaniel Philbrick notes in *The Heart of the Sea*, 110. But even several years later, any ship carrying a single chronometer might be unable to use it effectively for longitudinal determinations because the enormous duration of whaling voyages seriously affected the instrument's "rate," or error quotient, over time, thereby degrading the accuracy of navigational readings. See Ian R. Bartky's *Selling the True Time*, 11–13.
30. Bulson remarks that in the face of the story's absence of any sequel, it is precisely "Moby-Dick's escape that resists closure" (63).
31. David Chidester and Edward T. Linenthal, in their editorial Introduction to *American Sacred Space*, point out that "If sacred places could be battlefields [i.e., culturally contested sites], battlefields could also be sacred places" (3).
32. Sears, *Sacred Places*, 99–121; and David Charles Sloane, *The Last Great Necessity*, 13–95.
33. Sears, *Sacred Places*, 100.
34. William Ellery Channing's "Sleepy Hollow" and Ralph Waldo Emerson's "Address," both in *Miscellanies*, Vol. 11 of *The Complete Works of Ralph Waldo Emerson*, 428, 429–430, 433–434, 431.
35. See James L. Cotton Jr., *The Greatest Speech, Ever*, esp. 143, 127–154; and Gabor Boritt, *The Gettysburg Gospel*, esp. 33–48. In their Introduction to *American Sacred Space*, David Chidester and Edward T. Linenthal consider how the USS Arizona Memorial at Pearl Harbor likewise serves as both battle "shrine" and "tomb" of slain combatants (3–4).
36. Lincoln, cited in *The Portable Abraham Lincoln*, 295.
37. For accounts and text of the dedication ceremony, see Cotton, *The Greatest Speech, Ever*, 202–219; Gary Wills, *Lincoln at Gettysburg*, 34–35; John Russell Bartlett, *The Soldier's National Cemetery at Gettysburg*; and http://thisweekinthecivilwar.com/?p=1694.

Following Lincoln's speech, the proceedings included a choral dirge and a Benediction delivered by the Rev. H. L. Baugher.
38. Everett cited in Cotton, 212–213. In ways that Linenthal discusses at length (87–126), the process of venerating and commemorating Gettysburg as sacred ground also continued well beyond Lincoln's day.
39. Although there is little doubt that Lincoln included the phrase in his spoken remarks, debate persists about whether it appeared in previous text or was added spontaneously upon delivery. A. E. Elmore discusses the issue at length in *Lincoln's Gettysburg Address*, 121–122, 129–148.
40. Although I think it fair to say that the Address contains no *overt* biblical allusions, any number of subtler references have been identified, including a parallel to the language of Psalm 90 by means of the familiar King James translation, in Lincoln's opening words. The most detailed argument for how Lincoln presumably applied his knowledge of the King James Bible, together with the Book of Common Prayer, in phrasing the Address appears in Elmore, *Lincoln's Gettysburg Address*.
41. Peter Brown's seminal assessment of *The Cult of the Saints* describes how cultic devotion to saints first arose in the ancient Mediterranean world in association with cemetery rituals honoring the bodily remains of Christian martyrs. Edward Everett, in his address at Gettysburg, actually referred to the honored dead as "martyrs." And in *The Sacred Remains*, Gary Laderman suggests how the "language of martyrdom" served more broadly to address or deflect the otherwise intolerable horror of the war's immense death counts.
42. Cotton, 154.
43. Gary Wills, 22.
44. Present-day efforts to preserve if not augment the National Park's hallowed atmosphere can nonetheless present complications. Historian John McCardell points out, for example, an unexpected result of the project undertaken in 2007 to clear away extensive tree and weed growth from the battlefield so as better to "resemble what those who fought there actually saw and experienced" ("Introduction: Charged with the Grandeur of God," 19). Ironically, though, the intended beautification ended up

freshly exposing visitors to anachronistic artifacts such as the Pennsylvania Monument and park maintenance sheds.
45. Mark S. Schantz, "Death and the Gettysburg Address," in *The Gettysburg Address: Perspectives on Lincoln's Greatest Speech*, ed. Sean Conant (New York: Oxford University Press, 2015), 107.
46. In contrast to the tactful reticence about the South that here informed the rhetoric of Lincoln, who was already looking ahead toward winning the peace as well as the war, both the Reverend Stockton and Edward Everett condemned the southern cause—and especially its leaders—quite explicitly in their addresses to the crowd. Even in the context of his prayer, Stockton bemoaned the prideful aggression of "our enemies," those who were "prepared to cast the chain of slavery around the form of Freedom." Still more pointedly, Everett denounced the southern cause as a "crime," a "stupendous rebellion," and a "monstrous conspiracy against the American Union." This "scourge of an aggressive and wicked war," he charged, was attributable to "hard-hearted men" driven by a "cruel lust of power."
47. Samuel Weaver, directly responsible for superintending the reinterment process, insisted that no such mistakes had been made. But Linenthal points out in *Sacred Ground* that "Such beliefs notwithstanding, several Confederates were reportedly buried in the cemetery" (93).
48. See Linenthal, 93–118, who also describes the eventual construction of southern monuments at Gettysburg.
49. Bobbie Ann Mason, "Shiloh," in *Shiloh and Other Stories*.
50. Belden Lane, *The Solace of Fierce Landscapes*.
51. Abbey, *Desert Solitaire*, 33.
52. Stoll, *Inherit the Holy Mountain*, 188–190. James M. Cahalan, in *Edward Abbey: A Life* (6, 8) points out that although Abbey's mother served as an elder in the Presbyterian church, Abbey himself attended Sunday school only briefly before stomping out in disgust, and thus replicated his father's rejection of organized religion.
53. Thoreau, *Walden*, 91. Abbey discourses more fully on his appreciative relation to Thoreau in a later essay titled "Down the River With Henry Thoreau," in Abbey's *Down the River*.

54. Calvin's appreciative view of Creation receives fuller discussion in Belden C. Lane's *Ravished by Beauty*, and in Mark Stoll's *Inherit the Mountain*, 15–22.
55. On Abbey's kinship with Robinson Jeffers and endorsement of the radically ecocentric, religious but non-creedal worldview Jeffers called "inhumanism," see Stoll's, *Inherit the Mountain*, 184–189; and Bron Taylor's essay on "Resacralizing Earth: Pagan Environmentalism and the Restoration of Turtle Island," in *American Sacred Space*, 105–110.
56. Terry Tempest Williams, *Refuge*, 3, 243.
57. Kathleen Norris, *Dakota: A Spiritual Geography*, 91.
58. Dorothy Day, *The Long Loneliness*, 44, 333, 11.
59. Although Maurin did work closely with Day in Manhattan, Day points out that "We looked at things differently" because "He was a peasant; I was a city product" so that "He knew the soil; I the city" (175).
60. James Baldwin, "Fifth Avenue, Uptown: A Letter from Harlem," in *Nobody Knows My Name*, 57.
61. Baldwin, "Fifth Avenue, Uptown," 65.
62. Baldwin thus records his having resolved "never to make my peace with the ghetto but to die and go to Hell before I would let any man spit on me, before I would accept my 'place' in this republic," from "Down at the Cross: Letter from a Region in my Mind," in *The Fire Next Time*, 37.
63. Baldwin, "Fifth Avenue, Uptown," 63.
64. See David Leeming, *James Baldwin*, 24–31; Baldwin in *The Fire Next Time*; and Dale M. Coulter's blog entry, "James Baldwin Was a Preacher: We Can Learn From Him Still" in *First Things*.
65. Baldwin, *Go Tell It On the Mountain*, 15.
66. Baldwin, *The Fire Next Time*, 38.
67. Baldwin, *The Fire Next Time*, 44.
68. Raboteau, "Balm in Gilead," 96.
69. Baldwin, *The Fire Next Time*, 47.
70. Alfred Kazin, *A Walker in the City*, 39.
71. In later life, as reflected in other autobiographical writings, Kazin continued to feel absorbed by religious aspirations and questions. He thus concludes his subsequent self-chronicling in *New York*

Jew declaring that "I want my God back. I will never give up until it is too late to expect you" (295). As indicated by his commentary on a dozen or so canonical, exclusively Gentile authors in *God and the American Writer* (1997), his fascination with God-haunted writers and thinkers also extended well beyond Jewish cultural contexts.

72. "The Custom-House" Preface to *The Scarlet Letter*, 35. The allusion here is to Hawthorne's self-determined exile from his birthplace in Salem, Massachusetts.

Chapter 5

1. See "The Value of University: Where's Best?" in *The Economist*.
2. In response to questions about the goals of America's colleges and universities for a study conducted by UCLA's Higher Education Research Institute (HERI) in 2003–2004, less than three-fourths of those surveyed deemed it "essential" or "very important" for their institutions to help undergraduates "develop moral character" (66.7%) or to "help students develop personal values" (64.5%). An even smaller proportion of faculty (30%) agreed strongly or somewhat that "Colleges should be concerned with facilitating students' spiritual development." Granted, these surveys may reflect the professoriate's understandable resistance to compromising a primary commitment to academic rigor for the sake of potentially moralistic oversight, in an era when colleges had long since abandoned any claim to serve *in loco parentis* for their students. See *Spirituality and the Professoriate: A National Survey of Faculty Beliefs, Attitudes, and Behaviors,* http://spirituality.ucla.edu/docs/results/faculty/spirit_professoriate.pdf
3. McClay, "The Tocquevillean Moment," 54.
4. McClay, "The Tocquevillean Moment," 54.
5. See Richard Arum and Josipa Roka, *Academically Adrift*; and Derek Bok, *Our Underachieving Colleges*, 116–117.
6. Bok, *Our Underachieving Colleges*, 8.
7. Louis Menand, *The Marketplace of Ideas*, 17, 157.
8. Bok, *Our Underachieving Colleges*, 146–151.

9. Baker and Bilbro, *Wendell Berry and Higher Education*, 1. In contrast to the utilitarian remedies often proposed for the current ills of higher education, this volume as a whole sets forth what I take to be a refreshing countervision of learning in which the formation of virtue and character plays a prominent role.
10. Christie, *The Blue Sapphire of the Mind*, 20, ix, 12, 22.
11. Christie, in *Blue Sapphire of the Mind*, reflects on the notion of place-making as contemplative practice (114–188), crediting in turn anthropologist Keith Basso for bringing the term "place-making" into currency. See also Douglas Burton-Christie's article, "Place-Making as Contemplative Practice."
12. I discuss these matters more fully in "Meditation on the Creatures: Ecoliterary Uses of an Ancient Tradition." See also Barbara Lewalski, *Protestant Poetics and the Seventeenth-Century Religion Lyric*, 148, 150–151, 162–169.
13. I discuss this expression of Levertov's commitment to poetic meditation more fully in *Making Nature Sacred*, 239–243.
14. Berry, from poem VI. of "Sabbaths 2007," in *Leavings*, 91.
15. Berry, in his Preface to *A Timbered Choir*, recommends that these poems be read in much the same way he had composed them: ideally "in silence, in solitude, mainly out of doors" (xvii).
16. Stewart, *Names on the Land*, 3–4.
17. The reference guide I have in mind is Smith and Suarez, *Sewanee Places*.
18. Haskell, *The Songs of Trees*.
19. "The Secret Life of Trees," 16–25.
20. *Ely: An Autobiography*, 67.
21. Cather, *My Ántonia*, in *Willa Cather: Early Novels and Stories*, 722.
22. In addition to information provided by the administration of this Tennessee State Archaeological Park, relevant archaeological commentary is available in Charles H. Faulkner, *The Old Stone Fort*; and C. Ward Weems. "The Old Stone Fort Site."
23. Thus Michael S. Northcott points out in *Place, Ecology and the Sacred* how in many cultures places perceived to have been "hallowed by the Creator Spirit" are often "places where natural powers seem to gather the forces of nature together in particularly powerful combinations" including "waterfalls" and "the meeting point of two rivers" (27).

24. Faulkner, *The Old Stone Fort*, 30.
25. Lines from Gardiner L. Tucker's "Sewanee," cited in Waring McCrady and Thomas Ward, *All Saints' Chapel*, 111.
26. A key source of information about the Chapel's history and character, in addition to pamphlet material circulated by the Chapel itself, can be found in McCrady and Ward, *All Saints' Chapel*, including Ward's revealing Introduction to that volume.
27. Like other elements of the Chapel's architectural design, the modeling of these aspects is directly attributable to the interests and initiative of former Vice Chancellor Edward McGrady.
28. There can be little doubt that at the Great Vigil of Easter, celebrated liturgically each year in the Chapel, the opening ritual of lighting the Great Fire is meant to stir primordial memory. But the comparative statement must remain tentative because much remains uncertain about whatever communal practices once took place at Old Stone Fort. Although there is reason to believe fires may have been set in trenches near the mounds as part of the solstice rituals there, archaeological evidence does not reveal just how these rituals were performed.
29. William Porcher DuBose, "Sermon Preached in the University Chapel, Sewanee, on the Feast of the Transfiguration, 1911," in *Turning Points in My Life*, 123.
30. T. S. Eliot, Little Gidding" section of *Four Quartets*, in *T. S. Eliot: The Complete Poems and Plays*, 145.

BIBLIOGRAPHY

Abbey, Edward. *Desert Solitaire: A Season in the Wilderness.* New York: Ballantine Books, 1968.
Abbey, Edward. *Down the River.* New York: Penguin, 1982.
Anon. "The Secret Life of Trees." *Sewanee Magazine*, Fall 2010, 16–25.
Anon. "The Value of University: Where's Best?" *The Economist*, October 31, 2015.
Arum, Richard and Roka, Josipa. *Academically Adrift: Limited Learning on College Campuses.* Chicago: University of Chicago Press, 2011.
Bachelard, Gaston. *The Poetics of Space.* Translated by Maria Jolas. New York: Orion, 1964.
Baker, Jack R. and Bilbro, Jeffrey. *Wendell Berry and Higher Education: Cultivating Virtues of Place.* Lexington: University Press of Kentucky, 2017.
Baldwin, James. *The Fire Next Time.* New York: Dell, 1963.
Baldwin, James. *Go Tell It On the Mountain.* New York: Vintage-Random House, 1981.
Baldwin, James. *Nobody Knows My Name: More Notes of a Native Son.* New York: Dial Press, 1961.
Barnhill, David Landis. "The Spiritual Dimension of Nature Writing." In *The Oxford Handbook of Religion and Ecology.* Edited by Roger S. Gottlieb, 419–445. New York: Oxford University Press, 2006.

Bartholomew, Craig G. *Where Mortals Dwell: A Christian View of Place for Today*. Grand Rapids, MI: Baker Academic, 2011.

Bartky, Ian R. *Selling the True Time: Nineteenth-Century Timekeeping in America*. Stanford, CA: Stanford University Press, 2000.

Bartlett, John Russell. *The Soldiers' National Cemetery at Gettysburg: With the Proceedings at its Consecration; at the Laying of the Corner-Stone of the Monument, and at Its Dedication*. Providence, RI: Providence Press, 1874.

Beecher, Lyman. *The Autobiography of Lyman Beecher*, Vol. 1. Edited by Barbara M. Cross. Cambridge, MA: Harvard University Press, 1961.

Behringer, Maggie. "Gone from Litchfield, Saint's Efforts Go On." *The Register Citizen*, February 21, 2009.

Berry, Wendell. *The Art of the Commonplace: The Agrarian Essays of Wendell Berry*. Edited by Norman Wirzba. Berkeley, CA: Counterpoint, 2002.

Berry, Wendell. *Home Economics*. New York: North Point Press, 1987

Berry, Wendell. *Imagination in Place*. Berkeley, CA: Counterpoint, 2010.

Berry, Wendell. *Leavings: Poems*. Berkeley, CA: Counterpoint, 2010.

Berry, Wendell. *Recollected Essays: 1965–1980*. San Francisco: North Point Press, 1981.

Berry, Wendell. *Remembering: A Novel*. Berkeley, CA: Counterpoint, 2008.

Berry, Wendell. "Sabbaths 2013, XIV." *Sewanee Review* 122 (2014): 559.

Berry, Wendell. *Sex, Economy, Freedom & Community*. New York: Pantheon, 1993.

Berry, Wendell. *That Distant Land: The Collected Stories*. Berkeley, CA: Counterpoint, 2004.

Berry, Wendell. *A Timbered Choir: The Sabbath Poems 1979–1997*. Washington, DC: Counterpoint, 1998.

Berry, Wendell. *What Are People for?* New York: North Point Press, 1990.

Bilbro, Jeffrey. *Loving God's Wildness: The Christian Roots of Ecological Ethics in American Literature*. Tuscaloosa: University of Alabama Press, 2015.

Black Elk. *The Sacred Pipe: Black Elk's Account of the Seven Rites of the Oglala Sioux*. Edited and recorded by Joseph Epes Brown. Norman: University of Oklahoma Press, 1989.

Bok, Derek. *Our Underachieving Colleges: A Candid Look at How Much Students Learn and Why They Should Be Learning More.* Princeton, NJ: Princeton University Press, 2006.

Boritt, Gabor. *The Gettysburg Gospel: The Lincoln Speech That Nobody Knows.* New York: Simon & Schuster, 2006.

Bradford, William. *Of Plymouth Plantation, 1620–1647.* Edited by Samuel Eliot Morison. New York: Modern Library, 1952.

Bratton, Susan Power. *The Spirit of the Appalachian Trail: Community, Environment, and Belief on a Long-Distance Hiking Path.* Knoxville: University of Tennessee Press, 2012.

Bronowski, Jacob. "The Reach of Imagination." *The American Scholar* 36 (Spring 1967): 193–201.

Brown, David. *God and Enchantment of Place: Reclaiming Human Experience.* New York: Oxford University Press, 2004.

Brown, Peter. *The Cult of the Saints: Its Rise and Function in Latin Christianity.* Chicago: University of Chicago Press, 1981.

Buell, Lawrence. *The Environmental Imagination: Thoreau, Nature Writing, and the Formation of American Culture.* Cambridge, MA: Harvard University Press, 1995.

Buell, Lawrence. "*Moby-Dick* as Sacred Text." In *New Essays on Moby-Dick*. Edited by Richard Brodhead, 53–72. New York: Cambridge University Press, 1986.

Buell, Lawrence. *New England Literary Culture: From Revolution Through Renaissance.* New York: Cambridge University Press, 1986.

Buell, Lawrence. *Writing for an Endangered World: Literature, Culture, and Environment in the U.S. and Beyond.* Cambridge, MA: Harvard University Press, 2001.

Bulson, Eric. *Novels, Maps, Modernity: The Spatial Imagination, 1850–2000.* New York: Routledge, 2007.

Burton-Christie, Douglas. "Place-Making as Contemplative Practice." *Anglican Theological Review* 3 (Summer 2009): 347–372.

Burton, Lloyd. *Worship and Wilderness: Culture, Religion, and Law in Public Lands Management.* Madison: University of Wisconsin Press, 2002.

Cahalan, James M. *Edward Abbey: A Life.* Tucson: University of Arizona Press, 2001.

Casey, Edward E. *Getting Back Into Place: Toward a Renewed Understanding of the Place-World.* Bloomington: Indiana University Press, 2009.

Cather, Willa. *My Ántonia*. In *Willa Cather: Early Novels and Stories*. New York: Library of America, 1987.

Cather, Willa. *The Professor's House*. In *Willa Cather: Later Novels*. New York: Library of America, 1990.

Cather, Willa. *The Selected Letters of Willa Cather*. Edited by Andrew Jewell and Janis Stout. New York: Knopf, 2013.

Chandler, Marilyn R. *Dwelling in the Text: Houses in American Fiction*. Berkeley: University of California Press, 1991.

Charles, Eleanor. "Harriet Beecher Stowe's Link to Litchfield for Sale." *New York Times*, August 25, 1996.

Christie, Douglas E. *The Blue Sapphire of the Mind: Notes for a Contemplative Ecology*. New York: Oxford University Press, 2013.

Christie, John S. *Latino Fiction and the Modernist Imagination: Literature of the Borderlands*. New York: Garland, 1998.

Chidester, David and Linenthal, Edward T., eds. *American Sacred Space*. Bloomington: Indiana University Press, 1995.

Coleridge, Samuel Taylor. *Biographia Literaria*. 2 Vols. Edited by J. Shawcross. 1818. Reprint, Oxford: Oxford University Press, 1973.

Cotton, James L. Jr., *The Greatest Speech, Ever: The Remarkable Story of Abraham Lincoln and His Gettysburg Address*. Palisades, NY: History, 2013.

Coulter, Dale M. "James Baldwin Was a Preacher: We Can Learn from Him Still." Blog entry in *First Things: A Monthly Journal for Religion and Public Life* (June 2014), https://www.firstthings.com/blogs/firstthoughts/2014/06/james-baldwin-and-the-tensions-of-holiness.

Core, George and H. L. Weatherby. *Place in American Fiction: Excursions and Explorations*. Columbia: University of Missouri Press, 2004.

Crane, Hart. "To Brooklyn Bridge," from *The Bridge*. In *Hart Crane: Complete Poems and Selected Letters*. Edited by Langdon Hammer. New York: Library of America, 2006.

Crèvecoeur, Hector St. John de. *Letters From an American Farmer and Sketches of Eighteenth-Century America*. Edited by Albert E. Stone. New York: Viking Penguin, 1981.

Day, Dorothy. *The Long Loneliness: The Autobiography of the Legendary Catholic Social Activist*. New York: HarperCollins, 1980.

Dillard, Annie. *Pilgrim at Tinker Creek*. New York: HarperCollins, 1974.

Donnelly, Phillip J. "Biblical Convocation in Wendell Berry's *Remembering.*" *Christianity and Literature* 56 (2007): 275–296.
Dougherty, James. "House-Building and House-Holding at Walden." *Christianity and Literature* 57 (2007): 225–250.
DuBose, William Porcher. *Turning Points in My Life.* New York: Longmans, Green, 1912.
Eberle, Gary. *The Geography of Nowhere: Finding One's Self in the Postmodern World.* Kansas City, MO: Sheed & Ward, 1994.
Eliade, Mircea. *The Sacred and the Profane: The Nature of Religion.* Translated by Willard R. Trask. New York: Harcourt, 1957.
Eliot, T. S. *The Complete Poems and Plays, 1909–1950.* New York: Harcourt Brace, 1962.
Elmore, A. E. *Lincoln's Gettysburg Address: Echoes of the Bible and Book of Common Prayer.* Carbondale: Southern Illinois University Press, 2009.
Emerson, Ralph Waldo. "Address" together with William Ellery Channing's "Sleepy Hollow." Vol. 11, *Miscellanies,* of *The Complete Works of Ralph Waldo Emerson.* Edited by Edward W. Emerson, 427–436. Boston: Houghton Mifflin, 1932.
Emerson, Ralph Waldo. *Emerson: Essays and Lectures.* Edited by Joel Porte. New York: Library of America, 1983.
Engell, James. *The Creative Imagination: Enlightenment to Romanticism.* Cambridge: Harvard University Press, 1981.
Faulkner, Charles H. *The Old Stone Fort: Exploring an Archaeological Mystery.* Knoxville: University of Tennessee Press, 1968.
Frost, Robert. *Collected Poems, Prose, & Plays.* New York: Library of America, 1995.
Gaines, Ernest J. *In My Father's House.* New York: Knopf, 1978.
Gatta, John. *American Madonna: Images of the Divine Woman in American Literary Culture.* New York: Oxford University Press, 1997.
Gatta, John. "Coleridge's 'Fears in Solitude' and the Prospect of Social Redemption." *Cithara* 26 (1986): 36–43.
Gatta, John. *Making Nature Sacred.* New York: Oxford University Press, 2004.
Gatta, John. "Meditation on the Creatures: Ecoliterary Uses of an Ancient Tradition." In *Early Modern Ecostudies: From the Florentine*

Codex to Shakespeare. Edited by Thomas Hallock, Ivo Kamps, and Karen L. Raber, 181–192. New York: Palgrave Macmillan, 2008.

Gatta, John. "'Not a Tame Lion': Animal Compassion and the Ecotheology of Human Imagination in Four Anglican Thinkers." In *Ecotheology in the Humanities*. Edited by Melissa J. Brotton, 193–207. Lanham, MD: Lexington, 2016.

Gatta, John. "Progress and Providence in *The House of the Seven Gables*." *American Literature* 50 (1978): 37–48.

Gatta, John. "Rediscovering the Earth." *Sewanee Review* 112 (Fall 2004): 618–625.

Gatta, John. "Toward a Theology of Pilgrimage." In *Traveling Well: Christian Reflection, A Series in Faith and Ethics*. Edited by Robert B. Krushwitz, 89–93. Waco, TX: Baylor University Institute for Faith and Learning, 2016.

Green, Ely. *Ely: An Autobiography*. 1966. Reprint, Athens: University of Georgia Press, 1990.

Haltunen, Karen. "Gothic Imagination and Social Reform: The Haunted Houses of Lyman Beecher, Henry Ward Beecher, and Harriet Beecher Stowe." In *New Essays on Uncle Tom's Cabin*. Edited by Eric J. Sundquist, 107–134. Cambridge and New York: Cambridge University Press, 1986.

Haskell, David George. *The Forest Unseen: A Year's Watch in Nature*. New York: Viking Penguin, 2012.

Haskell, David George. *The Songs of Trees: Stories from Nature's Great Connectors*. New York: Penguin Random House, 2017.

Hawthorne, Nathaniel. "The Ambitious Guest." In *Twice-Told Tales*. Vol. 9 of *The Centenary Edition of the Works of Nathaniel Hawthorne*. Edited by William Charvat et al., 324–333. Columbus: Ohio State University Press, 1963–1987.

Hawthorne, Nathaniel. "Fire-Worship." In *Mosses From an Old Manse*. Vol. 2 of *The Centenary Edition of the Works of Nathaniel Hawthorne*. Edited by William Charvat et al., 138–147. Columbus: Ohio State University Press, 1963–1987.

Hawthorne, Nathaniel. *The House of the Seven Gables*. Edited by Seymour Gross. New York: Norton, 1967.

Hawthorne, Nathaniel. *The Letters, 1843–1858*. Vol. 16 of *The Centenary Edition of the Works of Nathaniel Hawthorne*. Edited by William Charvat et al. Columbus: Ohio State University Press, 1963–1987.

Hawthorne, Nathaniel. *The Marble Faun: Or, The Romance of Monte Beni*. New York: Viking Penguin, 1990.
Hawthorne, Nathaniel. *The Scarlet Letter and Other Writings*. Edited by Leland S. Person. New York: Norton, 2005.
Hawthorne, Nathaniel. *Tales and Sketches*. New York: Library of America, 1982.
Hedrick, Joan D. *Harriet Beecher Stowe: A Life*. New York: Oxford University Press, 1994.
Heidegger, Martin. "Building Dwelling Thinking," In *Basic Writings*. Edited by David Farrell Krell. San Francisco: HarperCollins, 1993.
Heise, Ursula K. *Sense of Place and Sense of Planet: The Environmental Imagination of the Global*. New York: Oxford University Press, 2008.
Hitt, Jack. *Off the Road: A Modern-Day Walk Down the Pilgrim's Route Into Spain*. New York: Simon & Schuster, 1994.
Hokum, Matt. "Cather's Use of Genius in O Pioneers." Online Newsletter of the Cather Colloquium, Willa Cather Archives at the University of Nebraska, Lincoln. Last accessed July 24, 2017. http://cather.unl.edu/mt.spr04.05.html
Hubbard, Phil, Kitchin, Rob, and Valentine, Gill, eds. *Key Thinkers on Space and Place*. Los Angeles: Sage, 2004.
Huber, J. Parker. *Elevating Ourselves: Henry David Thoreau on Mountains*. Boston: Houghton Mifflin, 1999.
Hunt, James B. *Restless Fires: Young John Muir's Thousand-Mile Walk to the Gulf in 1867–68*. Macon, GA: Mercer University Press, 2012.
Husserl, Edmund. *The Essential Husserl: Basic Writings in Transcendental Phenomenology*. Edited by Donn Welton. Bloomington: Indiana University Press, 1999.
Ignatius of Loyola. *The Spiritual Exercises of St. Ignatius*. Translated by Louis J. Puhl, S. J. New York: Vintage-Random House, 2000.
Inge, John. *A Christian Theology of Place*. Farnham, UK: Ashgate, 2003.
Jackson, Wes. *Becoming Native to This Place*. Lexington: University of Kentucky Press, 1994.
James, Henry. *Complete Letters of Henry James, 1855–1872*. Edited by Pierre A. Walker et al. Lincoln: University of Nebraska Press, 2006.
Jefferson, Thomas. *The Portable Thomas Jefferson*. Edited by Merrill D. Peterson. New York: Viking, 1975.
Johnson, Edward. "Wonder-Working Providence of Sions Saviour." Vol. 1, In *The Puritans: A Sourcebook of Their Writings*. Edited by

Perry Miller and Thomas M. Johnson, 143–162. New York: Harper and Row, 1963.

Karnes, Michelle. *Imagination, Meditation, and Cognition in the Middle Ages.* Chicago: University of Chicago Press, 2011.

Kazin, Alfred. *God and the American Writer.* New York: Knopf, 1997.

Kazin, Alfred. *New York Jew.* New York: Knopf, 1978.

Kazin, Alfred. *A Walker in the City.* New York: Grove Press, 1951.

Koester, Nancy. *Harriet Beecher Stowe: A Spiritual Life.* Grand Rapids, MI: Eerdmans, 2014.

Laderman, Gary. *The Sacred Remains: American Attitudes Toward Death, 1799–1883.* New Haven, CT: Yale University Press, 1996.

Lane, Belden C. *Landscapes of the Sacred: Geography and Narrative in American Spirituality.* Baltimore: Johns Hopkins University Press, 2001.

Lane, Belden C. *Ravished by Beauty: The Surprising Legacy of Reformed Spirituality.* New York: Oxford University Press, 2011.

Lane, Belden C. *The Solace of Fierce Landscapes.* New York: Oxford University Press, 2007.

Lang, Joel. "Who is Chandler Saint, And Why Did He Hide Harriet Beecher Stowe's Birthplace?" *Hartford Courant*, April 8, 2001.

Leeming, David. *James Baldwin: A Biography.* New York: Knopf, 1994.

Levertov, Denise. *New and Selected Essays.* New York: New Directions, 1992.

Lewalski, Barbara. *Protestant Poetics and the Seventeenth-Centry Religious Lyric.* Princeton, NJ: Princeton University Press, 1979.

Lincoln, Abraham. *The Portable Abraham Lincoln.* Edited by Andrew Delbanco. New York: Viking Penguin, 1992.

Linenthal, Edward Taylor. *Sacred Ground: Americans and Their Battlefields.* Urbana: University of Illinois Press, 1991.

Lopez, Barry. *Arctic Dreams: Imagination and Desire in a Northern Landscape.* New York: Random House, 1986.

Lopez, Barry. *Crossing Open Ground.* New York: Random House, 1988.

Lopez, Barry. "The Language of Animals." In *A Place on Earth: An Anthology of Nature Writing From Australia and North America.* Edited by Mark Tredinnick, 159–166. Lincoln: University of Nebraska Press, 2003.

Lopez, Barry. *Vintage Lopez.* New York: Random House, 2004.

Lopez, Barry. *Winter Count.* New York: Random House, 1981.

Lytle, Andrew Nelson. *Nathan Bedford Forrest and His Critter Company.* New York: Minton, Black, 1931.

Martz, Louis. *The Poetry of Meditation: A Study in English Religious Literature of the Seventeenth Century.* New Haven, CT: Yale University Press, 1963.

Mason, Bobbie Ann. *Shiloh and Other Stories.* New York: Harper & Row, 1982.

McCardell, John M. Jr., "Introduction: Charged with the Grandeur of God." *Sewanee Theological Review* 58:1 (Christmas 2014): 19–21.

McClay, Wilfred M. "Their Tocquevillean Moment . . . and Ours." *Wilson Quarterly* 36 (Summer 2012): 48–55.

McClay, Wilfred M. and McAllister, Ted, eds. *Why Place Matters: Geography, Identity, and Civic Life in Modern America.* New York: Encounter Books, 2014.

McCrady, J. Waring and Ward, Thomas R. Jr., *All Saints' Chapel: In the Sesquicentennial Year of the University of the South.* Prospect, KY: Harmony House, 2008.

McKibben, Bill. *The End of Nature.* New York: Random House, 1989.

Mellow, James Robert. *Nathaniel Hawthorne in His Times.* Boston: Houghton Mifflin, 1980.

Melville, Herman. *Moby-Dick.* Edited by Hershel Parker and Harrison Hayford. New York: Norton, 2002.

Melville, Herman. *Pierre or The Ambiguities.* In *Melville.* Edited by Harrison Hayford. New York: Library of America, 1984.

Menand, Louis. *The Marketplace of Ideas: Reform and Resistance in the American University.* New York: Norton, 2010.

Merleau-Ponty, Maurice. *Phenomenology of Perception.* New York: Humanities Press, 1962.

Miller, Perry. *Nature's Nation.* Cambridge, MA: Harvard University Press, 1967.

Momaday, N. Scott. *The Way to Rainy Mountain.* New York: Ballantine, 1970.

Moore, Margaret B. *The Salem World of Nathaniel Hawthorne.* Columbia: University of Missouri Press, 1998.

Moyers, Bill. *The Language of Life: A Festival of Poets.* Edited by James Haba. New York: Doubleday, 1995.

Muir, John. *A Thousand-Mile Walk to the Gulf.* 1916. Reprint, Boston and New York: Houghton Mifflin, 1998.

Murphy, John. J., ed. *Willa Cather and the Culture of Belief*. Provo, UT: Brigham Young University Press, 2002.
Nelson, Marilyn. *Carver: A Life in Poems*. Asheville, NC: Front Street, 2001.
Nelson, Marilyn. *Faster Than Light: New and Selected Poems, 1996–2011*. Baton Rouge: Lousiiana State University Press, 2012.
Nelson, Marilyn. "The Fruit of Silence." Center for Contemplative Mind in Society. Last accessed July 24, 2017. http://www.contemplativemind.org/files/nelson-fruit-of-silence.pdf
Nelson, Marilyn. *The Homeplace*. Baton Rouge: Louisiana State University Press, 1990.
Nitzsche, Jane Chance. *The Genius Figure in Antiquity and the Middle Ages*. New York: Columbia University Press, 1975.
Norris, Kathleen. *Dakota: A Spiritual Geography*. Boston: Houghton Mifflin, 1993.
Northcott, Michael S. *Place, Ecology and the Sacred: The Moral Geography of Sustainable Communities*. London: Bloomsbury, 2015.
Perkins, David, ed. *English Romantic Writers*. New York: Harcourt Brace, 1967.
Philbrick, Nathaniel. *In The Heart of the Sea: The Tragedy of the Whaleship Essex*. New York: Viking, 2000.
Pickering, Sam. *Autumn Spring*. Knoxville: University of Tennessee Press, 2007.
Raboteau, Albert J. "Balm in Gilead: Memory, Mourning, and Healing in African American Autobiography." In *Invisible Conversations: Religion in the Literature of America*. Edited by Roger Lundin, 83–99. Waco, TX: Baylor University Press, 2009.
Ransome, Joyce. *The Web of Friendship: Nicholas Ferrar and Lttle Gidding*. Cambridge, England: James Clarke, 2011.
Raycraft, Patrick. "History in the Unmaking: Dedicated Workers are Dismantling Harriet Beecher Stowe's Litchfield Birthplace . . . Very Carefully." *Hartford Courant*, May 17, 1998.
Reynolds, David S. *Mightier Than the Sword: Uncle Tom's Cabin and the Battle for America*. New York: Norton, 2011.
Robinson, Marilynne. *Gilead*. New York: Farrar, Straus and Giroux, 2004.
Robinson, Marilynne. *Home*. New York: Farrar, Straus and Giroux, 2008.

Robinson, Marilynne. *Housekeeping*. New York: Farrar, Strauss and Giroux, 1980.
Robinson, Marilynne. *Lila*. New York: Picador, 2014.
Rosen, Christine. "The New Meaning of Mobility." In *Why Place Matters: Geography, Identity, and Civic Life in Modern America*. Edited by Wilfred M. McClay and Ted V. McAllister. New York: New Atlantic Books, 2014.
Sausner, Rebecca. "Beecher Stowe's Birthplace: A Discarded Bit of History." *Hartford Courant*, August 11, 1996.
Schama, Simon. *Landscape and Memory*. New York: Knopf, 1995.
Schantz, Mark S. "Death and the Gettysburg Address." In *The Gettysburg Address: Perspectives on Lincoln's Greatest Speech*. Edited by Sean Conant. New York: Oxford University Press, 2015.
Seamon, David. "Situated Cognition and the Phenomenology of Place: Lifeworld, Environmental Embodiment, and Immersion-in-World." *Cognitive Processing: International Quarterly of Cognitive Science* 16 Supplement 1 (2015): 389–392.
Sears, John F. *Sacred Places: American Tourist Attractions in the Nineteenth Century*. New York: Oxford University Press, 1989.
Servid, Carolyn. *Of Landscape and Longing: Finding a Home at the Water's Edge*. Minneapolis, MN: Milkweed Editions, 2000.
Shanley, J. Lyndon. *The Making of Walden: With the Text of the First Version*. Chicago: University of Chicago Press, 1957.
Shakespeare, William. *A Midsummer Night's Dream*. Edited by R. A. Foakes. Cambridge: Cambridge University Press, 1984.
Sheldrake, Philip. *Spaces for the Sacred: Place, Memory and Identity*. London: SCM Press, 2001.
Sloane, David Charles. *The Last Great Necessity: Cemeteries in American History*. Baltimore: Johns Hopkins University Press, 1991.
Smith, Gerald L. and Suarez, Sean T. *Sewanee Places: A Historical Gazeteer of the Domain and the Sewanee Area*. Sewanee, TN: University of the South, 2010.
Snyder, Gary. *Mountains and Rivers Without End*. Washington, DC: Counterpoint, 1996.
Snyder, Gary. "The Place, The Region, and the Commons," from *The Practice of the Wild*. In *The Gary Snyder Reader: Prose, Poetry, and Translations 1952–1998*. Washington, DC: Counterpoint, 1999.
Snyder, Gary. *Turtle Island*. New York: New Directions, 1974.

Sobel, Dava and Andrewes, William J. H. *The Illustrated Longitude.* New York: Walker, 1995.

Stegner, Wallace. *Where the Bluebird Sings to the Lemonade Springs:Living and Writing in the West.* New York, Random House, 1992.

Stewart, George R. *Names on the Land: A Historical Account of Place-Naming in the United States.* New York: Random House, 1945.

Stoll, Mark R. *Inherit the Holy Mountain: Religion and the Rise of American Environmentalism.* New York: Oxford University Press, 2015.

Stout, Janis. *Willa Cather: The Writer and Her World.* Charlottesville: University Press of Virginia, 2000.

Stowe, Harriet Beecher. *The Minister's Wooing.* 1859. Reprint, New York: Penguin, 1999.

Stowe, Harriet Beecher. *Poganuc People.* 1878. Reprint, Hartford, CT: Stowe-Day Foundation, 1987.

Stowe, Harriet Beecher. *Uncle Tom's Cabin: Authoritative Text, Backgrounds and Contexts, Criticism.* Edited by Elizabeth Ammons. New York: Norton, 1994.

Stowell, Robert F. *A Thoreau Gazeteer.* Edited by William L. Howarth. Princeton, NJ: Princeton University Press, 1970.

Tayor, Bron. "Resacralizing Earth: Pagan Environmentalism and the Restoration of Turtle Island." In *American Sacred Space.* Edited by David Chidester and Edward T. Linenthal. Bloomington: Indiana University Press, 1995.

Taylor, Bron et al. *The Encyclopedia of Religion and Nature.* London: Continuum, 2005.

Thoreau, Henry David. *I to Myself: An Annotated Selection From the Journals of Henry D. Thoreau.* Edited by Jeffrey S. Cramer. New Haven, CT: Yale University Press, 2007.

Thoreau, Henry David. *Journal.* Vol. 2 of *The Writings of Henry D. Thoreau: Journal.* Edited by John C. Broderick, Robert Sattelmeyer, Mark Patterson, and William Ross. Princeton, NJ: Princeton University Press, 1981.

Thoreau, Henry David. *The Maine Woods: A Fully Annotated Edition.* Edited by Jeffrey S. Cramer. New Haven, CT: Yale University Press, 2009.

Thoreau, Henry David. *Walden and Resistance to Civil Government.* Edited by William Rossi. New York: Norton, 1992.

Thoreau, Henry David. "Walking." In *Natural History Essays*. Edited by Robert Sattelmeyer. Salt Lake City, NV: Peregrine Smith, 1980.

Tillinghast, Richard. "Four Directions." *Sewanee Review* 123 (2015): 463–469.

Tuan, Yi-Fu. *Space and Place: The Perspective of Experience*. Minneapolis: University of Minnesota Press, 1977.

Tredinnick, Mark, ed. *A Place on Earth: An Anthology of Nature Writing From Australia and North America*. Lincoln: University of Nebraska Press, 2003.

Véa, Alfredo, Jr. *La Maravilla*. New York: Penguin, 1993.

Vella, Christina. *George Washington Carver: A Life*. Baton Rouge: Louisiana State University Press, 2015.

Turner, Victor and Turner, Edith. *Image and Pilgrimage in Christian Culture: Anthropological Perspectives*. New York: Columbia University Press, 1978.

Warren, Robert Penn. *All the King's Men*. New York: Modern Library, 1953.

Weems, C. Ward. "The Old Stone Fort Site: A History of the Early Descriptions and Maps and Their Relevance to Modern Research." *Tennessee Anthropologist* 20:2 (Fall 1995): 96–125.

Welty, Eudora. "Place in Fiction." In *The Eye of the Story: Selected Essays and Reviews*. New York: Random House, 1977.

Whitman, Walt. "Crossing Brooklyn Ferry." In *Leaves of Grass*. Edited by Sculley Bradley and Harold W. Blodgett. New York: Norton, 1973. 159–165

Whitman, Walt. "Song of the Open Road. In *Leaves of Grass*. Edited by Sculley Bradley and Harold W. Blodgett. New York: Norton, 1973. 149–159

Whitman, Walt. *Walt Whitman's Leaves of Grass: The First Edition* (1855). Edited by Malcolm Cowley. New York: Viking, 1959.

Williams, Terry Tempest. *Refuge: An Unnnatural History of Family and Place*. New York: Random House, 1991.

Wills, Gary. *Lincoln at Gettysburg: The Words That Remade America*. New York: Simon & Schuster, 1992.

Woodruff, Paul. *Reverence: Renewing a Forgotten Virtue*. New York: Oxford University Press, 2001.

Woods, Derek John. "Knowing When You're in Terra Incognita: Mapping, Vision, and Orientation in Ishmael's Anatomies." *Leviathan: A Journal of Melville Studies* 14 (2012): 24–41.

Wordsworth, William. "Lines Composed a Few Miles Above Tintern Abbey." In *William Wordsworth: Selected Poems and Prefaces*. Edited by Jack Stillinger. Boston: Houghton Mifflin, 1965.

Yellin, Emily. "A Confederate General's Final Stand Divides Memphis," *New York Times*, July 19, 2015.

INDEX

Abbey, Edward (*Desert Solitaire: A Season in the Wilderness*), 76, 114, 168–175
  appealing "inhumanism" of desert country, 174–175
  contemplative and ecospiritual aspects of, 168, 170–171, 174–175
  reverential apprehension of Delicate Arch, 172–175
Alaska, Sitka, as described by Carolyn Servid, 66–69
animism, 4–6, 172
Appalachian Trail, 82–83
Arches National Monument and Park (Utah), 168–175
Augustine of Hippo, Saint, 37, 92, 115, 236

Bachelard, Gaston, 8–9, 15, 55
Baldwin, James, 182, 186–192, 197, 197
  conflicted relation to Christian faith, 188–190, 192, 259n64
  home place in Harlem, 187–188, 259n62
  largely autobiographical account of conversion in *Go Tell It on the Mountain*, 189–192
Bartholomew, Craig, 11, 252n21
Battlegrounds and burial grounds, 158–167
  Gettysburg National Military Park, Pennsylvania, 160–167
  Shiloh National Park, Tennessee, 167
  Sleepy Hollow Cemetery, Concord, 159–160
  Stones River National Battlefield, Murfreesboro, Tennessee, 213
Bear's Lodge. *See* Devils Tower
Benedictine and Trappist monasticism, 58, 121, 178–180, 206
Berry, Wendell, 9, 54–55, 58, 69–70, 85, 89–101, 115, 127–128, 213, 216, 217, 238, 246n4
  economy and economics as key concepts in, 91–94
  imagination, place-grounded and theological conception of, 108–111

Berry, Wendell (cont.)
    membership, theologically-configured concept of, 54–55, 93–101
    reverence for life and land in, 69–70
    sacramental outlook of, 93
    works
        "The Boundary," 100–101
        "The Gift of Good Land," 93
        Hannah Coulter, 54–55
        Home Economics, 91–92
        Imagination in Place, 69–70, 108–111
        "The Making of a Marginal Farm," 89–91
        "A Native Hill," 97, 127–128
        Remembering, 95–100
        Sabbath Poems, 94, 115, 213
        "The Wild Birds," 95
Bilbro, Jeffrey, 92, 205, 261n9
bioregionalism, 2, 85
Black Elk, 150–152
Bok, Derek, 204–205
Bradford, William, 50–51, 60, 146, 236
Bradstreet, Anne ("Contemplations"), 79–80, 115, 207
Bratton, Susan Power, 82–83
Bronowski, Jacob ("The Reach of Imagination"), 250n6
Brooks, David, 205
Brown, David, 7–8, 82, 240n8
Brown, Peter, 257n41
Brueggemann, Walter, 68
Bryant, William Cullen ("Thanatopsis"), 158
Buckeye Road, Arizona, portrayal of in Véa's novel, 132, 134–135, 139

Buddhism, traditions of, relating to place and spirit, 80, 88, 89, 216
Buell, Lawrence, 106, 153, 240n6, 243n11, 246n1
"Building Dwelling Thinking" (Heidegger), 112–113
Bunyan, John, 28, 74, 248n28

Calvin, John and Calvinism, 50, 154, 158, 171–172, 259n54
Carson, Rachel, 70, 87, 144
Carver, George Washington, 129–132
Casey, Edward E., 111, 240n7
Cather, Willa, 43–49, 59, 197, 223–225
    alienation from character's current domicile, portrayal of in *The Professor's House*, 43–44
    author's professions of alienation from modern world, 49
    intertopological dynamic of representations in *My Ántonia*, 223–224
    patria, found by adoption in mesa terrain, as portrayed in *The Professor's House*, 47
    portrayal of sacred enchantment in relation to ancient cliff dwellers, 44–47
    works
        My Ántonia, 47, 223–225
        The Professor's House, 43–49
Catholic Worker Movement, 182, 185–186
Channing, William Ellery, 148, 159–160
Christie, Douglas, 11, 206
Coleridge, Samuel Taylor, 89, 105–107, 112
    and "Fears in Solitude," 89

prose discourse on Imagination,
primary and secondary,
105–107, 112
and "Rime of the Ancient
Mariner," 106–107
Concord, Massachusetts
and Old Manse dwelling
(Emerson and Hawthorne),
22, 24–25, 56
and Sleepy Hollow Cemetery,
159–160
and Thoreau, 19–20, 22
contemplation, 11, 18–19, 24, 30,
45, 50, 63, 65, 79, 81,
102–103, 114–116, 121,
148, 168, 174, 178–179,
181, 194, 208
and contemplative ecology, 206
and contemplative pedagogy or
learning, 11, 203–209
contemplative prayer, 121, 178
contrasted with meditation, 115
Core, George, 108, 251n11
Crane, Hart ("To Brooklyn Bridge"),
120, 184
Crèvecoeur, Hector St. Jean de, 61

Dakota: A Spiritual Geography
(Kathleen Norris), 114,
178–181
Dante, Aligheri, 28, 98–100
Day, Dorothy (*The Long Loneliness*),
182–186
conversion of, 183
grace of community-amid-
affliction, as felt in
Manhattan, 184–186
launch with Peter Maurin
of Catholic Worker
Movement, 185

Desert Fathers and Mothers in early
Christian tradition, 167–168,
178–180
desert landscapes, hallowed
character of, 167–181
*Desert Solitaire: A Season in the
Wilderness*. See Abbey,
Edward
Devils Tower (Bear's Lodge),
Wyoming as contested
sacred site, 142–144
Dickinson, Emily, 29, 58, 115, 197
Dillard, Annie (*Pilgrim at Tinker
Creek*), 74, 114, 144, 150
domestic dwellings, 2, 4–5, 9, 15–56
Dougherty, James, 17, 242n4
Dreiser, Theodore, 181
DuBose, William Porcher ("Sermon
Preached . . . on the Feast of
the Transfiguration"), 231

Eberle, Gary, 240n9
ecocriticism, 2, 84, 106, 108, 181
definition of, 2
ecospirituality, 4, 170, 241n12
education, collegiate
a case-study in localized learning,
209–233
challenges to residential model
of, in present-day America,
198–200
and contemplative pedagogy or
learning, 203–209, 216
place-based learning programs in,
10–13, 201–203
spiritual and religious dimensions
of place-based education,
202–209
Eliot, T. S. (*Four Quartets*), 56, 79,
115–116, 232–233, 236

Emerson, Ralph Waldo, 8, 15–16, 19, 21, 22–24, 107, 147–149, 159, 185, 197
  works
    "Consecration of Sleepy Hollow," 159–160
    "Experience," 21
    "Hamatreya," 242n10
    Nature, 8, 15–16, 18, 22, 24
Engell, James, 105–106
Everett, Edward, 162

Faulkner, William, 58, 111, 197
Ferrar, Nicholas, 56, 78–79
The Forest Unseen: A Year's Watch in Nature (Haskell), 101–104, 213
Forrest, Nathan Bedford, 124–125, 253nn35–36
Four Quartets (T.S. Eliot), 56, 79, 115–116, 232–233, 236
Francis, Pope (Francis Mario Bergoglio), 235
Franklin, Benjamin, 59
Frost, Robert, 70, 219, 237–238

Gaines, Ernest (*In My Father's House*), 49, 51–54
genius loci, 4–7, 46, 65, 134, 140–141, 157, 172, 173, 178, 197, 236, 241nn17–18
  and sacramentality, 7
Gettysburg National Military Park and Lincoln's Address, 160–167
Go Tell It On the Mountain. *See* Baldwin, James
Green, Ely (*Ely: An Autobiography*), 213, 220–223

Hall, Joseph, 206
Haskell, David George (*The Forest Unseen, The Songs of Trees*), 101–104, 218–219, 233

haunted houses, 6
Hawthorne, Nathaniel, 5–6, 22–29, 31, 43, 56, 73, 128, 144, 159, 196, 197
  domestic piety, shown in contentment at the Old Manse and other domiciles, 22–25, 27
  estrangement from Salem, 25, 28–29, 196
  Gables as figure for explotative and possessive prosperity of America's majority culture, 26
  Gables as setting for spiritually redemptive progress of Clifford, Hepzibah, Holgrave, 28
  pilgrimage theme in works of, 28
  residence in Lenox, 25
  spirituality, attributed to hearth fire, reflected in writing, 31
  works
    "The Ambitious Guest," 5–6
    "Fire Worship," 23, 31
    The House of the Seven Gables, 25–29
    The Marble Faun, 73, 128
    "My Visit to Niagara," 144–145
    "The Old Manse," 24, 56
    Our Old Home, 23
    The Scarlet Letter, 25
Heidegger, Martin, 112–113
Heise, Ursuala, K., 84–87, 239n1
Herbert, George, 78–79, 206, 236
Holmes, Oliver Wendell, 16, 22
home, concept of, 235–238
  homelessness, and deformations of home, 27, 31, 42, 43–55, 89, 98, 142, 221, 237
Homer, *The Odyssey*, 237
The Homeplace. *See* Nelson, Marilyn

Housekeeping (Robinson), 49–51, 245n43
The House of the Seven Gables (Hawthorne), 25–29
Hudson River School, painters of, 146
Husserl, Edmund, 111–112

idolatry of place, 8, 82, 83
imagination, creative, 3, 9, 20, 105–140
   Berry's concept of "imagination in place," 108–111
   earthiness of, 9
   Emerson's view of, 107
   as expounded by Coleridge and other English Romantics, 105–108, 112
   Levertov's description of, 107
   philosophic formulations and implications of, 111–114
   place-grounded character of, 108–114
   as represented by Thoreau in *Walden*, 107, 114
   Shakespeare's representation of, 108–109, 251n11
   Welty's representation of, 108–109
Inge, John, 113–114, 240n7
In My Father's House (Ernest Gaines), 49, 51–54
Irving, Washington, 241n17
Islam and tradition of the hajj, 7, 8, 59, 72

James, Henry, 43, 124
Jeffers, Robinson, 259n55
Jefferson, Thomas, 27, 61, 73, 85, 181, 253n37
Jerusalem, 8, 15, 59, 128, 142, 156, 194, 231, 242n2
Jewett, Sarah Orne, 197
Judaism, 7, 56, 59, 84, 145, 164, 182, 192–196, 227

Kazin, Alfred (*A Walker in the City*), 182, 192–196
   and Brownsville's intertopological linkage to other places, 195–196
   conflicted religiosity of, 193–195, 259n57
   diasporic identity of, 196
Kerouac, Jack, 49, 75

Of Landscape and Longing: Finding a Home at the Water's Edge (Servid), 66–69
Lane, Belden C., 7, 141, 168, 251n17, 259n54
Lenox, Massachusetts, 25, 29
Levertov, Denise, 3, 107, 115–116, 207
liminality of place, 101, 138, 145, 152, 255n23
Lincoln, Abraham (Gettysburg Address), 161–167
   The Address, place-relevant features of, 162–163, 165–167
   and his rationale for avoiding all reference to Confederate dead, 165–167
Litchfield, Connecticut, Stowe's residence in, 30, 31, 39–43, 244n22
Little Gidding, 56, 78–79
localism versus globalism, 83–104
The Long Loneliness: The Autobiography of the Legendary Catholic Social Activist. *See* Day, Dorothy
Lopez, Barry, 3, 13, 62–66, 69, 127, 216, 238
   and alternative ways of knowing the world, 63–65
   on developing intimate knowledge of place, 13, 62–64

Lopez, Barry (cont.)
    on reverential and sacramental apprehensions of place, 65–66
    and travel writing, 62–64
    works
        "The American Geographies," 64
        Arctic Dreams, 62, 66
        Crossing Open Ground, 64
        "Landscape and Narrative," 64, 65, 248n20
        "The Language of Animals," 65, 247–248n18
        "Learning to See," 63
        "The Naturalist," 63–64
        "The Stone Horse," 66
        Winter Count, 65
Loyola, Saint Ignatius (*Spiritual Exercises*), 116
Lyell, Charles, 253n38

"The Making of a Marginal Farm" (Berry), 89–91
Mandarin, Florida, Stowe's residence in, 35–36
La Maravilla. See Véa, Alfredo
Mason, Bobbie Ann ("Shiloh"), 167
Maurin, Peter, 184–186
McClay, Wilfred, 83, 199–200, 216, 239n3
McKibben, Bill (*The End of Nature*), 87
meditation
    contrasted with contemplation, 115
    place-based application, and meditation on the creatures, 80, 102, 206–207, 261nn11–13
    poetry of, 78, 115–127, 207, 252n24
    practice and discipline of, 18, 64, 83, 115, 207–209
    Thoreau's disposition toward, 18
    walking mode of, 79–80, 115, 207
Melville, Herman (*Moby-Dick*), 23, 144, 152–157
    and challenge of navigating with quadrant and chronometer, 156–157, 256n29
    and liminality of place, 152, 255n23
    and *Pierre*, 156
    and problematic locating of the white whale, 154–157
Menand, Louis, 204–205
Merleau-Ponty, Maurice, 111–112
Merton, Thomas, 235
Michael, Jennifer, 208–209
Miller, Perry, 254n1
Milton, John, 75, 241n18
Moby-Dick. See Melville, Herman
Momaday, N. Scott (*The Way to Rainy Mountain*), 77–78, 84, 238
Monadnock, Mountain (New Hampshire), 146–149
Mormonism (Church of Latter-Day Saints), 76–77, 175–176, 178
Morrison, Toni (*Song of Solomon*), 140
Morton, Thomas, 146
mountain heights and ascents, 145–149
Muir, John, 3, 59, 75, 80, 107, 127, 144, 171, 185, 197, 253n38
    A Thousand-Mile Walk to the Gulf, 75

Native American conceptions of place-identity
    disputes concerning sacral status of Devils Tower (Bear's Lodge), 142–144

and Kiowa perceptions of place and memory (Momaday), 77–78
and Lakota Sioux attitudes (Black Elk), 150–152
in Véa's *La Marvilla*, 133
Nature (Emerson), 8, 15–16, 18, 22, 24
Nebraska, as evoked in writings by Willa Cather, 59, 197, 223–225
Nelson, Marilyn, 121–127, 129–132
  complex relation to African American heritage, 123–125
  portrayal of George Washington Carver and Tuskegee Institute, 129–132
  relation to father's service as Tuskegee Airman, 124, 126, 129, 132
  works
    Carver: A Life in Poems, 129–132
    The Homeplace, 121–127
New York City, 49, 75, 88, 155, 179, 182–196
  and Baldwin, James, 182, 186–192
  and Cather, Willa, 49, 224
  and Day, Dorothy, 182, 184–186
  and Kazin, Alfred, 192–196
  and Norris, Kathleen, 179
  and Williams, Terry Tempest, 179
  and Whitman, Walt, 117–118, 119–121
Niagara Falls, 141, 144–145, 241n12, 247n12
Norris, Kathleen (*Dakota: A Spiritual Geography*), 114, 178–181
Northcott, Michael, 11, 15, 261n23

O'Connor, Flannery, 58
Old Stone Fort (pre-Columbian site of ceremonial ritual, Manchester, Tennessee), 225–231
Oliver, Mary, 115
Otey, Bishop James Hervey, 230

palimpsest, place as, 10, 127–140
  association with Lyell and the "new geology," 253n38
  explicit mention of, in writings by Berry, Lopez, Muir, 127–128
pantheism, 106, 113, 172
Paul, Saint, 60, 94, 98–99, 192, 246n45
phenomenology of place, 2–3, 111–114
Pickering, Sam (*Autumn Spring*), 148–149
pilgrimage, diverse religious and spiritual practices of, 8–9, 22, 27, 28, 37, 51, 61, 72–83, 144, 146, 159, 177, 179, 203, 236, 243n11, 248n24
  anthropological and theological rationale for, 72, 78–79
  modes of in America, without definite destination, 81–83
  traditional pilgrimage destinations, 72–73, 78–79, 144
place-based educational programs. *See* education, collegiate
place-making, 11–12, 111, 197–198, 203, 206
  as allied by Douglas Christie to contemplative practice, 206, 261n11
  as conceived by noteworthy theologians, 11
"Place in Fiction" (Welty), 9, 108–109
"The Place, the Region, and the Commons" (Snyder), 4, 244n25, 247n7

polytheism, 4, 172
Potter, Bran, 173, 202, 213
Puritans, of colonial New England, 23, 24, 26, 33, 37, 50–51, 60, 74, 79–80, 114–115, 146, 207

Quakerism (Society of Friends), 33, 114

Raboteau, Albert J., 190
Refuge: An Unnatural History of Family and Place (Williams), 175–178
Remembering. *See* Berry, Wendell
reverence, place-directed, 45, 65, 66, 69, 70, 192–193, 216, 238
  and Abbey, Ed, 172–175
  and Berry, Wendell, 69–70
  and Kazin, Alfred, 192–193
  and Lopez, Barry, 65, 69
  and Norris, Kathleen, 180
  and Schweitzer, Albert, 70
  and Servid, Carolyn, 69–70
  and Woodruff, Paul, critically defined by, 65
Reynolds, David, 244n33
Robinson, Marilynne, 49–51, 53, 141–142, 235, 237
  dramatization of humanity's ultimately homeless state in *Housekeeping*, 50
  evocation of forest's wilder darkness in *Housekeeping*, 50
  linkage to Calvinist tradition, 50–51
  works
    Gilead, 141–142
    Home, 235–237
    Housekeeping, 49–51, 245n43
    Lila, 141–142
Rome, and ancient tradition of the *genius loci*, 4–5, 6, 22, 47, 128

sacramentality of place, 7, 9, 17, 33–34, 68, 87, 93, 101, 110, 113–114, 118, 120, 136–138, 183, 230–231, 238, 242n6
  as envisioned by Berry, 93, 101, 110
  as envisioned by Brown, in theological perspective, 7
  as envisioned by Hawthorne at "The Old Manse," 24
  as envisioned by Kazin, 193
  by Lopez, 65–66
  by Servid, 68
  by Stowe, especially through food rituals, 4, 33–34
  by Thoreau, 17–18, 193
  by Alfredo Véa, 136–138
  by Whitman, 118, 120
sacred geography and directionality, 3, 37, 76, 145, 149–157
The Sacred Pipe: Black Elk's Account of the Seven Rites of the Oglala Sioux, 150–152
saints
  communion of, 95, 99
  as embodied by George Washington Carver, 130–131
  and martyrdom, 164, 257n41
  with place-identified standing, 5, 7, 36, 60, 90–191, 164, 190–191, 225, 228, 236, 241n18
Salem, Massachusetts, 25–29
San Francisco, as represented in Wendell Berry's *Remembering*, 95, 98–99
Santiago, Spain, pilgrimage to, 72, 78, 203, 248n33
Schama, Simon, 254–255n9
Schantz, Mark S., 165
Schweitzer, Albert, 70
Sears, John, 144, 159, 247n12

INDEX | 285

Seeger, Pete, 42
Servid, Carolyn (*Of Landscape and Longing*), 66–69
Sewanee, Tennessee and University of the South, 6, 11–12, 56, 71–72, 101–104, 173, 201–203, 208–223, 228–233
  All Saints' Chapel, campus focal point, 228–233
Shakespeare, William, 108–110, 251n11
Sheldrake, Philip, 252n21
shrines, of Our Lady of Guadalupe and of St. Anne de Beaupré, 73
Snyder, Gary, 4, 12, 58–59, 80, 85, 87–89, 115
  on attaining global consciousness through place-based identity, 88–89
  on becoming native to North America, 58–59
  on knowing "the spirit of a place," 4, 12
  on North America as Turtle Island, 59
  "The Place, the Region, and the Commons," 4, 244n25, 247n7
Spenser, Edmund, 26
Stegner, Wallace, 58
Stewart, George R., 218
Stoll, Mark, 171, 259n54
Stowe, Harriet Beecher, 4, 29–43, 56, 236–237
  her portrayal of the spiritual solace possible in a home place, 34, 38
  later residence of, in Mandarin, Florida, 35–36
  residence of, in Hartford, 38–39
  residence of, in Litchfield and present-day controversy about homesite, 30, 31, 39–43, 244n22
  and sacramental rituals of food preparation and consumption, 4, 33–34
  theological resonance of "home" references in, 34, 36, 236–237
  Tom's cabin in UTC as hallowed domestic space, 32–33, 56
  works
    The Minister's Wooing, 31, 34, 244n32
    Poganuc People, 30
    Uncle Tom's Cabin, 29–39, 41, 43, 56
syncretism and polytheism, 4, 138, 172

Taylor, Bron, 241n12, 259n55
Taylor, Edward, 115, 207
Te Deum Laudamus hymn, 231
Thoreau, Henry, 3, 8, 1–22, 23, 58, 73, 80–82, 88, 91–92, 107, 114, 144, 146–148, 150, 159, 168, 171–172, 185, 197, 219, 230, 242–243n10
  attraction to mountainous terrain including Katahdin and Monadnock, 146–148
  encounter with numinous center of cosmos at Walden, 21–22
  his house at Walden, as porous and as portal to sacred space of surrounding nature, 17–19
  his practice of walking meditation, 80–82
  place-centered contemplation at Walden, 19–20

286 | INDEX

Thoreau, Henry (cont.)
   works
      Journals, 147–148, 255n13, 255n15
      The Maine Woods, 146–147, 255n11
      Walden, 8, 16–22, 107, 114
      "Walking," 80–82, 150
      A Week on the Concord and Merrimack Rivers, 20
      See also sacramentality of place
Tillinghast, Richard ("Four Directions), 149–150
topophilia (love of place), 68, 197
tourism, as linked to or contrasted with homage and sanctification of place, 73, 141, 144–145, 171, 214, 254n2
Traherne, Thomas, 206
travel writing, 9, 23, 58, 61, 62–64, 75, 82–83, 144–145
Tuan, Yi-Fu, 1, 216
Turner, Victor, 72, 73, 248n26
Tuskegee, Alabama and Tuskegee Airmen, 124, 126–127, 129–132
Twain, Mark, 49, 75–76, 150–151, 241n17

Uncle Tom's Cabin. See Stowe, Harriet Beecher
University of the South. *See* Sewanee
urban environmentalism, 99, 181–196, 240n6

Véa, Alfredo (*La Maravilla*), 132–140
   interlayering of ethnicities and religious traditions in, 132–136, 138
   permeability of place in, 134, 138
   sacramentality represented in, 136–138
   See also Buckeye Road, Arizona
Virgil, 5, 47

Walden. See Thoreau, Henry
A Walker in the City. See Kazin, Alfred
walking meditation (*kinhin*), 79–83, 115, 207
Warren, Robert Penn (*All the King's Men*), 150
Washington, Booker T., 129
watercourses, prominent representations in American literary and religious culture, 144–145, 227, 230, 261n23
The Way to Rainy Mountain. See Momaday, N. Scott
Weber, Max, 3
Weil Simone, 84
Welty, Eudora, 9, 108–109, 111
Whitman, Walt, 75, 116–121, 144, 207. *See also* sacramentality of place
   works
      "Crossing Brooklyn Ferry," 119–121
      Preface to 1855 *Leaves of Grass,* 118
      "Song of Myself," 116–119
Williams, Rowan, 78
Williams, Terry Tempest (*Refuge*), 114, 175–178, 238
   familial and religious lineage of, 175–176, 179
   perceived holiness of Utah's salt desert, testimony to, 176–178
Woodruff, Paul, 65, 238
Wordsworth, William, 9, 97, 108, 142, 175–176

Yosemite, California, esp. as memorialized by John Muir, 3, 141, 197